The Hebrew Orient

The Hebrew Orient

Palestine in Jewish American
Visual Culture, 1901–1938

Jessica L. Carr

Cover art: "Mystic Safed" from the June–August 1934/5694 NFTS Art Calendar; used by permission.

Published by State University of New York Press, Albany

© 2020 State University of New York

All rights reserved

No part of this book may be used or reproduced in any manner whatsoever without written permission. No part of this book may be stored in a retrieval system or transmitted in any form or by any means including electronic, electrostatic, magnetic tape, mechanical, photocopying, recording, or otherwise without the prior permission in writing of the publisher.

For information, contact State University of New York Press, Albany, NY
www.sunypress.edu

Library of Congress Cataloging-in-Publication Data

Name: Carr, Jessica L., author.
Title: The Hebrew orient : Palestine in Jewish American visual culture, 1901–1938 / Jessica L. Carr
Description: Albany : State University of New York Press, [2020] | Includes bibliographical references and index.
Identifiers: ISBN 9781438480831 (hardcover : alk. paper) | ISBN 9781438480824 (pbk. : alk. paper) | ISBN 9781438480848 (ebook)
Further information is available at the Library of Congress.

10 9 8 7 6 5 4 3 2 1

Contents

List of Illustrations		vii
Acknowledgments		xi
Introduction		1
Chapter 1	"The Orient" as Jewish Heritage	29
Chapter 2	The Place of Relics and Pioneers: Periodicals of the Zionist Organization of America	43
Chapter 3	Reviewing the Past: Jewish Art Calendars of the National Federation of Temple Sisterhoods	89
Chapter 4	Reconstructing History: The *Jewish Encyclopedia*	133
Chapter 5	Envisioning Citizenship: The Jewish Exhibit and Jewish Day at the 1933 World's Fair	171
Chapter 6	Making a Difference: Maternalism in Hadassah's "Propaganda"	205
Conclusion		231
Notes		245
Bibliography		265
Index		281

Illustrations

I.1a, I.1b	Images accompanying Ittamar Ben-Avi, "We Young Palestinians: To the Jewish Youth of America"	2
1.1	Advertisement in *The New Palestine*	30
2.1	"Give Today and Build For Ever!"	44
2.2	"A Survivor of Old Palestine"	50
2.3	"To Liberate the Smaller Nationalities"	53
2.4	Baltimore Convention Number cover of *The Maccabaean*	54
2.5	"Herzl as Moses"	55
2.6	"Greetings to Dr. Weizmann"	56
2.7	"Son of the Ancient Race" and "Samaria from the South"	58–59
2.8	"HOW UNJEWISH!"	62
2.9	"Whither?" and "On the March"	63
2.10	"Weary Wanderers" and "Goluth"	65
2.11	"For Whom?"	66
2.12	"Zion: Out of the Jungle!"	67
2.13	"A Picturesque Group in Jerusalem: A Turkestan Jew, a Moroccan (Magrabi) Jew and a Yemenite Jew"	69
2.14	*Yemenite Jew*	69
2.15	"Primitive Arab Farming," "Modern Jewish Farming Methods," and "A Farm of the New Era"	70–71

2.16	"Images of Chassidism" and "Scenes of Palestine Life"	78
2.17	"Bringing Health to Palestine" and "Corps of Nurses, Hadassah Medical Organization"	84–85
3.1	*Michelangelo's Moses*	90
3.2	*In the Synagog*	99
3.3	*The Crowning of Esther*	101
3.4	*The Destruction of Jerusalem*	105
3.5	*Ezechiel*	106
3.6	*Jochebed*	110
3.7	*Jews Taken Captive into Babylon*	112
3.8	*Jeremiah on the Ruins of Jerusalem*	113
3.9	*By the Waters of Babylon*	115
3.10	*Midnight Prayer*	116
3.11	*Boris Schatz*	117
3.12	*The Boy David*	118
3.13	*Mystic Safed*	120
3.14	*Gypsy Arabs in Sephardic Quarter—Jerusalem*	121
3.15	*Old Jewish Quarter*	123
3.16	*David's Tower in Jerusalem*	125
3.17	*Haluzah*	125
3.18	*Fervently We Invoke Thy Blessing*	127
3.19	*The Workers' Village*	130
4.1	"Court of Priests"	134
4.2	"Holy of Holies"	139
4.3	"The Temple at Jerusalem"	141
4.4	"Substructure of Temple of Herod, Now Called 'Solomon's Stables'"	145

4.5	"View of the Temple of Solomon"	145
4.6	"The Hereford Mappa Mundi, 1280, Showing Jerusalem in the Center of the World"	151
4.7	"Jerusalem—Modern"	153
4.8	"Zion Gate"	154
4.9	"A Typical Street in Jerusalem"	156
4.10	"General View of Rehoboth Colony, Palestine"	159
4.11	"Division of Fields in Modern Palestine"	160
4.12	"Plowing in Palestine"	161
4.13	"Bedouin Tent" and "Jews of Tunis in Native Costume"	163
4.14	"Tunisian Jewess"	165
4.15	"The Jewish Type Composite Portraits of Ten Jewish Boys, New York"	167
5.1	Stage as pictured in Chicago World's Fair guidebook	172
5.2	"The Ark"	177
5.3	"Israel's Contribution to Social Service"	179
5.4	"Israel's Contribution to Agriculture"	181
5.5	"Russian Cossack, in Days of Czar, Beats a Jew"	188
5.6	"Dudele"	189
5.7	Americanization scene	190
5.8	Two postcards from the Oriental Village	201
6.1, 6.2	"Join the Circle of Palestine's Children"	206–207
6.3	"Interior of a Health Welfare Station"	215
6.4	*Doorway to Life . . .*	216
6.5	*Hadassah Mothers the Children of Erez-Israel*	219
6.6	Four girls eating at a table	226

6.7	Cover with return address and stamp	227
C.1	"Replica of Western Wall Planned in Kansas"	238

Acknowledgments

An earlier version of chapter 3 appeared in the *American Jewish Archives Journal* 66, nos. 1 and 2 (2014) with the title "Picturing Palestine: Visual Narrative in the Jewish Art Calendars of National Federation of Temple Sisterhoods."

Images reprinted in *The Hebrew Orient* were scanned from the collections of the American Jewish Historical Society, Chicago Jewish Historical Society, Hadassah, University of Illinois at Chicago Special Collections, Women of Reform Judaism, and the YIVO Institute for Jewish Research.

Thank you to all of the research institutions who have made it possible for me to complete my book. This of course begins with the Indiana University library staff, particularly in the Wells and Fine Arts libraries, including everyone who sold me coffee and made me sushi or sandwiches. The staff at the American Jewish Archives and the Klau Library at Hebrew Union College are some of the most skilled and friendliest archivists and librarians anyone could ever hope to work with, and I am extraordinarily thankful for all that they did for me. Thanks to the Chicago Public Library, the Art Institute of Chicago, and Spertus for allowing me to view their materials, with a special thanks to the University of Illinois at Chicago library and special collections for being so cooperative and for their careful preservation of ephemera from 1933. Thank you to the excellent staff at the Center for Jewish History and the New York Public Library. Finally, thank you to State University of New York Press for bringing this book to the world, and especially to Rafael Chaiken for being the best editor imaginable. I received a fellowship as a scholar-in-residence with the Hadassah-Brandeis Institute at Brandeis University, where I wrote chapter 6 on Hadassah and benefited from conversations about my research and the study of gender with students, colleagues, and members of Hadassah.

Acknowledgments

Many colleagues over the years have influenced my ability to articulate what I want to say in this book. David Levenson convinced me that studying religion was the only, best path in life. Martin Kavka, the ineffable: teacher, mentor, friend, rock. Amanda Porterfield and John Corrigan guided me throughout my master's in the American Religious History program at Florida State University. My dissertation committee was outstanding, and I owe them many thanks for helping me begin this project: Constance Furey and Sylvester Johnson were insightful readers. Jeff Veidlinger not only read carefully but also initiated me into the professional world of Jewish studies. Katie Lofton left Indiana but never left me, throughout graduate school or my career. Shaul Magid has remained an adviser, guide, and friend from my arrival at Indiana to the completion of my book. My fellow Religious Studies graduate students at Indiana University know the value of the Wheel: Geoffrey Goble, Diane Fruchtman, Aimee Hamilton, Erik Hammerström, Amy Hirschtick, Nicole Karapanagiotis, and Brad Storin. Jigga Jigsu enthralled me Jewish Studies at Indiana: Gabi Berlinger, Leah Cover, Joseph Hayden, Ilana McQuinn, Avi Lang, Allison Posner, Anya Quilitzsch, Sebastian Schulman, and Asya Schulman (honorary member). Kenyon College Religious Studies gave me my first professional home: Joseph Adler, Miriam Dean-Otting, Ennis Edmonds, Royal Rhodes, Vernon Schubel, and Mary Suydam. A special debt of gratitude goes to my department at Lafayette College for bringing me into their world: Rob Blunt, Brett Hendrickson, Youshaa Patel, Robin Rinehart, Herman Tull, and Eric Ziolkowski. Laura McKee has truly made my life run. Alex Hendrickson is chaplain to the stars. Thank you to Ilan Peleg and Bob Weiner for welcoming me to the Jewish Studies program. Many others have been constants, occasional, or some whom I barely know but who answered an email or question at a key moment that allowed me to keep going. Or maybe you just grew a plant, caught me for a laugh in the hallway, bought me a drink at a conference (the greatest gifts scholars offer to one another): Jennifer Adler, Mary Armstrong, Betsy Barre, Jessica Cooperman, Evie Dean-Olmsted, Shawntel Ensminger, Bianca Falbo, Jodi Eichler-Levine, Michelle Geoffrion-Vinci, Peter Gildenhuys, Alessandro Giovanelli, Rachel Gross, Liora Halperin, Sarah Imhoff, Jenna Weissman Joselit, Dov-Ber Kerler, Rebecca Kamholz, Ken Koltun-Fromm, Barbara Krawcowicz, Hartley Lachter, Nitzan Lebovic, Matthias Lehman, Nancy Levene, Laura Levitt, Samira Mehta, Owen McLeod, Eva Mroczek, George Panichas, Sarah Panter, Mike Pasquier, Josh Sanborn, Sasha Senderovich, Ben Schreier, Josh Schreier, Caleb Simmons, Ida Sinkevic, Josh Smith,

Sarah Stein, Shayna Weiss, Steve Weitzman, and Wendy Wilson-Fall. It's my great fortune to have Erin Corber and Devi Mays as my flowerz frenz, intellectuals who have always been by my side, even from afar: Who could count the tears of laughter and solidarity we have shared?

I have found a community at Lafayette College with intellectuals turned friends who not only engage my work but make my life worth living. I have appreciated and learned with too many students to name, but I want to express how deeply comments in class or chats in office hours have made this profession worth pursuing and defined what I consider to be the most purposeful aspect of my career. Academia can be weird so often, but friends in Easton have made my time beautiful and special with jokes, hikes, animals, and kindness. Academic life is as often as volatile, unkind, and transient as it is rewarding and fulfilling, so I thank you as part of my community, whether the job market or life has allowed you to stay near or not: Aseel Bala, Angela Bell, Andrew Brandon, Leigh Campoamor, Lindsay Ceballos, Ben Cohen, Rob Guroff, Amauri Gutierrez Coto, Jess Hejny, Ben Jahre, Michaela Kelly, Maggie Levantovskaya, Emily McGinn, Sarah Morris, Margaret Page, Jeremy Roth, Amir Sadovnik, Jen Talarico, Simon Tonev, Sue Wenze, Joe Woo, and Jenny Zallen. Jeremy Zallen was my friend and colleague from day one, and our conversations have bridged political, professional, personal, and puppies in the most ideal, sustaining way. Tamara Carley became my Powerhouse one blizzard, cementing a relationship destined by professional outlook, love of science—citizen or official, and a care that never required saying too much. Meg Fernandes and Brent Utter appeared early in my life at Lafayette, but I cannot fathom what it would have been like to experience fallout without you. So glad to be celebrating better days with you now. I'm grateful to all these people for the ways they have made my life complete, in and out of work.

My friends and family have been deeply important to my life and fulfillment throughout graduate school, and I offer my most profound gratitude to the following. Colyar Pridgen has been not just a cousin but a friend since high school and across the country. Louis Lavoie sat with me through French, an introduction to Judaism, and so much more. Doug, Beryl, and Leo Storch, for fun and offering love that few people get to experience. Melissa Storch has been my best friend since high school, and I feel lucky to have a friendship that always picks up exactly where we left off. Kristine, Emmie, and Adler Schwab for the artwork that has brightened my life and walls. Del Schwab crosses the boundary between colleague and friend, and I am deeply grateful for the countless number of drafts he read of every chapter. Rachel Rosner and Jesse Gabriel, though we go long periods without each other, I never forget how much encouragement and empathy they've offered me. Kenny Draper offered a decade of love, respect, intellect, and encouragement that kept me together even though life took us in different directions. I'm grateful for the new form our friendship has taken as we move forward. Ana Theophilo and Luiza Ramos literally took me in, and their friendship renewed my love for the world. My Aunt Deedee and Uncle Skip and their families have been steady parts of my life for as long as I can remember. I'm so grateful that my work brought me nearer to my Aunt Judy and Uncle Richard and my cousins Christian, Megan, Wyatt, Aidan, and Gavin. Thank you to my brother Nathan and his family, Bethany, Austin, Evan, Tutu, and Jia-Jia Carr, for giving me such happiness at every break. Your love has kept me going through everything. Thank you so much to my parents, Walter and Jenny Carr, who taught me the value of education. You have loved me and supported me whether you understood what I was doing or why, and this is a rare gift in the world. You were the first, most intelligent people I knew, but more importantly, I have always known I could turn to you.

Annie, la verdadera esposa, thank you for everything. You are the love of my life.

Introduction

In the summer of 1917, a collection of photographs in the journal *The Maccabaean* (hereafter, *TM*) conjured images of the landscape and life of the Holy Land for Zionist Americans (fig. I.1). A postcard image of the heart of the old city of Jerusalem shows its domes and courtyards. Another image shows Herzliah, Palestine's first Hebrew high school "with its harmonious blend . . . of Oriental lavishness and Occidental comfort," designed by Joseph Barsky (1876–1943) and inspired by architectural descriptions of Solomon's Temple. Alongside this new Temple educating the children to establish the new epoch of Jewish civilization, *chalutzim*—Zionist pioneers—work the fields of the first Jewish agricultural school in Palestine, Mikveh-Israel. In other images, children lead the way to an agricultural fair celebrating the Jewish New Year for trees, while adults labor in the Bezalel school for the arts, in recently constructed factories, and in boats on the Mediterranean.[1] Ancient architecture—and its contemporary reinterpretations—invigorated by modern technology and communion with nature created a stage for the Jewish American imagination.

These images visualized "the Orient" for American viewers, creating the possibility for Jewish Americans to understand themselves through imagining "Oriental" counterparts. Through these images, Ittamar Ben-Avi (1882–1943) issued a call to Jewish American youth to hear the strength and regeneration of the voice of Palestine. "If you only were to lay aside your daily interests for a little while; if you were—no, not to travel to Canaan, for the hour has not yet struck—if you were to let your fancy fly towards the Hebrew Orient . . . then indeed you would be amazed at the panorama which unfolded itself before you."[2] Ben-Avi was a Zionist activist and, in Jewish nationalist heritage, the first native speaker of Modern Hebrew. Born Ben-Zion Ben Yehuda, he was the son of celebrated figure Eliezer

We Young Palestinians

To the Jewish Youth of America
By ITTAMAR BEN-AVI

THERE is a voice calling from afar, young and strong, fresh and vigorous; and you, the Jewish youth of free America, lend us your ears, if only for a moment, and hearken to the message of this ringing voice. For, although it calls from the far away East, and although some of you will not grasp immediately its true meaning, yet it is a voice not wholly unknown to you.

For it is the voice of your brethren, the voice of the younger generation of modern Palestine, which echoes from mountains as lofty as Hermon, which fords torrents as mighty as the Jordan, which leaps over valleys as fertile as Sharon, which sweeps over vast seas as the Mediterranean and the Atlantic, until it reaches the shores of America, America the happy and the prosperous.

It is the voice of your brethren, which has burst from that very land so dear and so cherished to each Hebrew heart, the land which was once the possession of your renowned forefathers, and which a new generation, proud and resolute, is striving to make the land of the Jewish people in the not far distant future.

Surely you know it now, that voice of young Zion, that voice of new Canaan.

For after all you also are Jews. If you were to respond to this appealing voice, which brings you a hearty greeting, a resounding and oriental "Shalom"; if only you were to lay aside your daily interests for a little while; if you were—no, not to travel to Canaan, for the hour has not yet struck — if you were to let your fancy fly towards the Hebrew Orient,

ITTAMAR BEN-AVI
of Jerusalem

fly and wander to and fro throughout the country, for at least a few days, then indeed you would be amazed at the panorama which unfolded itself before you. In all the principal cities, from Beer-Sheba in the south to Sidon in the north, and in the forty-seven Jewish colonies, from Ruchamah in the desert of Idumaea as far as Metullah in the crags of Upper Galilee, there you would find a hundred and fifty thousand Jews who are courageously continuing the life of the ancient nation. After the destruction of the land at the hand of the Roman Emperor Titus, and after two thousand years of black and bitter exile for the great majority of the people of Israel, this is perhaps the greatest event in the history of our people, — that history which is already so rich in incidents of tremendous import. Babylon and Egypt, Assyria and Persia, ancient Greece and mighty Rome have passed from the face of the earth, they who believed that they had completely annihilated this, our little nation,— but they were mistaken; for, to this very day, this same nation still exists on the same consecrated soil.

You will surely recognize Mikveh-Israel . . .

. . . And what is that which rises before us in white splendor?

Figure I.1a. Images accompanying Ittamar Ben-Avi, "We Young Palestinians: To the Jewish Youth of America."

THE MACCABAEAN

They are all here to attend the famous yearly agricultural fair

It is only thirty years since the first Jewish child opened his small mouth to pronounce the endearing term of "Abbah" (papa), in that same tongue in which the child Isaac spoke to his father Abraham; and today, thirty thousand boys and girls, most of them born in Palestine, fill our two hundred schools with their noisy chatter, our Kindergartens and Hadarim, our Talmud Torahs and High Schools. It is a great host, a powerful host the like of which our land has not seen since the time of Shimeon Ben-Shetah, the inspired founder of the first schools in Palestine,—until the beginning of our new epoch, the epoch of the Hebrew renascence and the pride of the Jew in Zion. It is in truth an army, our army of boy scouts and young soldiers, of whom each one, the baby of three, the girl of seven, the Bar Mitzvah boy, the adolescent of over sixteen, bears in his hand the banner of the nation, blue and white, consecrated through a generation of renewed Hebrew vigor; and that army of our Palestinian youth, be sure, will not relinquish it until it breathes its last.

Only two years before the beginning of this terrible war, the young Palestinians demonstrated to the whole world what stuff they were made of, and what the nation might expect from them,—when, one fine day, thousands of the pupils of Palestine deserted their schools because their teachers wanted to replace their beloved Hebrew by German, a foreign language. Jerusalem will never forget, and the Hebrew Diaspora will ever remember, that moving episode when the little orphan girls in the picturesque "Rehov Ha-Habbashim" (Abyssinian Street), children of five and six, defied their principal, whom they loved intensely because of her former devotion to Hebrew, as she was trying to have them remain true to her new theories, and submit to her sudden German words of command. They cried bitterly, for they had to leave their school house; but no matter, they clung to their older schoolmates, who left the Germanized institution never to return, thus proclaiming in their childish voices:
"We will not be traitors to the Hebrew tongue! We will not be traitors!"

* * *

What is that commotion in the streets of Jerusalem? What is that long, almost endless procession? What is the meaning of these columns of boys and girls passing towards the outskirts of the city? They are all dressed in white, with blue bands across their chests. There are fresh flowers in the boys' buttonholes, and the girls are crowned with gay wreaths. Each group carries its standard and the band at the head of the procession urges them on with martial tunes. Where are they going, these care-free children, notwithstanding the war and their unprecedented isolation? What can be the cause of their singing so joyfully psalms of the past and songs of the future?

It is the fifteenth of Shebat,—not a Shebat of Europe or America with its February winds and snows, with its freezing cold, with its stormy skies, with its bare trees, but a Shebat of Jerusalem, of all Eretz-Israel. It is the New Year of the Trees, because between the Mediterranean and the Jordan, and especially between the Jordan and the Euphrates, the winter has come to an end at last, the rains and the hail have almost ceased. The sun has resumed its glorious dominion; the kindly winds announce the approach of Spring, the trees are bourgeoning once more, and the fragrance of myriads of wild flowers, daisies and lillies and anemones, saturates the clear atmosphere.

This is why the city is rejoicing. This is why the young generation of rejuvenated Jerusalem is happy; for they love the light and the sun, the warmth and the verdure. For they see in that festival of the

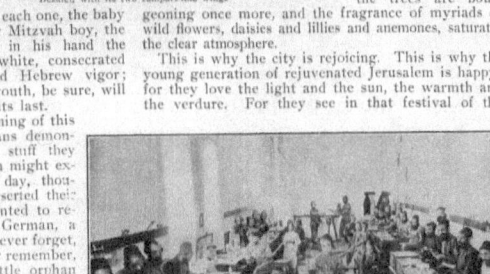

Bezalel, with its two rampart-like wings

Over a hundred and fifty artisans are sitting at their tables . . .

Two-sixty

June-July, 1917

Figure I.1b. Images accompanying Ittamar Ben-Avi, "We Young Palestinians: To the Jewish Youth of America."

Ben Yehuda (1858–1922), who is credited as the driving force behind the revival of Modern Hebrew. His call had the authority of the reborn Jewish nation, and he announced that Jewish Americans did not have to travel to Palestine for "the Orient" to influence their lives. Ben-Avi petitioned Jewish American youth to exit space and time momentarily to enter an imaginary world. Jewish Americans who saw a variety of different futures for Jews, the United States, and Palestine heard this call to imagine an idealized "Orient" rather than to physically enter Palestine during World War I. Accordingly, their visions were of an imagined "Orient," not of Palestine: they saw themselves and life in the United States by creatively picturing "the Orient" as a laboratory for understanding the Jewish past, present, and future. The idea of "the Orient" as the geographic place of Jewish origin has been important to many Jewish Americans as a means of articulating an authentic heritage as a community, even though many never set foot in Palestine and could not point concretely to ancestors who hailed from the Middle East. Jews themselves or those whose parents, grandparents, or older progenitors hailed primarily from Europe made themselves over in their visions of "the Orient" as homeland. Paradoxically, imagining "the Orient" as heritage made many Jewish Americans feel more "at home" in the United States.

This book lays out the panoramas of "the Orient" that Jewish Americans could imagine through the visual culture of multiple organizations and movements, revealing the complex issues of time and materiality for Jewish Americans in the early twentieth century. Given the cultural embeddedness of Jewish Americans in the United States and their shared political, religious, and social practices with non-Jews, I use the term "Jewish Americans," despite the popularity of the term "American Jew" with many scholars. In other words, I do not consider a goal of my work to be to demonstrate the "Americanness" of those whom I study. They are American. Many of those who produced, circulated, and viewed the visual culture I analyze were not just second generation, but third, fourth, and so on. However, no matter how recently immigrants arrived or stayed, or whether they had received legal citizenship, I consider their presence a key influence on life in the United States and their contributions as significant and as American as anyone else. While acknowledging the significant place for Jewishness in their lives, the word order of "Jewish American" affirms the belonging, cultural rootedness, and sociopolitical structures of the Jews I study in the United States.[3]

For Jewish Americans, looking toward "the Orient" was explorative and aspirational: through this visual culture, they imagined themselves by imagining others. They looked for how they wished to see themselves and to be seen by other Americans. By envisioning "the Orient," Jewish Americans created a tangible heritage to cite as their central role in world history and American society. Such heritage and roles never became a given in the United States, but they were continually created and maintained through visual culture. "The Orient" offered Jewish Americans a homeland, countering antisemitic ideas of Jews as rootless or parasitic. By visualizing this heritage, Jewish Americans could also map themselves onto American history and values. By doing so, Jewish Americans not only saw a place for themselves in the United States and the world, but they also constructed new ways that all Americans might see inclusion in citizenship and heritage. Jewish American visual culture imagining "the Orient" not only pictured Jews as part of the United States. Jewish American visual culture redrew ways that any minority could be seen in the United States. Jewish Americans revised concepts such as race, gender, and American culture, even as imagining "the Orient" had limits in deconstructing traditional ways of viewing those concepts within the many competing visions of Jewish and non-Jewish American heritage.

New technologies in the twentieth century transformed how Jewish Americans and so many others understood space and time. It is an obvious point in physics that distance equals speed multiplied by time. The change of speed technology, therefore, inevitably altered how Jewish Americans calculated the values of distance and time. Enda Duffy shows that "access to new speeds . . . has been the most empowering and excruciating new experience for people everywhere in twentieth-century modernity." Moreover, these new speeds are political.[4] Duffy emphasizes both the pleasure and the pain of moving in new ways never before experienced and in ways that are uncommon to the human body. Speed can be exhilarating, from ship to car to airplane. But speed is also terrifying, always threatening injury or death in its deviation from control of movement and our expectations thereof.[5] "The very notion of life as the capacity for energetic movement . . . took on a new valence." This new valence took multiple forms, from nostalgia for a different form of life energy to "need for new levels of visual alertness." New technologies of speed transformed possibilities for representation and vision; film, the moving image, epitomized this transformation, but this should not distract from how this transformation permeated twentieth-century human experience technologies for viewing. As a political issue, movement and energy related to the new ways that people in the twentieth century could access speed, an access that must be understood intersectionally, looking at ability to financially afford travel (physical or simulated); the spaces and methods of movement available to different genders; and the institutional regulation of movement, from nation-states to religious and ethnic organizations.[6]

Heritage is spatialized because of the conceptual link of time and space, mediated by changes in technology.[7] Space is neither obvious nor natural. However, visual culture such as photographs, drawings, and reconstructions of historical spaces can cover over the ways that connections to these spaces are mediated. Speed transformed how people in the twentieth century could understand place. Because it became possible to move quickly between places, whether a person actually could access that travel or not, place and space collapsed.[8] By this I mean that the very difference between once place and another became muddied and intertwined. Twentieth-century technology, from photography to travel, allowed people in one place to quickly experience another place. This experience was so fast as to be simultaneous: in this way, photography offered a spectacle of movement more immediate even than technologies such as the steamboat, railroad, car, or airplane. The intertwining of two places through new technologies necessarily affected new experiences and imaginations of time. The ability to experience two or more places seemingly at once collapsed not just space but time. Time and space are constitutive elements of each other, inextricably linked in how we understand human experience. And if it was felt possibly to be in two or more places at once, why not two or more times at once? New speeds, and the ways people understood the benefits and experience of those speeds, led to new views not only of local and global distance but also historical time and its relevance to the construction of "heritage." These speeds made history seem like it was not cut off from the present.

Through new technologies, humans had amazing but dangerous access to all kinds of places and times. However, the simultaneity of speed is merely a spectacle. No matter how fast the speed, no one can be in multiple places at once. The strength of the spectacle of speed depended especially on vision, seeing oneself in these places. This new and unfettered access was dangerous not only because of the possibility for physical disaster, but perhaps more importantly because of the unfettered access to the concept of speed. Visual culture in particular brought speed to the masses. The politicization of speed resulted from institutional attempts to control and regulate this democratization of speed. Even for those who could not travel, they could see what was afar. I use visual culture as a methodology in this book because it offers a window into the public culture that Jewish organizations formed in the early twentieth century and because it provides a glimpse into what everyday people saw when Palestine-turned-"the Orient" was presented to them. What people thought of the images before them is hard to recover, but this project seeks to see what Jewish Americans saw and how that structured their possibilities for interpreting "the Orient," whether they took up the ideologies of institutions or not. Nation-states began to issue increasingly complicated passports and track human movement.

Photographs in particular play an important role in many of the images discussed throughout the following chapters. The word "photograph" simplifies the many different methods for capturing an image through some type of camera, and the linguistic roots of "photograph" literally conveyed these images as writing with light.[9] At first glance, it seemed "photography confirmed the image as natural, for was not the process instantaneous and automatic, unmediated by hand?" But humans construct the camera, the lens, and the framing of the shot. This leads Hubert Damisch to argue against seeing photographs as natural or unmediated. "It is a product of human labor, a cultural object whose being . . . cannot be dissociated from its historical meaning and from the necessarily datable project in which it originates."[10] If photographs themselves are human products, all the more so is their circulation and (re-)use historically and socially located. "Destined by the medium's technology to represent a specific moment in the past, they are also free to serve any representational function desired by a photographer and his audience."[11] Photographers select the visual context of a photograph's frame, but viewers continuously recontextualize the photographer's choice with every display and observation. Photographs are simultaneously timeless—a certain moment is frozen, it documents the past, a moment that happened at a certain point in history—and they are futuristic—they represent a new technology that offers a distancing lens from the subjects and they allow the moment to be endlessly reexamined in the future. Why take a photograph if not with the expectation that it will be viewed in the future, for myriad reasons? But while photographs may seem to document a particular moment, they are never unmediated presentations. Instead, photographs are always mediated representations. Even "documentary" photographs, images that seem or seek to present "the real," cannot do so without framing, without perspective—though photographs, their photographers, and others who circulate the images may nevertheless claim access to "the real" through them.[12]

Photographs and all images' meanings are not solely defined by the agency, vision, or interpretation of their original artist. Once in circulation, viewers interpret the photographs themselves based on their own personal and communal experiences, sometimes with little or no knowledge of the photographer, and it is to these recontextualizations that I turn my attention. Images and especially photographs have become a key artifact of the production of heritage precisely because they appear "natural" or even "unmediated," as if their meanings are reproduced in each copy citation. "Images become history, more than traces of a specific event in the past, when they are used to interpret the present in light of the past, when they are presented and received as explanatory accounts of collective reality." New contexts continually reframe photographs.[13] A dialectic between past and present, which produces imagined futures, constitutes the production of heritage.

Reimagining Orientalism

From 1901 to 1938, Orientalism was a key means of the construction of Jewish American "imagined community."[14] As described by Benedict Anderson, any community might be considered an imagined community. The continual process of articulating the shared values and practices of an in-group, however large or small, as well as of articulating boundaries between two groups, is the very construction of community. Accordingly, I consider all of the sets and characters within the Jewish American panorama equally "Oriental," that is, equally integral to Jewish American heritage construction. Some may closer resemble "Western" ideals and some may serve more clearly as foils; some may be overtly "modern" while others are "ancient," and yet others a collapse or hybrid. That is to say, complicated and contradictory representations of "Orients" and "Orientals" are prolific in these constructions.

Ivan Davidson Kalmar and Derek Penslar's collection *Orientalism and the Jews* looks at cases of Orientalism that have not been readily categorized or whose categorizations have shifted. They ask, what about groups such as Jews who fit ambiguously? How has their intellectual and cultural interaction with the discourse of Orientalism shaped their subjectivities? And how have Jews in turn engaged, suffered, or benefited from and generally influenced Orientalism? Jews were both objects and viewers of these Orientalisms, and multiple "Orients" and "Wests" were manifested through these Orientalisms. Such "Orients" included East European Jews, and Sephardic and Mizrahi Jews, Byzantium and the Eastern Church, Turkey and Turks, and the Middle East and Arabs. Such "Wests" and "Westerners" included Europe, Western Europe, Christianity, Judaism, Zionism, Ashkenazi Jews, secularism, and nationalism. Their collection illuminates the ambivalent place of Jews in Europe, Palestine, and elsewhere in the Middle East, but each chapter tends to show one focal position of viewers and one object of their Orientalist imagination. My research reveals to me messy, contradictory uses of multiple Orientalist visions. At the same time, Jewish Americans had to pick and choose the ways they wanted to see themselves in contradistinction to Europe. Palestine provided an imaginary panorama that served as a cipher for "the Orient," Europe, and the United States and the relationship between Jewishness and each space.

My definition of Orientalism refers to the construction of heritage, especially through visual culture, and the continuous revision of communal identities. The process of constructing "heritage" is ongoing, disputed, and creative. Constructing Orientalism is, at its core, a process of "Westerners" looking at others to understand themselves (as "Westerners") by creating a narrative about where they came from, whether they have been to that imaginary homeland or not. This narrative is neither preexisting nor natural: calling it "heritage" distinguishes the stories people tell about themselves from history. History, in part, seeks to uncover and interrogate the implications of the very ways that people have constructed heritage by selecting and excluding details that they consider desirable or representative of their values and how they wish to be seen. The idea of the "West" is produced through imagining "the Orient." "The West" exists nowhere but imagination, just like "the Orient." Orientalism is the practice through which those in Europe and America have imagined "the Orient" to understand themselves as members of various European and American nations and subgroups within those nations. This process depends on a treatment of those inhabiting "the Orient" as somehow existing differently in time than those from "the West." Orientalism is a very specific form of heritage, one that became possible in new ways in the specific sociohistorical context of the late nineteenth and especially early twentieth centuries, although Orientalism dates back to the end of the Crusades, the moment of Christian Europe's military loss and abandonment of attempting to seize Jerusalem from the Muslim Ottoman Empire. This book shows how Jewish American views of Palestine engage Jewish traditions to value "heritage" while revising specific historical moments and their integration into, exclusion from, and contours in Jewish life in the United States from 1901 to 1938.

In other words, though Orientalism depends on engagement with the lives and spaces of the Middle East, it treats the lives of those who inhabit "the Orient" as "contemporaneous" but not truly "contemporary." Barbara Kirshenblatt-Gimblett defines this distinction. "Contemporaneous" describes "those in the present who are valued for their pastness" and "contemporary" as "those of the present who relate to their past as heritage."[15] This process of Orientalism, sorting that which matters as "heritage" and that which matters as "modern," has aided Jewish Americans in defining themselves exactly as such: simultaneously Jewish and American. Jewish Orientalism creates a "heritage" that depends on the East, a sense that Jews have a history related to the Holy Land but not trapped in it or the past. Jewish Orientalism contrasts sharply with Christian Orientalism, which has depended on treating Jews as contemporaneous people, valued only as living proof of the supersession of the Old Testament by the New. Jewish and Christian Orientalisms share practices of looking toward the East and defining a "West" against romanticized visions of various "Orientals," including Jews and Muslims, Arabs and Bedouins, and other groups sometimes melded together as a single group and sometimes arranged in a hierarchy "proving" that "the West" belongs atop that hierarchy as an organizing, civilizing force. Moreover, Orientalism posed as irredentism. Among Jews and non-Jews, "the Orient" was imagined as a rightful homeland and state for Jews, although Jews had not constituted a majority in the territory for nearly two thousand years. The only way to see "the Orient" as a homeland for Jews was to envision its inhabitants as contemporaneous relics of the past waiting to be replaced or improved by civilized contemporary Ashkenazi Jews. This often froze the politics of "the Orient" in what many imagined as the biblical era.

Jewish Americans, like many immigrants and especially those not presumed to be white prior to their arrival in the United States, had to walk a tightrope between being able to claim a heritage in order to seem "normal" and not allowing that heritage to compromise their perception as loyal Americans. The new concept of cultural pluralism paved the way for new practices of Americanism that allowed Jewish Americans to do this. Popularized by Horace Kallen and Louis Brandeis, cultural pluralism denounced the need for assimilation in the United States, instead asserting that connections to other nations and culture do not threaten a person's status as a loyal United States citizen. Cultural pluralism also became a dominant language for hegemonic conceptions of the role of immigrants among established and recently arrived Americans. Accusations of rootlessness had weighed heavily on Jews in Europe and influenced the development of what Jewish Americans in the early twentieth century called cultural pluralism. However, rather than looking to various European countries as their homelands, Jewish Americans constructed "the Orient" as a homeland, though most Jewish Americans had not lived there in the past or even visited. Increasingly in the twentieth century, being in the US was a choice *not* to be in Palestine. Many did not have pleasant memories of their political and social status in European countries, and they sought a "homeland" with a solely and explicitly Jewish nature. "The Orient"-as-homeland allowed them to look structurally like other immigrant groups without grouping themselves along with non-Jews who hailed from the same places of origin in Europe.

Therefore "the Orient" as heritage simultaneously distanced Jewish Americans from other immigrants arriving from the same Central and East European regions, places that Jewish Americans sought to reject as homelands from which they or their ancestors had emigrated. Moreover, "the Orient" as heritage produced Jewish difference through a pseudo-immigrant status for generations to come. Even if Jewish Americans' families had been in the United States for decades or over a century, envisioning "the Orient" engaged a type of ongoing immigrant status, including those born in the United States. Nostalgia for "the Orient" marked Jewish Americans as somehow native and foreign at the same time. In this way, imagining "the Orient" helped situate Jews as part of a pan-ethnic whiteness that perhaps enabled the inclusion of other groups as white, such as Irish and Italians, by the 1940s and 1950s. Inventing a new nationalism requires "plausibly" "rediscovering" a past. This presents constructions of national and religious heritage not as new but old. Orientalism offered a perception of Jewish heritage as ancient. This had historically been problematic for Jews, othering them as less-than compared to non-Jewish Europeans and Americans who characterized Jews as "Oriental."[16] By appropriating and adapting Orientalism, Jewish Americas could benefit from the value of oldness in validating Jewish nationalism while attempting to dispense with the negative ways that non-Jewish Orientalism often portrayed Jews as inherently unable to "modernize."

Studying Orientalism as a scholarly approach at once opens a perspective of the role of "the Orient" in the United States beyond Zionism and shifts away from measuring the "success" of American Zionism by goals formed outside of the United States. This forms a new assessment of the nature of American engagement with both the politics of Palestine and the imagined "Orient." I argue that the two are difficult or impossible to disentangle fully. But the richness of Jewish American visual culture differs from such scholarship as that of Naomi Cohen's assessment of American Zionism as reduced to weak and watered-down "Palestinianism" as compared to robust European Zionism. "Palestinianism" as a frame for understanding Jewish American history suggests that Jewish Americans were less engaged with Palestine than other Jews throughout the world. Instead I assert that all Jews viewed Palestine through the lenses of their local contexts and ideological visions of Jewishness. Seen this way, Palestine is always mediated, informed by an imagined "Orient." My analysis takes up this process of imaginative Orientalism to better see Jewish American visual culture from 1901 to 1938.

Envisioning Jewish Heritage

Analyzing the construction of "heritage" interrogates the place of the past—both time and space—in the performance, maintenance, and dispute of contemporary identities. Each chapter in this book demonstrates how a different group of Jewish Americans participated in and deployed Orientalism as Jewish heritage in their vision of the future of Jewishness, in the United States and in the world. In this way, "heritage" points to a subsection of memory, which is multifaceted. My sources in this book, for example, largely cannot speak to subjectivity or reception. However, I read how Jewish American visual culture representing "the Orient" created a specific and tangible heritage in the United States in the early twentieth century, mediating potential conflicts in contemporary Jewish conceptions of heritage among various interpretations of Jewishness, Palestine, and the United States. Jewish Americans in the nineteenth century argued for the compatibility of Judaism and democracy, a compatibility so successfully established that Jewish Americans have taken this construction to be a timeless natural fact in the twentieth and twenty-first centuries. Beth Wenger argues, "What they produced was not history but heritage."[17] With qualifications, Wenger borrows the concept of heritage from David Lowenthal, who argues that through heritage, "we tell ourselves who we are, where we came from, and to what we belong."[18] Jewish Americans "designed their Jewish past as an expression of their own interests and expectations for Jewish life in the United States."[19] Through the production of heritage, Jewish Americans argued for their place in the United States and Jewishness. I commonly refer to "Jewishness" rather than "Judaism" to point to broader performances and identities not limited to interpretations of halakha or Jewish law. If "Judaism" seems to refer to some engagement with the Hebrew Bible and the Talmud as commanding, "Jewishness" offers vistas that engage practices that offer new centers of Jewish heritage, such as early Jewish history or extra-synagogue communal organizations.

To create and debate their heritage, Jewish Americans produced a great number of images from 1901 to 1938. The study of the images of the "the Orient" is a matter of visual culture, meaning an analysis of the contexts in which anything we see is produced, presented, and perceived. The study of visual culture includes the content of any single image; the study of iconography or how certain topics are depicted over time; the technology and media by which anything visible is produced; artists' intentions and actions to create an image; the various political, social, religious, and other contexts in which the image is produced; identifications brought to bear on the image, such as nation, race, ethnicity, gender, sexuality, and religion; the presentation of any image, including verbal and nonverbal texts and environments; the influence, funding, or exhibition, by various institutions; and various audiences, including the moments different people view images as well as critical and popular responses to images. All of these may be difficult to trace for any single image or group of images, and visual culture should not be limited to what consumers, practitioners, critics, and scholars might label "art." Visual culture includes anything the eye can see, as well as all the mental processes brought to bear at the moment of seeing. S. Brent Plate defines these many different factors as the "field of vision." The "message" or meaning of any image is not stable or predetermined but the result of the interactions of the many factors of the field of vision at play for an individual or community.[20] Similarly, David Morgan considers visual culture a method rather than a discipline. It is not separate from other historical interpretations, but only a new emphasis on evidence that might expand all disciplines. "Visual culture refers to the images and objects that deploy particular ways of seeing and therefore contribute to the social, intellectual, and perceptual construction of reality." This definition privileges attention to the social construction of reality; in other words, individual images and experiences of viewing those images are placed in a social and cultural context. Religious practice could not be the same without images, sites, and sights, and the goals of visual religion might include any of several practices: to "order space and time, imagine community, communicate with the divine and transcendent, embody forms of communion with the divine, collaborate with other forms of representation, influence thought and behavior by persuasion or magic, [and] displace rival images and ideologies." The goals and functions of religion are not discrete; practices typically display a combination.[21]

Scholars such as Rachel Gross and Ken Koltun-Fromm have analyzed Jewish anxieties about authenticity. Like Gross and Koltun-Fromm, I do not seek to confer authenticity on any examples of visual culture. Gross analyzes how the emotional aspects of nostalgia confer authenticity on Jewish constructions of heritage from "historical synagogues" to food.[22] The sources I have gathered do not belie the emotional reactions of their historical viewers or the meanings Jewish Americans made with these visions. I agree with Koltun-Fromm's description of "visual authenticity" as "a *rhetorical activity*—it is a mode of argument and persuasion—in which visual discourse, images, and bodies critically inform and anxiously produce the authentic self." Visual culture is a central mechanism by which Jewish Americans "[cultivate] Jewish bodies, texts, images, and faces."[23] By focusing on the formal constructs in visual culture, I assert that images and visual culture are texts as significant as verbal texts, that verbal texts are also visual texts, and that verbal and visual texts interact with each other in ways that can complicate, contradict, embellish, amplify, or undermine any given text seen in isolation.

Visual texts have their own "grammar," or set of rules by which the world may be organized and categories may relate to each other. Part of the reason it is important to examine Jewish American visual culture representing "the Orient" is to analyze how texts form new grammars when combining multiple grammars. This is not to claim that any texts ever follow the rules of a single grammar. Rather, visual and verbal texts always integrate multiple grammars. Jewish American visual culture representing "the Orient" combines grammars and tropes of Orientalism, Judaism, and Americanism to create new grammars. Jewish Americans combining these grammars did not agree as to the new rules, thus each of the following chapters addresses a different visual grammar and vision of Jewish Americanness through the cipher of "the Orient." Additionally, even if a text seeks to cite or reproduce a certain grammar, that text inevitably alters the grammar. Joan W. Scott's attention to "grammar" in her argument for the usefulness of gender as "a useful category of historical analysis" calls attention to more than just "discourse," as Foucault frames the evolving meaning of words. Discourse matters, but the formal grammar or rules of the larger context and multiple relations are an essential piece of how texts attempt to shape meaning. Moreover, the combination of grammars may lead to the subversion of one or more of those grammars. Jewish Americans combined Orientalism with Judaism and Americanism to subvert aspects of all three grammars. This produced new rules in those grammars that formally positioned Jews in places of authority and power, attempting to remedy Jewish insecurity in the United States and abroad.

Rather than toggle between concepts such as "grammar" or "discourse" to encapsulate the goals of Jewish Americans or any community, I turn to the larger category of "heritage." The production of knowledge of individual or communal heritage depends upon grammar, rhetoric, and discourse. "Heritage" is a version of the past created in a community's own image and vision, knowledge that Jewish American Orientalist visual culture produced in the first half of the twentieth century. Jewish Americans in the nineteenth century knowingly constructed the compatibility of Jewishness and democracy in the United States, a compatibility so successfully established that Jewish Americans have taken this construction to be a timeless natural fact in the twentieth and twenty-first centuries. In the diverse ways that Jews in the United States have made this argument, they drew heavily on the Jewish past. Jewish Americans did not have unmediated access to the past. Rather they turned to the production of heritage, meaning that Jewish Americans "designed their Jewish past as an expression of their own interests and expectations for Jewish life in the United States."[24] Invoking this notion of heritage—centrally about communal myth-making—Beth Wenger focuses not on the history of academics, but on popular narratives and understanding circulated throughout Jewish communities in the United States. In telling these stories, two myths have been central: 1) Europe served as a foil to the possibilities for Jews in the United States, and "the mantra that 'America is different' emerged as perhaps the most fundamental axiom of American life." 2) The Hebrew Bible as a foundation for American culture—first articulated in the Puritan vision of America as the New Israel—became a space for Jews to insert themselves into American historical narratives and traditions.[25] Through civic celebrations, Jewish Americans performed and produced identities that incorporated these myths and asserted the place for Jews in American democracy. Many groups attempted to envision themselves as part of American heritage and to claim their own stake in the Revolution and its resulting rights. Such efforts were as much about molding the heritage of minority groups as remolding the fabric of the United States as a whole.

Gender and Jewish American Visual Culture

Women's and gender studies, as academic pursuits, are intertwined with but conceptually separable from feminism. Narratives of Jewishness in the United States are incomplete without a complex analysis of the many roles gender has played in the construction of Jewish heritage. Although feminism as a political ideology can be separated from the study of gender, I echo Rita Gross (and many other scholars) in arguing that scholarship that omits women for an androcentric version of history obfuscates the reality of historical experience. It is androcentric history, not intersectional feminist history, that skews our vision. Gross specifically advocates for feminist scholarship because it creates a less biased view, not a skewed vision.[26] In this book, I pursue the goal of including women in the study of Jewish American visual culture in order to better understand both women and men. This is in service of both my academic and feminist goals of telling a more inclusive account of Jewish life. As Judith Plaskow asserts, "'Judaism' has always been richer, more complex, and more diverse than either 'normative' sources or most branches of modern Judaism would admit."[27] While Plaskow focuses on rabbinic texts to argue for the need to make women visible in Jewish history, she points to the need to find new methods of uncovering women's roles. It is not that women were ever absent from Jewish life, but certain normative texts have simply not considered women's lives important to record or integrate in the telling of Jewish heritage. The study of visual culture is an especially strong methodology for making women visible precisely because it is more or less nonnormative, quotidian, and gives us a window onto the images that Jewish men and women used to imagine themselves. I am wary of falling into the trap of a study of gender that suggests women's worlds are created by men as a result of the hierarchical and relational nature of men's and women's lives.[28] For this reason, I begin each chapter with a brief history of the movement that led to the production of the examples of visual culture at hand. This background shows how men and women created the worlds in which the primary visual sources existed and helps fill out how I understand the field of vision that each example of visual culture (re)presents. Chapter 3 on the National Federation of Temple Sisterhoods and chapter 6 on Hadassah pay particular attention to the ways that women created their own worlds through these groups and how women turned to the production of visual culture to materialize the power they sought through organizing.

Furthermore, the question of feminism is relevant not only on the second-order level of my own motivations as a scholar and author, but also on the first-order level of the people I study. Most of the women in the National Federation of Temple Sisterhoods and Hadassah did not consider themselves or their work to be "feminist," including these organizations' projects that I discuss in chapters 3 and 6. However, that subjects of study would not use terms such as "feminism" does not preclude scholars from using those terms to understand their subjects. Many of these women engaged in what could be labeled either "feminism" or at least "protofeminism," most minimally defined as the belief that women are equal to, if not the same as, men in their ability to contribute to communal life. And although these women may not have considered themselves feminists, contemporary feminists look back to the work of women in the early twentieth century as laying a base for feminist projects in the late twentieth and twenty-first centuries. Scholars such as R. Marie Griffith and Saba Mahmood provide excellent models for research that shifts from "feminism" to how women have always negotiated their positions in various religious communities, even those who have defined themselves against feminism. Even when women appear to reinforce a hierarchy with men at the top, they may create space and power for themselves.[29] Rather than spend space in this book arguing for or against the feminist nature of any Jewish Americans, I focus not on drawing this boundary but rather on the ways that men and women included or excluded women from Jewish American visual culture and various visions of Jewish heritage and future. Envisioning roles for women necessitated looking toward the future. But this view toward the future is interwoven with imaginations of the past or Jewish heritage. Men and women argued for what they considered the future of Jews in part through a focus on the future of Jewish women, and Jewish heritage plays a central role in how Jewish Americans in the early twentieth century attempted to authenticate various visions of women.

In primary sources, gender is not necessarily explicitly invoked through language marking "men" and "women" or "masculine and feminine," though it sometimes is. Joan W. Scott succinctly addresses an assumption now prominent in gender studies, that "figurative allusions by employing grammatical terms to evoke traits of character or sexuality" must be dissected.[30] These allusions may cite known tropes such as supposedly positive concepts of motherhood and "the fairer sex" or derogatory critiques of women as "hysterical" and "shrill," all of which place women lower than men in a gender hierarchy. I examine the visual grammar through which Jewish Americans have figured gender, attending to the ways that gender may be detached from the physical bodies of males and females. Riv-Ellen Prell has demonstrated how Jewish and non-Jewish Americans detached the stereotype of the JAP (Jewish American Princess) from women and from Jewishness to use as a critique of capitalism or questions of assimilation.[31] In studying gender, we must examine how masculinity and femininity are both constructed in connection with and apart from physical bodies. This idea of not only malleable but gloating gender constructions detached from the supposed physical sex of the subject plays an important role in Orientalism. For one, "women have long served as a template for Jewish and Muslim apologists seeking acceptance in European and American societies, and as lightning rods for those seeking to exclude Jews and Muslims." Addressing gender norms, in other words, is a key part of ongoing arguments for social belonging and political citizenship. Jewish Americans have continuously surveilled gender performance and sought to represent Jewish gender in ways that were acceptable according to Jewish and non-Jewish Americans. Visual culture has been a particularly powerful mode for negotiating Jewish American norms because of the mobility of visual culture and the ability of visual culture to serve as an aspiration, ideal, or fantasy rather than to present reality. Moreover, "the treatment of women became an index for the degree of 'orientalism' marking Judaism in the nineteenth century, and of 'fanaticism' and 'irrationality' marking Islam in more recent decades."[32] Non-Jews in Europe and the United States have othered Jews and Muslims via Orientalism, and the mechanism for that Orientalizing is often gender. A sophisticated study of gender shows "how gender inequality structures all other inequalities," making connections that do not seem obvious, such as between internal Jewish hierarchies of gender and external relationships and representations of non-Jews.[33] Gender is a means to better understand Jewish American men and women, but also to see how Jewish American men and women used gender in Orientalism to, for example, feminize Arab men as a foil to Jewish masculinity (chapters 1, 3, 4, and 6) or to discredit "Oriental" women as mothers (chapter 6). Jewish Americans turned to Orientalism to construct social hierarchies that placed Jews at the top. These hierarchies also reveal, however, the ways that Jewish men and women attempted to remedy their own social anxieties by perpetuating the inequality of others.

That women have gender can be obvious. Masculine visual culture—meaning representations of men, visual culture made or collated by men, visual culture designed to be consumed by men, or visual culture emphasizing masculine gender norms with or without the representation of men's bodies—is and was often assumed to be unmarked. To use a mathematical analogy, masculinity is the 1 before the x. Masculinity is assumed, it need not be marked, and marking it is frequently interpreted as unnecessary or even a mistake. It can be difficult to mark masculinity precisely because part of its power lies in being unmarked and therefore appearing as the "natural standard." An important aspect of gender studies is to tease out the embeddedness, embodiedness, learnedness, and malleability of all genders. Sarah Imhoff helpfully articulates that although a "construct," this does not mean that iterations of gender, or religion for that matter, are "simply acts of will."[34] Individuals and even groups cannot simply make changes to gender without a communal process of naturalization—of acceptance, rejection, and inculturation. Our worldviews are cumulative, and so instant change is difficult to accomplish. Accordingly, we tend to see what we expect to see and can only recognize what we have already been taught. In instances of cultural contact, misrecognition can fuel misunderstanding because vision is a cumulative process, dependent not only on the biological process of eyes sending messages to our brains, but our brains making sense of our eyes' messages given our experiences and knowledge to date.[35] For example, a news story spread in January 2010 of a flight out of LaGuardia Airport that a pilot grounded due to an airline attendant's alert that there was a potential bomb scare. She did not recognize a Jewish teenager's tefillin, small leather boxes that the boy had wrapped around his head and arm to perform morning prayers on the plane, as tools of prayer. The FBI met the plane in Philadelphia to investigate. Commenting on what was an unexpected experience for the teenager given the prevalence of tefillin in Orthodox Jewish visual culture, FBI agent J. J. Klaber explained the flight attendant's reaction by saying, "This is something most Americans probably have not seen before." Vision was key to interpreting the entire event. The FBI agent did not consider the flight attendant's lack of recognition of the tefillin as ritual tools to be a failure of vision or an unacceptable reaction. In contrast, *New York Daily News* writers who undoubtedly had prior knowledge of the common use of tefillin commented, "What schmucks."[36] Their language invoked Jewish vision through the use of the Yiddish insult. Multiple sets of visual knowledge collided here, indicating the possibility for entirely different interpretations of an interaction depending upon how people see visual culture.

Visual culture is useful for understanding the ways that gender, religion, heritage, and other "constructs" come into being because vision demonstrates the scientific and social processes taking place in moments of recognition. Moreover, primary sources of visual culture give us durable examples to follow changes in iconography. Attending to the formal changes in iconography can quickly condense the process of visual change over time right before our eyes, giving the opportunity to 1) notice that change more easily; 2) see how experiments arose, which are no less meaningful in their moments of appearance even if they did not continue to be cited; and 3) see continuities and how Jewish Americans and other groups introduced new traditions into visual culture and naturalized these new representations into conceptions of heritage.

All the members of the organizations or movements in this book were publicly labeled "men" and "women." The gender plurality that shapes subjectivity and public debate in the twenty-first century did not exist in the same way in the first half of the twentieth century. This is not to say gender plurality did not exist, however. Jews and non-Jews experimented with gender through secret or semi-public life worldwide. From clothing to fine arts, visual culture played a key role in these Jews lives. Their experimentation with and critique of gender norms likely haunts the firm gender binaries presented in the visual culture of "the Orient" that I analyze in this book. The masculinity and femininity that Jewish Americans emphasized in Orientalist visual culture actively and continuously worked to order the world according to a gender binary. Orientalism critiques Arab and Muslim culture as being backward for failing to live up to binary gender norms, but we might ask ourselves what other invisible anxieties underlay the heteronormativity in Jewish American Orientalism. This also does not mean that some members of the organizations and movements I discuss did not chafe at the norms of the very existence of binaries. Sexuality and the production of heteronormativity are also key aspects of the study of gender. Like masculinity and whiteness, heterosexuality also appears as a "1 before the x." Heterosexuality can appear so naturalized as to seem invisible, but this invisibility is of an entirely different nature from that of the invisibility of Jewish women in Jewish heritage. Jewish American women struggled to make themselves visible. As scholars, we struggle to make masculinity visible and interrogate its forms and intersectionality with other identities. We must analyze the implications of both masculinity and femininity, whether attached to "male" and "female" bodies or detached and tied to various representations of heritage.

The Ottoman Empire, the British Mandate, and the United States

The Ottoman Empire controlled the region of Palestine until World War I, and then the British Mandate gained control over the territory. Under

Ottoman rule, the empire's millet system granted a good deal of local jurisdiction to religious groups in their own courts over matters addressed in their traditions' religious law, especially family and relational issues such as marriage and divorce. The region of Palestine therefore went from the Ottoman millet system to the British Mandate system prior to becoming the State of Israel. Legal pluralism—coexistence of more than one court system in a single location—existed in both the Ottoman Empire and the British Empire. Although the British Empire claimed a policy of a " 'status quo' agreement," the legal possibilities for Jews and non-Jews living in Palestine of course changed during Ottoman reforms and under the Mandate system. Moreover, rabbinic authorities in Palestine at the time of the shift to the British Mandate claimed to "fix and impose" Jewish tradition in their courts, when actually they introduced new interpretations and versions of Jewish law into the operation of Jewish courts.[37] The British Empire used the Mandate system not only in Palestine but all over the globe in occupied territories. Although Britain presented the Mandate System as a shift from colonialism, Mandates imposed many similar structures to colonialism although reconfigured. However, the Mandate system was not at all monolithic. Many British people with power as legislators within the Mandate system believed in a hierarchy of peoples from most to least civilized, and this hierarchy structured the Mandate system. Rather than a system that included various territories and their inhabitants as equal members of the British Empire, the Mandate system was based on an ideology that the less civilized and those "incapable" of civilizing must be ruled undemocratically for their own good and for the good of the world.[38]

As the sociopolitical context in Palestine changed, several circumstances in the United States pushed "the Orient" to the fore as a *site* of Jewish heritage for Jewish Americans in the early twentieth century. Among the most visible displays of "the Orient" in early twentieth-century United States was the 1904 St. Louis World's Fair exhibition. The St. Louis replica of Jerusalem appeared in the middle of a massive wave of Jewish immigration to the United States. Many Christian Americans began to question the implications of the increasing number of Jews and other immigrants for their vision of Americanness. The ten-acre full-scale replica of buildings, streets, and "natives" included Jews, Christians, and Muslims. These Jerusalem "natives" staged a racial difference between "the Orient" and the United States, producing American whiteness and empire while also articulating the necessity of settler colonialism in Palestine. Though the latter work fell to Jewish Zionists, the exhibition implicitly asserted and naturalized what was an imaginative Protestant Christian frame of interpretation of "the Orient" and the United States.[39] The Christian replica of Jerusalem placed Jews in antiquity and in "the Orient," suggesting their contemporaneous status. The St. Louis Fair's image of "the Orient" reveals anxieties about national identity and interreligious contact. Though the Jerusalem exhibit was not the first or only Protestant Christian representation of "the Orient," its treatment of "natives" and emphasis on the material, especially visual, is archetypical. The exhibition both exemplified and embodied an ongoing Protestant American logic about the "Holy Land" and set a standard to which the full spectrum of later popular to elite visions of "the Orient" implicitly or explicitly responded.

Just as the 1904 St. Louis Fair took place in the midst of major changes in American views of immigration, so did the 1933 World's Fair. In 1921, the United States passed the Emergency Quota Act, limiting Jewish immigration along with that of many other groups. In 1924, the Johnson-Reed Act passed, further limiting immigration: no more than 2 percent of the number of immigrants who had lived in the United States in 1890 could enter the country following 1924. Technologically, it was faster and easier to move to the United States. Politically, however, United States laws made it harder than ever for many. The immigration acts legislated the anxieties and fears of immigrants among many Americans in the early twentieth century. The legislation also produced anxieties for Jewish Americans. Though Jewish Americans who had already entered the United States legally were equal to Christian American citizens, antisemitism was on the rise in the United States and the immigration acts created a sense that Jewish Americans needed to continue to prove their status as loyal Americans even after entry. The immigration acts also effectively closed the possibility for ongoing Jewish immigration to the United States. This meant that as antisemitism increased across Europe, Jews needed to seek new options for refuge for Jews who wished to leave Europe. Jewish Americans continued to present images of the United States as unique in world heritage for protecting Jews, which was somewhat true for those who had already arrived. But many Jewish Americans within the United States tried to make sense of the difference between their circumstances and Jews around the world. The indefinite end of Jewish immigration to the United States also suggested that Jews could no longer rely on the arrival of new immigrants to infuse Jewish American life with a sense of continuity with Jewish heritage. Jewish Americans would now have to maintain Jewishness on their own if they hoped to see Jewish heritage continue in the future.[40] Orientalism offered a schema for Jewish Americans to understand themselves in the United States, while also envisioning a place for Jews abroad.

Jewish organizations and individuals who made some use of representations of "the Orient" in their visual culture during the twentieth century are numerous. It would be impossible to include them all in one book; I have not attempted to compile an exhaustive assessment of all the forms of movements that had some stake in depicting "the Orient." Rather, I have selected a series of movements that might help us understand more about how Jewish Americans diffused "the Orient" throughout American life in the early twentieth century and how this can help us think about the complexities of Jewish American heritage. My goal is to show that there were many representations of an imagined "Orient" in the early twentieth-century United States, and I hope that additional studies will address other views. This study stretches from 1901 to 1938, with a focus on the interwar period. This time period saw an outpouring of Jewish visual culture in the United States. The earliest example that I analyze began in 1901, the first year that a volume of the *Jewish Encyclopedia* was published. Shortly thereafter, many different kinds of materials depicting "the Orient" became increasingly available. Political developments in Palestine and the United States prompted greater interest, and the printing of materials became steadily more available to the masses in the United States. This study concludes with 1938 as the bookend to a pre-state period when imagining "the Orient" was possible prior to the existence of explicit political roadmaps to a Jewish state in Palestine. Prior to 1938, many different Jewish Americans imagined "the Orient"—past, present, and future—in many different ways. Jewish Americans continued to picture "the Orient" in diverse ways after 1938, but these began to be pitted for or against more concrete geopolitical visions for the region. The Palestine Royal Commission, or Peel Commission, released a proposal for partitioning Palestine in 1938 that changed the largely speculative nature of Palestine politics, altering the sense that Palestine was anything that Jewish Americans could imagine it to be. Though the World Zionist Organization rejected the partition plan, against the pleading of the organization's head at the time, Chaim Weizmann (1874–1952), this plan established a tangible map and definition of statehood against which future visions of Palestine and "the Orient" would have to be compared. Furthermore, the outbreak of World War II added new complexities to the image of Jews worldwide as well as new limits for Jews and non-Jews. Though I address some images circulated in Jewish American visual culture after 1938 and even after the creation of the State of Israel by the United Nations in 1948, it is as comparison to materials produced prior to the Peel Commission, and a robust study of the post-1938 period is beyond the scope of this text.

Chapter Overview

In each of the following chapters, I bring to life the possibility for imagining "the Orient" by Jewish American organizations and the meanings of the characters and sets or landscapes that multiplied with each new representation. The first chapter lays out an analytical definition of Orientalism, complicating Edward Said's classic work, its interpretation by many other scholars since the publication of *Orientalism* in 1978, and analysis of Zionism and Jewish American life more broadly. For the purpose of my argument, Orientalism means the construction of heritage by looking to an imagined site of the "past" in "the Orient" to create a vision of the site of the future. "The Orient" simultaneously served as "model" and "other" for American Orientalists, so that the significance of the "Orient" is imaginative. By considering Orientalism as an imaginative visual process, this understanding of Orientalism calls attention to the mental images and boundaries constructed in conceptions of "the Orient." Like Said, I argue that Orientalism has less to do with the "East" than it does with the culture of the "West."[41] My use of Orientalism as a category offers an examination of the complex ways Americans, including Jews, imagined others in order to imagine themselves.[42] I consider all of the sets and characters within the Jewish American panorama equally "Oriental," that is, equally integral to Jewish American heritage construction. Complicated and contradictory representations of the "Orient" and "Orientals" are prolific in these constructions. This definition of Orientalism distinguishes the importance of images of Palestine as "the Orient" as a phenomenon with greater import beyond Zionism because Zionists were not the sole arbiters of the image of "the Orient" or the place of Palestine in Jewish heritage.

Chapter 2 looks at images of "the Orient" in the publications of the Zionist Organization of America (initially the Federation of American Zionists) from 1901 to 1938. First characterized as "old-new" by Theodor Herzl, the journals of the FAZ/ZOA carved out American Zionist visual culture by playing with concepts of time. Images of the Temple as well as architectural relics such as the Western Wall and Tower of David represented, on the one hand, idealized moments in the Jewish past, even though the connection to these particular landmarks was a development of the nineteenth century and many relics did not actually date to the moments their names implied. On the other hand, Zionist Americans constructed a timeless conception of the landscape and architecture of Palestine and Jewish Americans' connection to it, particularly as images of the Western Wall remained static even as chaotic political events unfolded on the ground. Additionally, feminized East European Jews, Mizrahi Jews, and Arabs along with hypermasculine chalutzim (pioneers) figured centrally in the visual culture and discourse of the FAZ/ZOA. Gender and race were interarticulated in these images, as Jewish American masculinity is explicitly constructed through looking toward "the Orient."

Chapter 3 analyzes the art calendars of the National Federation of Temple Sisterhoods, the organization for Reform Jewish women. Like the ZOA's periodicals, Reform women's art calendars primarily presented images of men when figuring Jewish bodies. But the production of calendars by Reform Jewish women reveals their construction of their own sense of heritage similar to Hadassah, as discussed later in chapter 6, even as the NFTS circulated images that did not make women visible in Jewish American visual culture. I discuss biennial conference yearbooks, letters, posters, and newsletters to establish how the NFTS created a new space for themselves in the practice of Reform Judaism in America that gave women important roles *without* challenging traditional leadership roles of men that were not available to women. The images of the art calendars suggest a narrative of increasing American exceptionalism, beginning with largely biblical images of "the Orient" and later incorporating more and more explicit critique of Europe as a place of decline for Jewish civilization. Visual representations of Jewish antiquity and biblical scenes and figures show how the NFTS calendars defined what it meant to be Jewish in the United States through a different vision of "the Orient" from the ZOA. The NFTS did use images that were also circulated by Zionists, but in very different contexts. This chapter places cultural exchange among Jews and between Jews and non-Jews at the center of what is at stake in Jewish Orientalism. The NFTS calendars recontextualized images that had appeared in other contexts, including Renaissance and modern Christian art, disarming Christian claims on "the Orient" and positioning the biblical past as the origin of Jewish American heritage that grounds "Western" civilization. The calendars also used images popularized at Zionist exhibits while recontextualizing those images in Reform values and practice rather than Zionist politics.

Through a study of Jewish scholarship in the United States as embodied in the *Jewish Encyclopedia* (*JE*), published from 1901 to 1906, chapter 4 argues that the academic study of Jewish history was a viable medium for Jewish memory that created a new normative Jewish community in the United States. The *JE* sought to historicize Jewish life in Palestine, and as a part of the *JE*'s contributions for Jewish and non-Jewish audiences, publishers of the *JE* touted its inclusion of thousands of images as a key aspect of its contribution to historical study; however, these images frequently undermined or complicated the goals of Jewish scholarship. Attention to the arrangement of verbal and visual text demonstrates that the encyclopedia at times fell short of a historicized study of Jewish life, often idealizing "the Orient" in ways similar to other Jewish American organizations. Images idealized the Temple, favored depictions of the "ancient" even in articles dedicated to "modern" Palestine, and "Orientalized" Jews and Arabs in the Middle East. Despite this, through its periodization of Jewish history in "the Orient," the *JE* did offer a narrative of Jewish heritage that differed from the nascent Zionist movement's conceptualization of the Holy Land as contemporaneous, that is, a neglected, static physical and political entity.

Questions about the performance of heritage take center stage in chapter 5, which shows how Jewish Americans transformed historical narratives into popular forms for a broader audience through visual culture at the 1933 "Century of Progress" World's Fair in Chicago. At that fair, the Synagogue Council of America (SCA) cultivated the Jewish exhibit at the Hall of Religion, and the ZOA orchestrated a "Jewish Day," which culminated in the pageant *The Romance of a People*. These performances belied an external struggle, performing cultural pluralism and justifying Jewish American citizenship to non-Jewish Americans, and an internal struggle, as the SCA and Jewish Day pageant offered competing visions of Jewish unity. The SCA represented the rabbinical and lay organizations of Reform, Conservative, and Orthodox Judaism in the United States. Tied to these movements, its display articulated a vision of transnational Judaism characterized primarily as "religion." This limited the activities and events on which the organization was willing to comment, excluding, for example, the release of various White Papers by the British Mandate in Palestine, which were deemed exclusively political. The SCA did include Palestine in its representation of Judaism for the Hall of Religion, but it did not explicitly depict the Jewish community in Palestine as exceptional in comparison to Jews living in any other international community. The Judaism exhibit offered Jewish contributions in "the Orient" as evidence of Jewish compatibility with and participation in modern democracy. *The Romance of a People* also avoided overt references to political rhetoric, instead seeking to create an emotional connection to "the Orient" through a spectacular performance of Jewish history by thousands of performers on a replica of the Temple that served as the pageant stage in Soldier Field. Both performances demonstrate the significance of envisioning of the Jewish past and present in general and the representation of "the Orient" in particular for the performance of Jewish heritage in the United States, yet each display selected and exhibited moments of Jewish history in ways that bolstered an argument for its movements' own vision of the future of Judaism.

Chapter 6 addresses Hadassah, the Zionist women's organization, founded in 1913. From the 1920s until World War II, Hadassah was both the largest Zionist organization in the United States—gaining more members than any men's organization, including the Zionist Organization of America—and the largest American women's volunteer organization with over one hundred thousand members by the 1940s. Hadassah funneled much of their efforts into a major "propaganda" campaign ("propaganda" being their own term). They sought to indisputably establish Zionism as a democratic movement and familiarize the "non-Zionist public" with their vision of "the Orient." However, Hadassah's conception of "the Orient" and democracy was specific, and the equality of men and women were central to Hadassah's democracy. Though Hadassah cooperated with the ZOA and eventually affiliated with it, Hadassah's visual culture in the "propaganda" campaign presented new images rather than sharing visual culture with the ZOA. Hadassah's "propaganda" shows women and children in "the Orient," a major difference from the organizations discussed in the previous chapters. Hadassah's visual culture showed several things at once: Jewish Americans as "modern"; women in Jewish life; and maternalism as essential to the upbuilding of "the Orient." Images of children stand in for "the Jewish people," as "innocence" provokes an emotional response. The youth of children mirrors that of "the Orient" as a *site* for Jewish nationhood, still in its gestation prior to the creation a new political entity following the Ottoman Empire and the British Mandate. Hadassah's "propaganda" visually links Jewish Americans as mothers to the children of "the Orient," visually asserting a metaphor of inhabitants of "the Orient" as immature children requiring the instruction of the mature "modern" "Westerners," Jewish Americans.

Chapter 1

"The Orient" as Jewish Heritage

And now, what's going to happen to us without barbarians?
They were, those people, a kind of solution.

—C. P. Cavafy, "Waiting for the Barbarians," 1904

An advertisement for a cruise to Palestine appeared in the Zionist Organization of America's (ZOA) magazine, *The New Palestine* (hereafter, *NP*), on January 22, 1926. The ad centers on an image of the Western Wall, the remnants of the Second Temple complex, destroyed in 70 CE. However, the advertisement does not identify it as the Western Wall, apparently assuming that the image would already resonate with the target audience of the advertisement. A handful of men stand in front of the wall in what might resonate as "biblical" attire—they wear long white robes, but no turbans or kaffiyehs. Three of them pray at the wall while another stands in the background. One man with a long white beard in the foreground looks up reverently.[1] Most Jewish Americans would not take the transatlantic cruise to the Mediterranean, though many Jews and non-Jews did, beginning in the late nineteenth century. The emotional nostalgia for Jerusalem, and the Western Wall specifically, is linked to Jewish American heritage in this advertisement, a link that would become more prominent as the 1920s continued. I call this nostalgia Orientalism, engaged in many ways but prominently through the production, circulation, and viewing of visual culture depicting Palestine *in* the past and present and *as* the past and present. Through this mediated process of visual representation and interpretation, Palestine became "the Orient." Even for those who would

Direct to Palestine

The Cunard's Annual Winter

Voyage to the MEDITERRANEAN

on the

MAURETANIA, Feb. 17

(The World's Fastest Steamer)

with short stops en route at several tourist's ports on the Mediterranean. Surroundings, accommodations in all classes, service and cuisine of the best.

A Trip of Real Pleasure Amidst Luxury

Special Kosher Kitchen for Jewish Travelers

Early Reservation Advisable

For Information and Itinerary Apply to any Cunard Agent, or to

Palestine and Oriental Tours
122 FIFTH AVENUE
NEW YORK
Tel. Chelsea 0651

or

CUNARD LINE
25 BROADWAY
NEW YORK

Figure 1.1. Advertisement in *The New Palestine*.

never make the trip, the advertisement invited Jewish Americans to imagine a journey to Palestine on the *Mauretania*. Was it a journey across space? Or time? This depended on a traveler's presumptions. The juxtaposition of the sketched image of the Western Wall juxtaposed with the verbal emphasis on the power of the *Mauretania*, "The World's Fastest Steamer," suggested that this modern technology was a portal to the past. The *Mauretania* was built with state-of-the-art steam turbines to be the fastest ship in the world. It held the record for fastest transatlantic crossing from 1907 to 1929, and its interior was luxuriously designed in the new Edwardian fashion. Even the name "Mauretania" gestured toward connections between past and future, as it commemorated the ancient Roman province in North Africa. New technology seemingly allowed momentary return to the past, not dissimilar from conventional Jewish ritual such as the haggadah as a tool at Passover. The ship and the haggadah do not just allow memory but insist on a return. The Cunard Line's advertisement turned the *Mauretania* into a tool that could fulfill the same goal as Passover, a step back into sacred time and place. The advertisement implies that new sailing technology could better fulfill this goal than the haggadah. The content and advertisements in the NP expanded the place for travel as Jewish ritual and a means to encounter Palestine as a way to embody Jewish heritage.

Images of Palestine contributed to a Jewish visual culture that intimately connected images of the Holy Land to a sense of Jewish community. I analyze how visual culture influenced historical narratives, including the ways that Palestine was depicted as a "geography of identity." Jewish visual culture in the first half of the twentieth century integrated new technologies and aesthetics with new historical methods and consciousness. Jewish Americans were not the only ones looking East to define themselves. Jennifer Axsom Adler refers to the abundance of materials to which Christians turned, at many time periods but especially beginning in the nineteenth century, as "material gospel." However, the practice of turning to material gospel did not begin with Protestant Americans but flourished at various points throughout history, such as among Renaissance Christians and the early church.[2] Jews created a visual heritage by sharing some Christian practices with images while subverting Christians' gospel claims about those images at the same time.

Palestine simultaneously served as "model" and "other," so the significance of "the Orient" is imaginative. It is the transformation of Palestine into an imaginative vision that constitutes the work of Orientalism and the difference between Palestine and "the Orient." Rather than territorial or colonial, this understanding of Orientalism calls attention to the mental images and boundaries constructed in conceptions of the East. Edward Said profoundly shaped our understanding(s) of Orientalism. I return to his articulation of Orientalism, but I also question some of his assumptions to take a broader view of the cultural forms possible in the first half of the twentieth century. I turn to various critiques at moments throughout this book, but those critiques are strongest when they come from a full picture of what has made Orientalism so compelling for some and how Orientalism itself has been diverse and fragmented.

Archaeological Heritage in Jewish Visual Culture

Palestine has been an imaginative screen for Jews in many times and places. I contextualize Jewish American Orientalism with a history of how Jews looked toward varying sites in Palestine to imagine Jewishness. Although this geographic imagination has frequently been a constitutive aspect of Judaism, Jews have not always constructed a "West" through that vision or seen themselves as part of the vision. Prior to the nineteenth century, "the Orient" played a role in seeing Jewishness in many more expansive ways beyond earthly politics. Jews have engaged the Jerusalem above and the Jerusalem below when looking to Palestine, leading them to different sights and sites. Understanding Jewish American Orientalism therefore requires a sense of how images of "the Orient" compare and contrast with Jewish constructions of heritage in the past. Rami Arav notes that the Western Wall (the wall revered as the only remnant of Herod's Temple in Jerusalem) has been "perhaps, the only real relic in the entire Land of Israel" throughout the bulk of Jewish history, though the supposed tombs of ancient figures have been popular pilgrimage sites.[3]

Images of remnants of ancient Israel, whether photographed or otherwise artistically produced, abound in publications from the first half of the twentieth century. The Western Wall, the Synagogue of Beth Alpha, the Tower of David, and Masada were and have continued to be especially popular images in the Yishuv (the pre-state Jewish colony in Palestine) and the State of Israel.[4] Knowledge of these remnants or "relics" sought by archaeologists in the nineteenth and twentieth centuries reveals the significance of archaeology for the construction of heritage and ideology in Jewish American practice.[5] The visual discourse of Jewish Americans turned to archaeology to create a heritage narrative that began in the land of Israel and culminated in the United States. Early symbols included the Tower of David and the Tomb of Rachel.[6] The Tower of David rests on the site of an ancient fortress built by Herod the Great, but it includes a minaret and mosque built by Muslims in the fourteenth century, which were incorporated as Ottoman symbols after the Turks captured Jerusalem in 1517. The Tomb of Rachel is also a Muslim structure, mythically viewed as the tomb of the matriarch. Though these names evoke a Jewish national past—but also a Christian or Muslim past, depending on the viewer—they were not historically tied to the ancestors that they invoke. Nevertheless, they became strong symbols in the visual culture of many different groups of Jews because of the popular appeal of their names and the proud identification that they made possible.[7]

Throughout the medieval period, the Western Wall was not a significant monument for Jewish pilgrims. As late as the fifteenth century, Jewish pilgrims to Jerusalem chose the Mount of Olives outside the city as their primary destination. The Western Wall courtyard only became a distinctly defined space in the sixteenth century under Ottoman Sultan Suleiman the Magnificent, and pilgrims began to record visits to the Wall and connect the space to the "Presence of God" during the early sixteenth century. Even the Israeli Defense Ministry has acknowledged the lack of significance of the Wall throughout the Middle Ages. The Wall became a powerful religious symbol during the nineteenth century.[8] In the nineteenth and twentieth centuries, many archaeological projects began as efforts conducted by West Europeans and Americans to expand knowledge of Palestine and to augment the status of Western nations, but these efforts also became significant for the construction of Jewish and Zionist heritage in the land of Israel and in the diaspora.[9] Jewish Americans shared images of the Western Wall with each other and with their non-Jewish American compatriots. However, Jewish American organizations constructed a unique heritage, each instance of which fused images of Jewish and United States history. Thereby Jewish Americans simultaneously experienced themselves as Jewish, and thus distinct from their fellow Americans, but also as sharing in practices of "Orientalism," or looking toward the Holy Land to understand life in the United States.

In 1839, photographers took the first daguerreotypes and print negatives of the Holy Land. Shortly thereafter, numerous images began to appear of the Holy Land, including Jerusalem, Palestine, and the larger Middle East. Primarily non-Jewish photographers from Western Europe produced the earliest photographic images, though their photographs became integral in the presentation of Jewish histories—not only in encyclopedias, but in museum exhibits, calendars, newspapers, and many other material acts of producing heritage. The earliest photographers of the Holy Land made daguerreotypes, but the oldest original work surviving today was captured by calotypists. More so than the daguerreotypists, the calotypists sought scientific and scholarly photographs. The length of exposure (seven minutes) made it quite difficult to capture any images of people. After 1851, new technology made photography much easier and more portable. These images, though revolutionary in their technology and ability to capture what was in front of the lens to be developed as portable photographs that could bring the Holy Land home to Europe and the United States, were not unmediated presentations of Palestine. Photographers saw Palestine through the lens not only of their camera but their worldview. In addition to technological restraints and advances, photographers' worldview influenced what they framed and how they framed it. Furthermore, audiences "back home" viewed these images from their own subjectivities, projecting onto the photographs the heritages, politics, and worldviews they brought to these representations of the East. Early photography was influenced deeply by other conventions in the arts, including romanticism and the picturesque.[10] Most importantly, though, photographers framed their images, and audiences viewed the reproductions through the lens of Orientalism. Orientalism mediated the entire production of photographs of Palestine: the choice of general location, the specific content of images, and their circulation and viewing by European and American audiences.

Historicizing the Multiplicity of "the Orient"

Said's thesis posits a singular Western Orientalism tied to colonialism, whereas the multiplicity of Jewish Orientalisms assures that Orientalism cannot be limited to a definition of colonialism or oppression. Western Orientalists could be motivated for reasons not even linked to positions of authority. John Efron argues that in addition to colonial expansion and domination, "Orientalism could also be a profound expression of one's own cultural anxiety and insecurity, one that could provoke deep-seated fears of inferiority."[11] For Jewish Europeans fighting for emancipation, romanticized conceptions of "Oriental Jews" provided a model for a new form of Jewishness that would negate their sense of flawed Ashkenazi history and Orthodoxy, i.e., critiques of how Jewishness should be practiced in the future, sometimes influenced by internalized antisemitism. By decoupling Orientalism from colonialism, we can highlight a significant aspect of Orientalism, whether linked to colonialism, a sense of superiority, oppression, or self-doubt. In both colonial and noncolonial instances of Orientalism, Orientalists work out concerns over heritage at home—whether home is the United States or Europe, Judaism or Christianity. Orientalism, then, is certainly not solely about colonialism, even when it is also that. Orientalism provides an opportunity for defining the self through the "other" and reveals a necessary romanticization of "others" when defining oneself.

Said's critique of those who may suggest Orientalism is inevitable in the human imagination begs a historicization of the development of Orientalism as a cognitive process.[12] In one sense, Said seeks precisely to understand how Orientalism has operated. But, as a literary scholar, Said does not engage historicism to an extent that would better contextualize development, complexity, and production of knowledge through and of Orientalism. Jeffrey Librett's understanding of the link between historicism and Orientalism undergirds his critique of Edward Said. Librett criticizes Said's choice to base his study on French and British Orientalism to the exclusion of German Orientalism, Said's self-reflection as part of the fabric of his methodology, produced a kind of distortion, "an underemphasis, and insufficient appreciation, of the inextricable involvement of modern Orientalism both with a metaphysics of absolute foundations in crisis and with Christian anti-Judaism (and typology in particular)."[13] Because Orientalism is linked to historicism but Said is not a historian, Librett argues that historicism is a methodological blind spot for Said. For Librett, historicism itself is entangled with imperialism and Said is thus unable to critique this element of historicism and therefore Orientalism. Linking the emergence of Orientalism and historicism as responses to the "groundlessness" of eighteenth-century identity (discussed later), Librett complicates Said's claim that the West was always in a position of power toward the East. Librett argues that the West "imposes its violence . . . on the Orient paradoxically out of a position of cultural weakness and need, though not a position of material or military weakness."[14]

Both historicism and attention to visual culture address blind spots in analyzing Orientalism. Yaron Peleg's *Orientalism and the Hebrew Imagination* takes up the role of Jewish imagination among Zionists and later Israelis. However, he argues that Zionism circumscribed Orientalism when not fantasizing about Jewish life in Israel but turning to local Arabs to create Hebrew national culture. He emphasizes writing in his methodology, as he sees the production of literature as the primary key to the ways that Zionists addressed the conflicts between their desire to remain distinct from Arabs while simultaneously appropriating Arabs' land and culture. His focus on writing and his tendency to see works centering on Arabs as somehow less imaginative than other works of Orientalism led Peleg to a narrow view of the pitfalls of Orientalism and even to assert that "Hebrew-Orientalist works . . . are not only few and far between, [but] many of them tend to be mediocre." Peleg pays astute attention to the central role of Arabs and Bedouins in Zionism. But his location of this attention outside of the bounds of Orientalism is odd, as Arabs occupy the central concern of Said in his classic analysis of representations of the Middle East. Moreover, Peleg does not stress the place of Bedouins and Arabs in Zionist imagination as teleological, though he helpfully points to the ways that Bedouins and Arabs led Jews traveling to Palestine to perceive something familiar in the unknown land. For years, Orientalists had used Bedouins to imagine the Bible in Europe, especially in visual culture but in writing as well. When increasing numbers of European travelers and immigrants found themselves in Palestine, they perceived Bedouins as people "whose religion, manners, and habitat evoked the Hebrew patriarchs."[15] Orientalists teleologically assumed they discovered something familiar, whereas the appropriation of Bedouin and Arab life to fill in the unknowns of the realities of Israelite antiquity had begun long before the expansion of Orientalist movement and travel in the late nineteenth and early twentieth centuries.

Orientalist representations operate for many purposes. Whether certain outcomes were "inadvertent or not" is not entirely, as Said argues, "beside the point." If we can recover primary goals and distinguish what may have been initially epiphenomenal but nevertheless became entrenched practices, we can understand something about the place of Orientalism in American heritage. For Said, European powers and Zionists decided the fate of "the Orient" in the early twentieth century. With reference to Joseph Conrad's *Heart of Darkness*, Said asserts of Zionism, "The important thing was to dignify simple conquest with an idea."[16] This begs the question: Is Zionism nothing other than rationalization of a brute conquest? In what other ways has Orientalism more broadly fit into Jewish practices and production of heritage? Understanding this, we can return to the question of whether and how Jewish Orientalism has affected and disempowered non-Jews in Palestine, and even some Jews, intentionally or not.

In addition to scholarly historicization of Orientalism, a historicization of temporality is essential to understanding the complexity of Orientalism as a whole and its various iterations because time creates both intimacy and distance. A complicated conception of time-as-space characterized American hopes for the future and understandings of Jewish ethnicity. A near obsession with space has been present in the institutions and social structure in the United States. In media and universities in the United States, James Carey argues, "even time was converted to space as the social sciences, enamored of prediction, characterized the future as a *frontier* to be conquered" (emphasis mine). Envisioning the future this way, Americans consciously competed to define what the future "should be." This attempt to "conquer" the future, as Carey puts it, was of course impossible. However, focusing on the future is a very distinct way of defining the present and constructing conceptions of the past. In other words, the future has not always had the same place in conceptions of heritage, and turning to the future changed how people in the twentieth century related to each other and the new technologies they used on a daily basis. National and international relations overtook local and regional concerns. The future became ever more significant than the present and a litmus test of success or failure of social groups and religious movements. If the course of society did not seem to fulfill idealist predictions, as it could not and did not in regard to the persistent problems of class, race, and religion as well as nationalism in the nineteenth and twentieth centuries, Americans constructed a new future to respond to the failures of previous futures. In this way, the future became a powerful tool for deflecting the problems of contemporary society. American society could be idealized because of its continuously soon-to-be-achieved future rather than because of its fully realized (or not) present.[17]

Jewish Americans contested the role of Israel in the practice of Orientalism during the early twentieth century, though by midcentury these practices were taken for granted as formations of Jewish heritage. By emphasizing the frequent and quotidian role of Israel in Jewish American culture, Emily Katz redirects our attention from being limited to extraordinary moments, such as the creation of the State in 1948 and the Six-Day War in 1967. Instead she fills in what Israel meant to Jewish Americans for all the days in between these major moments, filling in scholars' lesser attention to "less 'dramatic' moments." Katz rightly blurs the boundary between culture and politics, suggesting that even those organizations not understood to be political by themselves or others nevertheless participated in political discourse and structures. She highlights "the extensive promotion and consumption of Israel in the American Jewish cultural realm" during the two decades after the establishment of the State of Israel. Katz points to patterns of practice that predated the establishment of the State of Israel. When the United Nations established the State of Israel in 1948, Jewish Americans engaged with the state through conceptions of heritage in continuity with their worldviews and practices before the state's formal creation. Emphasizing "culture" over "politics" offered the means to bring in greater numbers of Jewish Americans, but this is not to say that culture was merely a means to an end. Jewish American practices related to Israel promoted pluralism, which they perceived and performed as a central American value. Jewish Americans continually posited engagement and consumption related to the land of Israel as an act of American identification, not a conflicting political position.[18]

Picturing the Future through the Past

After the Enlightenment, utopias that people might once have imagined in no place and no time were given a place and a time: the future. The period of 1901 to 1938 included the heights of modernism. Many were supremely optimistic for a future utopia impossible to achieve, others longed for a past that had never really existed, and most engaged in some of both.[19] A theory of social time underlay the conception of "the Orient." For those who envisioned "Oriental" Jews as bearers of the Jewish past, Mizrahi Jews represented a connection to Jewish antiquity. However, those same people often experienced anxiety about the perceived modernization of "Oriental" Jews and denigrated Mizrahim who lived like other Arabs, which was to say "backward" or "stuck in the past." The presence of "Oriental" Jews was a double-edged sword. On the one hand, "Oriental" Jews served as a link to a useful past, but on the other hand, "Oriental" Jews symbolized the many differences and utter lack of shared history among Jews who hailed from various locations across Europe and the Middle East. The use of the future to construct Jewish visual culture theoretically overcame this problem ideologically, even or especially as it exacerbated the denigrated position of Mizrahim. Ideally, distinctions between "Oriental" Jews and European Jews would disappear as a Jewish utopia emerged, but in the meantime Orientalism positioned Ashkenazim in a position to direct "the Orient" toward a necessary transformation to be "viable" and "modern."[20]

Through their citation of Orientalist images, Jewish Americans negotiated how they were like *and* unlike Jews and non-Jews in "the Orient" as well as "the West." This simultaneous comparison and contrast through Orientalism emerged in the context of the pitfalls of racial discourse and rapid social changes, from the Industrial Revolution to Jim Crow Laws, in the late-nineteenth and early twentieth centuries for Jews in the United States. Eric Goldstein shows the anxieties Jews and non-Jews felt about the discourse of race when describing Jews in the early twentieth century. For non-Jewish Americans, Jews "became a foil for speculation about the grave moral issues presented by a changing society," leaving Jewish Americans ambivalent about their status as "whites," especially to the extent that they saw similarities between Black suffering in the United States and pogroms against Jews in Europe. In this context, Jewish Americans of Western and Central European heritage began to use racial discourse, considering themselves white more and more, but in so doing, they compromised a strong sense of their own group distinctiveness. Jewish American immigrants from Eastern Europe resisted racial discourse before World War I, though they maintained a sense of their group distinctiveness.[21] Many Jewish and non-Jewish Americans constructed race as an indelible characteristic. If one's race was considered good (read: "white" or part of the "white family of races") or bad (read: black, or at least not "white"), nothing could theoretically be changed. In the context of anxiety over racial discourse and in contrast to this hierarchy of races, Jewish and non-Jewish Americans interrogated the nature of Jewishness and the advantages or disadvantages of seeing Jewishness as race. If race was indelible, it clearly marked Jews as different from other Americans. This sense of difference potentially came at the cost of envisioning the possibility of integration for Jews, if the American nation was seen as a monolithic racial body. Seeing Jewishness as religion or culture argued for the adaptability of Jews for integration in the United States, but both Jewish and non-Jewish Americans were sometimes troubled by the possibility that Jews would cease to be a recognizable group as they assimilated.

As East European Jews immigrated in larger numbers, Jewish Americans mainly of Western and Central European descent who had been in the United States for a longer period of time became anxious that East European Jews' practices would compromise the status of Jews as Americans. Both groups were Ashkenazi, but a hierarchy still emerged in the eyes of Jewish Americans whose ancestors hailed from Western Europe. This is to say that Jewish Americans perceived East European Jewish immigrants as "proximate others," whose complicated similarities and differences were dangerous and problematized binaries such as white/black, Jewish/non-Jewish, and American/foreign.[22] To conceptually absorb and transform East European Jewish Americans, West European Jewish Americans Orientalized Eastern Europe in structurally and visually similar ways as Mizrahim (and Arabs) in Palestine. Nevertheless, the image of "Oriental" Jews offered apparent links to tradition for Jewish Americans, especially to halakha and to life in insular Jewish communities with boundaries imagined to have been clear. Jewish Americans did not have to study and practice halakha or cut themselves off from non-Jews so much as project their heritage onto other Jewish communities who did. In this context, Orientalism took the form of a sort of cultural garment to be put on or taken off. For many Jewish Americans struggling to understand how they would juggle their sense of themselves as simultaneously Jewish and American, the garb offered a sense of a grounded heritage.

Through Orientalism, Jewish Americans could also critique the qualities of "Oriental" Jews that they did not see as falling in line with their vision for the Jewish future. Culture could change, in contrast to religion or race. Orientalism was a means of critiquing Jews from "the Orient" without threatening the integrated status of Jewish Americans in the United States. If East European Jews' "backwardness" was not a product of Jews' race but rather a malleable product of cultural conditions sure to change once they acculturated in the United States, assimilated Jewish Americans could argue they were not a threat to the values and loyalty of Jews as citizens or the integrity of American culture.

"The Orient" in Jewish American Imagination

Jewish Americans have looked to "the Orient" for as long as they have lived in the colonies and the United States to define themselves as both Jews and as Americans. Imaginations of "the Orient" reveal more about Jewish Americans than about Palestine, and it is useful to consider three distinct periods of Jewish American imagination of "the Orient" as laid out by Jonathan Sarna to contextualize the Orientalism that become so powerful in Jewish American life in the twentieth century. In the eighteenth to nineteenth centuries, Jewish Americans focused less on the land and more on the activities of the Jews in the land of Israel. When Jewish Americans shed their practices and study of Torah for pursuit of capitalism, they imagined Jews in Israel persisting in pious poverty to discover deeper truths of traditional Jewish texts. In the late nineteenth to early twentieth centuries, romantic images of Jewish pioneers—physically strong farmers—dominated. And in the 1920s, led especially by Zionists like Louis Brandeis, Jewish society in Israel represented a pluralistic utopia, an extension and perfection of American democracy. As mythical images evolved, Sarna argues Jewish Americans were "increasingly out of touch with reality back in Eretz Israel."[23]

Imagining "the Orient," Jewish Americans articulated cultural pluralism as one of their key ideas that grounded a new conceptualization of what it meant to be Jewish in the United States. During the early twentieth century, philosopher Horace Kallen (1882–1974) and the lawyer and later Supreme Court Justice Louis Brandeis (1856–1941) became leading intellectual advocates of cultural pluralism. Against an Enlightenment value of granting rights to individuals, Kallen argued that citizenship must entail the right of individuals to see themselves as part of groups or peoples with shared heritage. "No individual can be emancipated through, in, and for himself. He can only be emancipated for himself in and through his group."[24] Kallen connected the rights of groups to maintain their particular cultures even as they joined the American nation and thus argued for a need for Jewish American Zionism.[25]

Louis Brandeis became perhaps the most well-known face of Kallen's argument and an ardent supporter of Zionism.[26] Brandeis asserted that "loyalty to America demands that each American Jew become a Zionist." Brandeis and his many supporters believed that American Zionism would allow Jews to offer the American nation "the best that is in us and give to this country the full benefit of our great inheritance." Drawing on Kallen's conception of cultural pluralism and a sense that Zionism would ground Jewish heritage and culture in the United States, Brandeis proclaimed Zionism was consistent with American citizenship: "Every American Jew who aids in advancing the Jewish settlement in Palestine, though he feels that neither he nor his descendants will ever live there, will likewise be a better man and a better American for doing so." Brandeis argued that Jewish suffering and religion had prepared Jews for democracy, and thus fused the Jewish past with Jewish contributions and citizenship in the present. Further, Brandeis argued that Zionism would dispel rather than heighten suspicions of Jewish disloyalty to America. He reasoned that any group who chooses to live in America rather than "the land of [their] forefathers" must be loyal to America, and thus Jewish loyalty would be further proven when living in America was really a choice over living in a Jewish state.[27] For both Kallen and Brandeis, Zionism in early twentieth-century America called for group rights because belonging to a subculture allowed one to contribute to the nation by contributing to one's group. American Zionists therefore grounded their perspective of American heritage on "the Orient," suggesting it as equal to or better than Greece and Rome as the predecessors to American history.

Jewish American shifts in practices and ideologies of Zionism illuminate the Jewish American tendency in general for the United States and American culture to play a central role in early twentieth-century practice. Not all Jews in the United States participated in Zionism, though many more engaged in imagining Zion. Orientalism shifted Jewish Americans to allow those who disagreed with Zionist principles nevertheless to see themselves through a vision of "the Orient." Orientalism, across genders and practices of Jewishness, centered the construction of Jewish American heritage as starting with the vantage point of the United States. All others who thereby came into view spoke to a visual heritage that used "the Orient" to imagine what it meant to be Jewish in the United States without requiring that Jews ever leave the United States.

Chapter 2

The Place of Relics and Pioneers

Periodicals of the Zionist Organization of America

The cover of the February 24, 1928, issue of the Zionist Organization of America's (ZOA) magazine *The New Palestine* (*NP*), which reproduced the Greater New York United Palestine Appeal campaign poster, placed the Temple Mount in Jerusalem in the spotlight, or rather, the torchlight (fig. 2.1). The Statue of Liberty stood tall on the cover, and the light from her torch poured down over Jerusalem with the Temple Mount at the center: the Golden Light of the Mother of Exiles lights the Golden City, the negation of the exile. Like the United States and with its blessing—the Statue of Liberty is figured nearly divine here—Palestine will bring together immigrants, who will no longer be exiles in Palestine. The UPA campaign motto encouraged, "Give Today and Build For Ever!"[1] Both time and space collapse in this image. The visual text telescopes the gap between New York Harbor and the city of Jerusalem. In the campaign motto, the present and future contract. Modern machinery as well as camels depicted the old-new quality of the city of Jerusalem. Alongside the camels stood Bedouins. These native tribes, often conflated with Arabs in Zionist imagery, stand just outside the torchlight. The image suggests that camels are a legitimate aspect of "the Orient's" past for Jews to claim as heritage. At the same time, the picture delegitimizes Bedouins and Arabs as significant for contemporary heritage. Jewish American heritage is therefore envisioned through "the Orient" but with a clear sense that aspects of "the Orient" must be controlled. The Statue of Liberty, the quintessential symbol of the United States, shines light on the proper

Figure 2.1. "Give Today and Build For Ever!"

way to see how modern and ancient life in "the Orient" relate to the United States, and the marginalization of Bedouins and Arabs through the metaphor of darkness implies that Jewish Americans positioned Jews as the guiding light for contemporary citizenship by othering Bedouins and Arabs as irredeemably outside the process of modernization.

In the ZOA's panorama, East Europeans, Mizrahim, and Arabs figure as contemporaneous relics of the past, similar to American depictions of Native Americans as "noble savages." The ZOA referred to these people as "Orientals" in their own texts. That first-order consciousness of Orientalizing Jews is significant for revealing how the ZOA sought to argue for the difference between so-called "Orientals" and Zionists. Alongside these "primitives," the members of the new Jewish commonwealth in Palestine appear as the seeds of the future generation, an alternative vision of "the Orient." Though the ZOA's visual culture contrasted various inhabitants of "the Orient" with newcomer Zionist pioneers "returning" and "reviving" their "homeland," I argue that images such as those of Zionist pioneers working the land of Palestine are equally Orientalist in form and visual practice. The ZOA carefully curated images of them to construct an idealized argument about what it meant to be Jewish in the twentieth century, and the ZOA used these images to create an imagined panorama of "the Orient" through which they hoped Jewish Americans would come to understand themselves.

Founded in New York in 1898 as the Federation of American Zionists (FAZ), the ZOA reorganized in 1918. American Progressivism was a key context for the development of the FAZ/ZOA. Though it is difficult to define Progressivism precisely, David Levy's discussion of the diffuse interests of those considered part of Progressivism is helpful. Levy argues that it is not clear what Progressivism was or if it should be considered a movement. Interests included in Progressivism were world peace; the settlement movement; social work; ending prostitution; improving public health, education, family; prisoners' rights; abolishing child labor; improving urban housing; and ameliorating black American life. However, no single concern is essential. Instead, Levy suggests three main concerns: (1) corruption, especially as a result of materialism; (2) class tensions; and (3) enormous business growth and its entanglement with government in the late nineteenth and early twentieth centuries. Many who participated in American Progressivism imagined an earlier romanticized society in the United States in which republicanism and communal unity had held these issues at bay.[2] This nostalgic conception of American heritage is also present in the FAZ/ZOA's visual imagination of Jewish life. If Jewish unity had existed in the past, this vision of heritage indicated, then it could exist again in the future.

The FAZ/ZOA drew on a transnational Zionist worldview while simultaneously articulating a uniquely Jewish American understanding of the implications of the Zionist account of Jewish heritage. Yael Zerubavel categorizes Zionist collective memory as focused on two main periods: "Antiquity" and "Exile." Antiquity represents the vibrancy of Jewish life as a kingdom from ~1000 BCE until 586 BCE (destruction of Solomon's Temple) or 70 CE (destruction of Herod's Temple), depending on how one is counting. Exile is a long period that at best should have no import but at worst has led Jews into disintegrated communities and stale practices. The emergence of Zionism appears as the inauguration of the first new period in Jewish history since antiquity, "National Revival." This periodization or theory of Jewish history indicates that contemporary Jews must reach back beyond the negative aspects of exile to recover what was so strong about Jewish antiquity and bring it into the present.[3] In Palestine and later Israel, hegemonic Zionism tended to focus on the need for a majority of Jews to leave their lives in the exile of diaspora to "return" to their true national home. The bulk of Zionist Jewish Americans never espoused the need to move to Palestine themselves, though they asserted the importance of "the Orient" in Jewish heritage and as a site for other Jews to take refuge in the twentieth century. To bridge the gap between much of world Zionism and their uniquely American view, Zionist Jewish Americans focused on the spiritual side of the possibilities of imagining Palestine as a Jewish center. They subverted a common Zionist narrative claiming that the entire diaspora was exilic. Zionist Jewish Americans asserted a central role for the United States and Jewish Americans, as summarized by the Zionist Israel Friedländer's slogan "Zionism plus Diaspora, Palestine plus America."[4]

Influenced by Zionist vision and American Progressivism, which both articulated "correctives" to the problems of society's ills, the ZOA sought to tell Jews in the United States how best to live in the world as Jews. The February 24, 1928, *NP* cover revealed the oldness and newness of Jewish practices properly combined: the freedom of America combined with the ancient traditions of Jerusalem, synthesized to create the ideal new nation. By piecing these two things together, the ZOA's visual culture indicated that Judaism had access to the origins of the ancient spirituality so valued by Americans, yet that visual culture also asserted that Jewish Americans were not at all trapped in the past. ZOA visual cultural showed that Jewish Americans, as much as any non-Jewish Americans, embodied the values symbolized by the Statue of Liberty. Moreover, Jewish Americans could use Zionist values to bring the Holy Land out of its neglect and into the modern era. The calls for ever greater fundraising emphasized that Jewish Americans could only claim Jewish superiority in matters of the Holy Land and American citizenship so long as they engaged the ZOA's careful vision of Jewish heritage. The FAZ/ZOA depicted Jewish life in "the Orient" as stuck in the past, as a critique and as a key link to Jewish history. As such, Orientalism constituted a key form or portraying the FAZ/ZOA's vision of Jewish heritage: "the Orient" showed Jewish past, part good and part bad, and Zionism offered the key to correctly negotiating how to preserve or transform these components. Although Jewish Americans of East and West European descent reconciled in the newly reconsolidated ZOA after World War I, the denigration of various "Oriental Jews" was a critique not only of Eastern Europe but also of East European Jewish practices in the United States. This would not have been lost on the readership of *The Maccabaean*, relaunched as *NP* in 1921. Many Jewish Americans, influenced by the values of Progressivism, critiqued East European culture as the antithesis of society in the United States. Visually presenting real or perceived problems plaguing Jewish life in "the Orient" was not solely a means of critique. Like their European counterparts, Zionist Americans used "the romantic self-image of a noble Oriental Jew" to construct a new image of themselves and what it meant to be Jewish in the twentieth century.[5] Before World War I, Jewish Americans hailing from West Europe constructed themselves in contrast to "Oriental" East European and Mizrahi Jews. After the war as Jewish Americans of East European heritage increasingly acculturated in America, Mizrahim became the primary object of Jewish American Orientalist visions. But as the first generation of Zionist children grew up, Jewish *chalutzim*, or pioneers, embodied the strength and normalization of Jews possible through connection to the Holy Land, and after the Arab riots of 1929 and the rise of Nazism in the early 1930s, chalutzim became the leading characters of the Zionist panorama as the synthesis of the positive characteristics of "the Orient."

The "Muscular Christianity" movement flourished in the United States during this time period. The term and movement began in England in the mid-nineteenth century, but it became prominent in the United States from 1880 to 1920 in connection with the Social Gospel movement, psychology, and American nationhood. Participants in Muscular Christianity did not assert the natural strength of Christian bodies. Leaders of the movement expressed anxiety about physical strength—presented as the image of manhood—and sought to address the problem of Christian American men's "descent" into effeminate weakness. Anxiety about bodies expressed an underlying ambivalence about urbanization and other modern changes, as well as doubt about the future of Christianity in light of new philosophies, such as Nietzsche's, and modern science, especially Darwinism. Charles Kingsley, a leader in the English Muscular Christianity movement, argued that muscular strength would not only help forge a connection between body and soul but mold contemporary Christians as the proper heirs of the Israelite empire, implicitly rejecting Jews and Jewish bodies as the legacy of Israelites.

Others in the United States saw Muscular Christianity as an antidote to the "clannishness" of Jewish and Irish Americans. Using Mark 11: 15 and I Corinthians 6: 19–20 as prooftexts for the New Testament's endorsement of physical exercise and health, the movement altered conceptions not only of the images of Christianity but what practices were permitted to "good Christians." Colonial and antebellum Protestant churches had often denounced exercise as an idle waste, contributing neither to work nor the development of a Christian spirit. However, the place of women in Protestant Christianity—not only as the more numerous bodies in the pews but also as emerging leaders—also influenced the anxieties about masculinity embodied in Muscular Christianity. Across the United States, President Theodore Roosevelt advocated masculine physical strength and connected this to nature while expanding policy on national parks that was matched by increased popular writing on the outdoors. Camping in particular offered a new mode of shaping the bodies and views of boys and some girls, linking the importance of time in nature to education and upbringing. Similar changes expanded in US university education. The YMCA was founded in this time period, and its visual culture pictured bodily strength as an essential piece of masculinity and Christianity. During World War I, the YMCA's visual culture also argued that the Y prepared young men to be strong soldiers and to fulfill any call of duty.[6] Both Muscular Christianity and Zionism addressed an anxiety crisis over "modern" men's bodies and "modernity" in general. Zionists portrayed chalutzim in ways that paralleled Muscular Christianity while countering its explicit or implicit critiques of Jewish bodies.

"Oriental" Relics and Envisioning Jewish Future

The paradox of Palestine's simultaneous ancient and utterly new character pervades *The Maccabaean* and *The New Palestine*. Tel Aviv symbolized the new future, but Jerusalem was the epicenter of the old-new.[7] In the heart of the old city of Jerusalem stood the remnants of the Second Temple complex, destroyed in 70 CE by the Roman Empire. Remembering the Temple is a key aspect of rabbinic texts such as the Talmud and later Jewish practices throughout the medieval and modern periods. However, the Temple, or more specifically the remnants understood to be the Western Wall containing the Temple plaza, did not play a large role in Zionist American visual culture until the mid-twentieth century. The physical site of the Temple itself, although ancient, did not play a prominent role in Jewish visits to the land of Israel until the fifteenth century. The Mount of Olives was a much more popular site for the minority of Jews who chose and were able to make a pilgrimage to Jerusalem in the medieval period. Yet idealized images of the Temple played an important role in Jewish visual culture in the medieval period, such as in illuminated manuscripts and the texts Jews use during Passover seder, haggadahs.[8]

During the nineteenth century, the physical space of the Temple became increasingly emotionally and political salient for Jews and non-Jews alike. Archaeologists from Europe, the United States, and the Middle East began projects that sought to confirm various historical sites. These projects could confirm the truth of biblical texts, for example, and often therefore could be used as a claim to the holiness of a space or the political rights to a place. Christians, Jews, and Muslims from various cultural and national backgrounds increasingly contested each other's histories and representations of ancient relics.[9] The Temple Mount is an archetype of how powerful the images of ancient spaces became in contemporary politics and production of heritage. Twentieth-century Jewish American representations demonstrate an increasing concern for the Temple, even or especially among those who did not participate in halakha. The image of the Temple was not necessarily important for restoring the rituals described in the Torah. For Jewish Americans, its image helped establish a long and legitimate Jewish history that paralleled American histories connecting to ancient Greece and Rome as "civilizations." By presenting this history as the visual heritage of Jewish life in the United States, the FAZ/ZOA's visual culture portrayed the Temple through an ideological vision of the United States and "the Orient." Selecting certain moments of the past and multiple Orientalized sites as the history of Jews created a trajectory for how FAZ/ZOA visual culture envisioned hopes for the Jewish future. Zionism and a Jewish state appeared as a solution to Jewish problems in Europe, Palestine, and the United States even as *The Maccabaean* and *The New Palestine* articulated different problems in each locale.

The Western Wall and other ancient architecture were not, however, the only relics to be found in "the Orient." The visual culture of the FAZ/ZOA depicted Mizrahi Jews in Palestine as "contemporaneous" but not "contemporary" Jews, to use Kirshenblatt-Gimblett's distinction. "Contemporaneous" Jews are alive in the present but valued as unchanging relics of the past, rather than as people with histories that inform their understanding of heritage. Reaching back in time, the caption for an image of "A Survivor of Old Palestine" proclaimed, "This young man lives, as he dresses, like an Arab, but he claims not only to be a Jew but one whose ancestors never left Eretz Israel to wander in the Diaspora" (fig. 2.2).[10] The caption claimed this Jew wore his Orientalism on his sleeve. Not indelibly other, his Orientalism is cultural dress. His geographic and temporal differences were denoted by his garb: he lived in the land of Israel, but more importantly, he had never left, making him a direct link to ancient Jewish life. The *NP* valued and printed his image for his symbolic and imagined link to Jewish heritage, not in order to understand this man's day-to-day life as changing and a potential alternative modernity but to present Mizrahim as living relics of Ashkenazi heritage. Moreover, World War I had hurt Sephardim and Mizrahim more than Ashkenazim. Though some in Palestine had implored Jewish Americans to remedy this gap

Figure 2.2. "A Survivor of Old Palestine."

through relief funds directed more clearly toward Sephardic and Mizrahi communities, Zionist Americans funneled their contributions toward Ashkenazim, including relatives. Zionist American relief efforts may have actually exacerbated economic differences between Mizrahim and Ashkenazim. Although this image attributes the material and cultural condition of this "Oriental" "Survivor of Old Palestine" to living like an Arab, the reality is that the decline of the Ottoman Empire, outbreak of World War I, and intervention of Ashkenazim set back Mizrahi Jews like this man.[11] Jewish American visual culture romanticized Mizrahim as relics of the past while simultaneously invoking their need for Ashkenazi/Western/American "civilizing" cultural forces. Yet on the ground, Ashkenazi Jewish American "relief" practices—often carried out by only a handful of Jewish Americans recently arrived in Palestine—exacerbated Mizrahi suffering rather than uniting Jews and ameliorating "Oriental" Jews' problems in Palestine. Although a humanitarian failure, this contributed to the success of Jewish American visual culture in the United States, which used Sephardic and Mizrahi poverty in the "Orient" as a foil to the material, cultural, and civic success of Jewish Americans in the United States.

Rather than considering a multitude of Jewish practices as "modern," the ZOA's material culture presented its own vision of Jewish life as the only modern option. This contrasted to an imagined "tradition," made "real" through presenting images such as this "survivor" as historical and unchanging, if contemporaneous. This suggested Jewish history was not lost to Jewish Americans, even if and especially because they did not practice similarly to "Oriental" Jews. Through representations of "Orientals" such as these, Zionist Americans constructed a vision of Jewish Americans in temporal contrast to their "Oriental" counterparts. Eliyahu Stern argues that Jewish narratives of Europe, both popular and scholarly, have reified schemas of "tradition" and "modernity" as opposites. Within these schemas, many Jews see tradition as static. A "traditional" system has power when its practices are perceived to be "handed down from the past, [as they] have always been." East European Jews and Mizrahim were both treated as living heritage, their cultural relevance and difference simultaneously marked by their persistence in modes of past Jewish civilizations. But rather than perpetuate schemas that treat any instantiation of Jewish life as static, Stern argues that "modernity" is not just a *movement* based on a set of liberal philosophical principles. It is a *condition* "that restructured all aspects of European life and thought, in diverse and often contradictory ways."[12] These restructured sociopolitical forms extended to the United

States, including for example new means of funding Jewish communal practice, new concepts of public and private, and changing articulations of relationship between individuals, groups, and nation-states. East European Jews, Mizrahim, and Arabs were *all* modern, subject to the changes resulting from the decline of the Russian and Ottoman Empires and the rise in nationalism as a way to see and order the world in the nineteenth into the twentieth centuries. However, their voices and visions for the future are not transparent in the periodicals of the ZOA, wherein the ZOA envisioned them as part of the contemporaneous "Orient" and failed to see or allow them to represent their alternative self-understandings and views of their heritage.

Images of the authors of articles in *TM* and the *NP* and of events held by Zionist Americans in the United States contrast sharply with the images of East Europeans, Arabs, chaluzim, and Mizrahi Jews. Michael Berkowitz argues that a visual culture centered on figures such as Lord Balfour, Chaim Weizmann, Nahum Sokolow, Louis Brandeis, Henrietta Szold, and Albert Einstein appealed more broadly to Zionists in Europe and the United States than figures such as Vladimir Jabotinsky or Joseph Trumpeldor. Jabotinsky and Trumpeldor appealed only to limited audiences in the United States. Jabotinsky and especially Trumpeldor were constitutive figures of the new myths of nationhood in the culture of Jewish settlement in Palestine during the early twentieth century.[13] Jabotinsky and Trumpeldor became mythic figures in Palestine for an ethos of war and a war of defense, respectively. An ethos of war was not central to the visual culture of Zionists in Western Europe and the United States. Instead, Zionist Americans circulated images that emphasized "democratic values" and "civility."[14] Jewish American politicians and philanthropists look like many middle- and upper-class Americans and Brits: they do not work on the land. Images of "friends of Zionists" emphasized the likeness and thus implied "modernity" between the preceding figures and their non-Jewish "Western" counterparts, rather than between "Western" and "Oriental" Jews, such as in the 1917 feature "To Liberate the Smaller Nationalities," with images of Woodrow Wilson (US, 1856–1924), Lord Arthur Balfour (UK, 1848–1930), and René Viviani (France, 1863–1925) (fig. 2.3).[15] Their pictures tended to represent their faces especially, humanizing them and granting them in personality in contrast to the wider scenes that tended to depict "Orientals" in and thus as a part of their landscape.

Theodor Herzl and Chaim Weizmann were exemplary personalities, as much in the ZOA's visual culture as its political strategies. Before and

Figure 2.3. "To Liberate the Smaller Nationalities."

after World War I, Herzl figured prominently among Zionist heroes. An iconographic photograph taken in 1897 depicted Herzl at the First Zionist Congress in Basel, Switzerland (fig. 2.4).[16] Although the image dated to 1897 and was taken in the Diaspora, not Palestine, it remained a staple of Zionist visual culture. Many Zionists critiqued or moved beyond Herzl's

Figure 2.4. Baltimore Convention Number cover of *The Maccabaean*.

utopian Zionist imagination, but his image still remains ubiquitous in the State of Israel, from official media to graffiti. Herzl died young and early in the pre-state period, but reproducing his icon has been a central practice of Zionism, making him immortal in Palestine and later the State of Israel in his continuous reappearance. Iconography of Herzl in FAZ/ZOA publications paralleled Zionist practices not just in Palestine but all over the globe. For example, Ephraim Lilien's stained glass window in the B'nai B'rith House in Hamburg depicted *Herzl as Moses* (fig. 2.5), collapsing the contemporary politician with the mythic leader of the Exodus, secularizing the Exodus as a symbol of twentieth-century Zionist politics.[17]

Figure 2.5. "Herzl as Moses."

The covers and pages of *TM* and the *NP* repeat Chaim Weizmann's image perhaps more than any other figure (fig. 2.6). A British citizen with a doctorate, Weizmann was well respected within Jewish and non-Jewish political circles. Even more than Herzl, Weizmann's trimmed hair, tailored suits, and good social standing embodied that which Zionist Americans sought to achieve for themselves.[18] Weizmann fulfilled the aspirational imagination of Jewish Americans. His appearance showed that the image Jewish Americans sought for themselves through looking toward "the Orient" was achievable. An upper-class gentleman, successful in his profession, in politics, and in gaining international visibility, Weizmann signaled the accomplishment of the ZOA's goals for the image of Zionist Jews in "the West." The goal of many Jewish Americans to create an image of Jewish respectability or whiteness was achieved *before* the goal of statehood held by the World Zionist Organization, Labor Zionism, the Haganah, or other representations of the later Jewish State of Israel was achieved. Of course, the ZOA's repetition of his image helped create the very semblance of visibility that they sought. Though the periodicals of the ZOA imagine a Jewish state in "the Orient," Weizmann represented success in the diaspora, "the West." Weizmann appeared briefly at Jewish Day at the 1933 World's Fair, giving a five-minute address before the beginning of the pageant *The Romance of a People* discussed at length in

Figure 2.6. "Greetings to Dr. Weizmann."

chapter 5. Even then, Meyer Weisgal, producer of the ZOA-helmed event, only wanted Weizmann for his appearance in the United States. Weisgal recalled later that he promised to reduce the ZOA's $100,000 donation to Weizmann's Central Refugee Fund by half if Weizmann gave more than a single speech.[19] Weisgal sought Weizmann's appearance for the prestige and authenticity it would lend the pageant. Even if the recollection is apocryphal, it suggests the power that Weisgal saw in Weizmann's image rather than in the details of his politics. ZOA visual practices could transform even "Western" Jews into symbolic imagery rather than living Jews negotiating politics. Weizmann's image helped Zionist Americans establish their goal of depicting Jewish Americans as acceptable citizens as much as, if not more than, to negotiate Jewish territorial and national rights in Palestine.

Fitting Eastern Europe into a Vision of "the Orient"

The FAZ/ZOA's visual culture presented images of East European Jews as evidence that Jewish life needed repair after the effects of life in the diaspora and to show that Zionism offered an answer. Similar to the representation of Mizrahim as relics of antiquity, the FAZ/ZOA periodicals depicted East European Jews as pieces of visual heritage available to construct a personal and communal American heritage, rather than as interlocutors in a worldwide Jewish community. Of Jews in Eastern Europe, a story by Martha Wolfenstein recounted a vision of East Europe: "The *Gass* [Yiddish for 'street'] is a real Ghetto street, and the Ghetto Jews are really relics of the Middle Ages, with all their uncouthness and dread of the open air . . ."[20] Images positioned "Western" Jews in contrast to recipients of Zionist relief in East Europe, implicitly—though not epiphenomenally—invalidating East European Jewish claims about Zionism along the way. This suggested a simultaneous connection and difference. "Oriental" Jews appeared in forms of dress associated with East European Orthodox Jews or Middle Eastern culture. This clothing tended to appear in tatters. Many images of East Europeans, Mizrahim, and Arabs show a wide angle, leaving the impression that "Orientals" were part of their landscape rather than fully embodied modern Jews, or else images of "Orientals" portray them sitting on the ground, backs hunched under the weight of destitution and poverty (fig. 2.7).[21] The images explicitly critique Jewish life in "the Orient," whether in the derelict and violent environment of Eastern Europe or the immigration of East European Jews to Palestine.

Figure 2.7a. "Son of the Ancient Race."

Figure 2.7b. "Samaria from the South."

FAZ/ZOA visual culture transformed East European Jews before and after immigration to Palestine into images of "the Orient," romanticizing them as significant for the Jewish past but problematic as a vision for the Jewish future. Carol Zemel refers to Roman Vishniac's (1897–1990) photographs of East European Jews as a diasporic photo-eulogy. Zemel's analysis of his work suggests a way to see how photographs of Eastern Europe portrayed Jewish life as lifeless before and after the Holocaust. Regardless of whether viewers are Jewish or not, Zemel argues photos of Jewish life in Eastern Europe like Vishniac's "have become tokens of memory, emblems of a culture once thriving, now gone." This is not the only way to understand East European Jewish heritage, as Jewish life in Eastern Europe was ongoing even into the twenty-first century, and Jews in Eastern Europe did not see their own lives and futures in the same ways as Jewish Americans and Zionists.[22] Yet Jews who left Eastern Europe, or who never lived there, have often constructed a narrative of Eastern Europe as little more than killing fields and graveyards. The prewar magazines of the FAZ/ZOA pictured East European Jews as "*the* Jewish past." But the FAZ/ZOA's visual culture was ambivalent, not necessarily mourning the loss of that tradition but instead presenting it as an important memory in the panorama of Jewish heritage. The magazines of the FAZ/ZOA printed images implying that life in Eastern Europe amounted to destruction and Jews required a remedy for both the decay of internal Jewish life and the violence imposed externally by non-Jews in Eastern Europe. The FAZ/ZOA periodicals pictured non-Jews in Eastern Europe as irreconcilably antagonistic to Jewish life, quite different from the possibilities that the United States offered for Jewish Americans.

However, Jewish life in Eastern Europe continued to be diverse and vibrant, including not only small-town *shtetl* life and Jewish participation in the processes of urbanization and secularization that took place before and during the exodus of Jews from East European nations. Hasidim (Jewish "pietists"), *Mitnagdim* (literally "opponents," Orthodox Jews opposed to Hasidism), and *Maskilim* (Jews who embraced Enlightenment principles) continued to debate what it meant to be Jewish, generally envisioning their future in Eastern Europe. Alongside Bundists and Zionists who gained support in the 1890s, Jewish liberals in Russia hoped for the success of a democratic parliament (duma) and influenced national and international politics by calling attention to repressive policies, ultimately even shaping the Zionists' program. In Odessa, Jews attempted to become European, rather than turning inward to tradition or Russifying, leading them to emulate or even lead their neighbors in "modernization."[23] Many Jewish Americans were committed to a vision of Eastern Europe as a decayed and degrading past because this picture helped laud the significance of Jewish life in the United States. But this myopic image ignored the many ways that East European Jews also struggled to picture and improve the Jewish future and to see Jews as remaining in Eastern Europe.

In the years prior to World War I, coordinated outbreaks of violence against Jews continued, epitomized by the Kishinev pogrom in 1903. Zionists saw their sense of hopelessness for Jews in Europe confirmed in the devastating and widespread violence in Eastern Europe, and thus represented Jews in Eastern Europe through images of destruction and downtrodden, outdated religiosity. During World War I, the scarcity of resources affecting all involved in the war seemed particularly acute to Jews, and Zionists saw the escalation of violence as a signal of the necessary confrontation between Zionism and Jewish resistance to establishing a new Jewish life in a new Jewish state. A controversial cover image on the January 1916 issue of *TM* portrayed the confrontation: Moving in from the left, Jewish men (shaved and bearded) and women (heads uncovered) march in unified lines (fig. 2.8). On poles topped with Stars of David, they hold white banners with more stars of David and the slogans "NATIONALITY," "DEMOCRACY," and "ZION." Marching against them from the right, in dark suits and top hats with hands extended to halt these nationalists, several large, heavy men with hooked noses and pince-nez glasses prevent the nationalists from going forward.[24] The opening editorial described the delays in establishing a Jewish Congress, primarily attributing them to the hesitation of the American Jewish Committee—presumably the men halting the progress depicted on the cover—but also critiquing the National Workmen's Committee.[25] The cover drawing is a surprisingly overt expression of the Zionist view of other Jewish movements, and it did not pass without controversy. Because of the deployment of antisemitic stereotypes, "it was inexcusable, a number of Zionists argued [after the publication of the cover], for the magazine to depict its opinion to such means."[26] The cover thus reveals the underlying tension between Jewish Americans' purported interest in East European Jewish life, certainly genuine to a great extent. However, many Jewish Americans did not see a place for East European practices of political ideologies or Jewishness in the United States and sought to distance themselves from the negative images of socialism, for example, that had a significant space in East European Jewish life. Such politics did not characterize all of East European

Figure 2.8. "HOW UNJEWISH!"

Jewish life, but Jewish Americans, like some East European Jews, feared the repercussions of socialism or Jewish participation in or association with those politics by antisemites.

During World War I, images of destruction of East European homes and lives and the flight of Jews who survived the violence became a lasting motif in Zionist visual culture. Several images of Jews in Russia appeared in October 1915, including homes destroyed and Jewish fugitives from the violence of the war.²⁷ In November 1915 and January 1916, *TM* printed photographs depicting Jews driven out of their East European town with the titles "Whither?" and "On the March," respectively (fig. 2.9). The

Figure 2.9a. "Whither?"

Figure 2.9b. "On the March."

images appear to show the same town at slightly different moments, but the town is not named, suggesting that the images could represent any Jewish town throughout the region. In "Whither?" smoke floats upward in the background while soldiers look on as the fugitives flee from this small town. The image was printed in the middle of the article "Between the Hammer and the Anvil (An Appeal to the Hammer)," extracts from an address delivered to the Russian Duma protesting persecution of Jews by the Russian government before that iteration of the Duma was dismissed.[28] The appeal to liberal politics in Russia was absent in 1916, however, when the photograph "On the March" was located below the end of Leon M. Herbert's article, "Nationalism vs. Zionism," which concluded Jews need a nation of their own where they would no longer be parasites.[29] Both of these photographs are examples of what could be called journalistic photography, although their appearance in *TM* lacks the specificity of date and place details that we might associate with rigorous journalism. But photography was still developing in the early twentieth century and was not yet established as a reliable form of journalism. However, the journalistic nature of these photographs, capturing contemporary events, contrasts with the lack of images in the ZOA's periodicals capturing the events surrounding the controversy over the Western Wall of the Temple in the late 1920s. There, no images or romantic depictions of a peaceful Wall stood in for journalistic coverage of the disagreements at the Wall and the riots that followed. Herbert's conclusion in 1916 echoed similar sentiments to the images "Weary Wanderers" and "Goluth" that appeared in December 1915 courtesy of Dodd, Mead and Company and *Harper's Weekly*: these depicted Jews tired of living in Goluth, "exile" in non-Jewish lands. The appearance of journalistic photographs of Jewish suffering and artistic renderings of East European Jews created a visual argument that Eastern Europe was a place of violence and death, not a viable space for the Jewish future. These downtrodden Jews appear hopeless and helpless, in need of rescue and guidance. Picturing them this way contributed to the FAZ's argument that Jews in "the West" must intervene (fig. 2.10).[30]

As World War I dragged on, *TM* continued to cite such images, solidifying the connection between suffering in Eastern Europe of weak, downtrodden Jews and their future redemption in Palestine. In March 1916, a shtetl burned on the cover of the periodical. A lone bearded man, holding a gun with bayonet, stood in front of a ring of houses set on fire. The cover asked, "For Whom?" (fig. 2.11).[31] Shmarya Levin (1867–1935), a Russian-born Jew turned Zionist after he was elected to the First Duma before the Duma was dispersed, expanded on the topic of the destruction

Figure 2.10a. "Weary Wanderers."

Figure 2.10b. "Goluth."

Figure 2.11. "For Whom?"

of Jewish life in Eastern Europe in "The Living Dead." He recounted a secondhand tale of pogroms, "They lie there like tombstones upon their own graves. They do not stir. They have no desire to be pitied. They refuse all aid." As tombstones have taken a prominent role in twentieth- and twenty-first century representations of East Europe, in the early twentieth century, Jewish American visual and verbal Orientalism transformed *living Jews* themselves into tombstones. Levin called the burning of Jewish towns a "churbon," invoking the term used in Hebrew and Yiddish for the fall of the Temple and therefore the "catastrophe" that had created Jewish exile from national life in Palestine in antiquity. Yet Levin admitted that his friend's "account made no deep impression upon me," though he had steeled himself for emotionally devastating descriptions. This because of the lack of action or thought for the future he saw among Jews: while he expected Belgians, Poles, and Serbs to recover because they possess land and fields, he saw no such future for Jewish victims of the war.[32] Then the April 1916 cover of *TM* cried, "Zion: Out of the Jungle!" (fig. 2.12). One

Figure 2.12. "Zion: Out of the Jungle!"

large bearded man in stood in the center forefront, his hair disheveled, clothes tattered, and massive hands resting on a table. In the background, the cover depicted more indistinguishable workers and farmland.[33] In contrast to the listless life of Jews in Eastern Europe, Baer Epstein (1875–1923), a delegate to the Jewish National Fund office in the United States, argued that the Jewish National Fund had introduced "the most valuable element of a nation's existence" in Palestine, "the producer of wealth,—the Jewish workman," who could finally be successful. The National Fund provided communally owned land for Jews, a first opportunity distinct from a life of serfdom in Eastern Europe and directly contrasted with the life of Arabs in Palestine, "whose standard of living is unthinkable for a Jewish laborer," according to Epstein.[34] In the cover image, Zion appears as perhaps a mountaintop reached by East European Jews or a line in the sand, moving East European Jewish away from broader East Europeans' failure to "modernize."

Constructing Difference in "the Orient": Mizrahim and Arabs

After the FAZ reconsolidated as the ZOA following World War I, the organization changed the name of its magazine to *The New Palestine* (NP). The *NP* maintained some continuity with the visual culture of *TM*, though new figures became increasingly important in the ZOA's iconography of "the Orient." The pages of the *NP* show Mizrahim as contemporaneous remnants of ancient Jewish life. Mizrahi men wore large head coverings, often fezzes or kaffiyehs, and robes or linen clothing instead of "Western" suits or work uniforms (fig. 2.13). The artwork of Hermann Struck (1876–1944), a Jewish German artist and founder of the Mizrachi Religious Zionist movement who immigrated to Palestine in 1922, appeared frequently either as representative and archetypical authentic Jewish artwork or as simple illustration for stories imagined in the land of Palestine. Dark skin and "Oriental" head covering and clothing were the most prominent features of Struck's renderings of Yemenite Jews (fig. 2.14).[35] In other contexts, Noah Isenberg argues that because of the exotic appearance of East European Jews in Struck's artwork, "the Eastern Jew represents . . . the more authentic, primal Jew."[36] The same is easily said of Mizrahim, especially Yemenites, in Struck's art. Struck's images of East European Jews also appear frequently in the ZOA's publications, and his

Figure 2.13. "A Picturesque Group in Jerusalem: A Turkestan Jew, a Moroccan (Magrabi) Jew and a Yemenite Jew."

Figure 2.14. *Yemenite Jew.*

rendering of East European Jews often bears a striking resemblance to Mizrahim in terms of dress and his focus especially on the faces of older Jewish men, nearly merging the two "Oriental" types into one as a vision of Jewish Past in a linear imagination of Jewish heritage.[37]

Struck's work idealized "Oriental" Jews as an ancient root of authentic Jewish culture, but Arab influence on Jewish life in Palestine was depicted as the source of the downtrodden nature of contemporaneous "Oriental" life. Arab culture was contrasted with Jewish culture at times implicitly and at times explicitly, such as the article "Farming in Palestine," which juxtaposed images of "Primitive Arab Farming" with "Modern Jewish Farming Methods" and "A Farm of the New Era" (fig. 2.15).[38] An "Oriental" stood alone in a barren desert, downtrodden, with nothing but a donkey and a camel. In contrast to the ways that the FAZ/ZOA portrayed "Oriental" Jews and especially non-Jews as contemporaneous, the FAZ/ZOA magazines romanticized Zionist Jews as the modern antidote that could bring the land of Jewish past into the present. Jewish farmers banded together to grow bountiful crops with the use of modern technology, including motorized trucks and farming equipment.[39] As exemplified in the image of the Statue of Liberty that opens this chapter, the twentieth-century machine age, from farm equipment to telegraphs, stood in stark contrast to the "rigidly religious" rule of the Qur'an in "medieval" Wahabi life in the Arab desert.[40]

Figure 2.15a. "Primitive Arab Farming."

Figure 2.15b. "Modern Jewish Farming Methods."

Figure 2.15c. "A Farm of the New Era."

Yaron Peleg characterizes Zionist Orientalism as a "constructive blend of opposites" and a "retrospective anticipation." The former describes the paradoxical problems built into Orientalist desire, while the latter points to the tendency to interpret the land of Israel through a biblical lens. Following symbolic readings of the Hebrew Bible, Jewish and non-Jewish Orientalists view deserts as places devoid of life and empty. In the book of Exodus, the Hebrews leave Egypt and reside in the desert for forty years before God allows them into the land of Israel. The Hebrews had to shed their enslaved mind-set before taking on the rigors of national life, and the symbolic emptiness of the desert serves as the perfect transitional space wherein the Israelites learned they could depend on nothing but God. Zionists integrated the Hebrew Bible as a reliable historical document of Jewish territorial life, even if they did not all see it as a testament to Jewish covenant with God.[41] Seen this way rather than as a projection backward of imagined origins or a collection of allegorical tales constructed by Israelites in antiquity, Orientalists read the desert teleologically. If the desert is empty, then anything in it is barren. Bedouins live in the desert, and rather than perceive them as evidence to the contrary of the reading of desert-as-emptiness, Orientalists interpreted Bedouins through a logic of representation: Bedouin culture was empty because it was in the desert. Zionists could intervene in the desert and Bedouin culture to breathe vitality and richness into both.

The *NP* presented the institutions of the Jewish Yishuv as (the pre-state Jewish settlement in Palestine) evidence of the strength and normalization of Jews through their communal renaissance in "the Orient." The diversity of images presented is thus complex. In scenes reflecting Jewish farmers, many romantic images of farmers, including men and women, working to plant and harvest fields by hand or with animals existed, even as images of high-tech farming machinery were also printed in Zionist publications.[42] These romantic images emphasized the connection between Jews, the land, and physical labor—in other words, the "normalization" of Jewish life—while images of machinery proved the superior capability of Jewish farmers to care for the land over their Arab neighbors, who relied on their donkeys to work the land.[43] The apparent contradictions between these images and their implications seem to have coexisted effectively within Zionist public culture. While agricultural "modernization" represented the newly established strength of Jews, the images also required harmonization. Modernized agriculture represented Jewish return to the land, yet many institutions of the Yishuv, from Hebrew University to the shopping malls of Tel Aviv, tied Jews to urban centers and eschewed physical labor on the land. The *NP* juggled this tension, however, in addition to the tension between world Zionist rejection of the diaspora (the *Galut*, or exile, in their words) in comparison to the *NP*'s obvious connection to and support for Jewish life in the United States. In so doing, the paper constructed a Jewish heritage that asserted the physical and mental strength of Jews in the United States, presenting Jewish Americans and "the Orient" as mutual influences on each other in the emergence of a new era in Jewish life.

The attire of Middle Eastern Jews and Arabs, especially the kaffiyeh or headscarf, depicted in artwork and photographs in *TM* and the *NP*, must be located in the history of the representation of "the Orient" and the Bible in Euro-American artwork, and not solely considered as a product of the culture typical in the twentieth-century Middle East. Prior to the kaffiyeh, yellow conical hats in the early Middle Ages and then Turkish-style turbans beginning in the thirteenth to fifteenth centuries marked ancient Israelites in Christian European artwork.[44] Only in the nineteenth century, especially after the appearance of Gustave Doré's *Sainte Bible* in 1865, did representations of ancient Israelites mark biblical Jews by using the kaffiyeh popular among Arabs in the nineteenth and twentieth centuries.[45] Thus photographs of Jews or Arabs in this dress would have meshed easily with Jewish and non-Jewish American imaginations of the Holy Land, past and present. Even or especially Jewish chalutzim—immigrants to the region—appear in kaffiyehs, underscoring their connection to the past even as they build a future Jewish home.[46]

The similarity in appearance between Mizrahim and Arabs and even early Zionist pioneers requires a theoretical framework to explain how such similar images could function differently in the visual argument of the FAZ/ZOA's magazines. Contemplating how much people make of small differences, Jonathan Z. Smith discusses the construction of others as "a preoccupation with boundary." This preoccupation occurs precisely when a boundary is unclear and not objectively present. Constructions of others through focus on their supposed unfamiliar features create the possibility for defining the self as well as mastering the other. The experience of difference allows for the articulation of the self, and labeling others "barbarian" implies they are incapable of speech or reason. Without speech or reason, the other is rendered nonhuman, animallike in lack of reasoning and communication. "Westerners" thus master "Oriental" Others because, unable to speak for themselves, barbarian Others need "Westerners" to speak for them. This sets up the necessity for "remote others"—those whom "Western" selves are radically defined against, such as Arabs and Muslims—but also the danger of "proximate others," such as "Oriental" Jews, who muddy the waters in the construction of difference and threaten to compromise the pure superiority of "Western" selves.[47] To maintain the integrity of the similarity between "Westerners" and proximate others, such as the similarities between Jewish Americans and Mizrahi Jews, "Westerners" must speak on the behalf of proximate others.

By speaking for proximate others such as those living in Muslim cultures, Zionist Americans critiqued Muslims and Mizrahi Jews at once, though there is a clear distinction between the two. Per the FAZ/ZOA, Mizrahi Jews had become like animals in Muslim lands, but only because they have assimilated to the "habits" of Muslims and Arabs. *TM* and the *NP* presented these habits as a matter of malleable culture rather than an unchangeable characteristic preventing Mizrahi Jews from joining "modern" society. The presence of this visual argument suggests an anxiety that Zionists felt in incorporating Mizrahim into their vision for Jewish society. On the one hand, Zionists used Mizrahim as a link to Jewish heritage that had been "lost" in the diaspora and as a claim for Jewish rights to live in Palestine. But the FAZ/ZOA's portrayal of Mizrahim as timeless or ancient compromised their claim that Jews as a whole were a "modern" group deserving to join the upper echelons of a hierarchy of world cultures. Though Mizrahim and Muslims may have been characterized as primitives or animals, unable to think or communicate rationally, the implications of the differences between the "proximate other" and the "remote other" result in varying responses to each type of "other." While Mizrahim may be relics of ancient Judaism, not yet "modernized" and enlightened, the *NP* portrayed Arabs and Muslims as hopelessly backward, unable to modernize, and responsible for the deterioration of Jews in Palestine and the land itself.

Seeing Mizrahim as relics of Jewish heritage in "the Orient" blurred the line that Zionist Americans sought to draw between themselves and a non-"Western" life. In order represent Jews in "the Orient" as evidence of a Jewish heritage that rooted Jewish Americans but did not define them, the periodicals of the FAZ/ZOA presented Arabs as "remote others," that is, excessively dangerous and a visual boundary that marked the difference between Jews and an unchanging vision of "the Orient." In 1929, Zionists responded to riots in Palestine by representing Arabs as savages and terrorists. Unlike "Oriental" Jews, for whom Orientalism was a cultural garb that might be altered or removed when necessary to be guided into

"Western" civilization, Arab "Orientals'" primitive or childlike qualities were marked as racially "Oriental," fundamentally Other. But even during the riots, Zionists did not always characterize Arabs as so irrational as to be unable to understand anything but violence. However, especially after the 1929 riots, Arabs were characterized as violent fanatics. Prior to 1920, Zionist Americans such as Stephen Wise had pointed to negotiations with Arabs to suggest Arab support for Jewish settlement, if not statehood, in Palestine. As late as 1919, negotiations with Amir Feisal (1885–1933, King of the Arab Kingdom of Syria in 1920 and King of Iraq, 1921–1933) left the door open for Jewish and Arab cooperation. Initially, according to Zionists, Arabs and Jews were collaborators in removing British colonial power from the region and restoring it to biblical greatness.

But after the League of Nations officially ceded Palestine to Britain in the spring of 1920, despite the Balfour Declaration's (1917) rhetoric ensuring Jewish and Arab rights, a trajectory toward some measure of Jewish autonomy seemed more certain, and many Arabs became more willing to struggle, even violently, to protect their land rights. When American media reported casualties in the 1929 riots, they explained that the violence was not evidence of Arab dissatisfaction with growing Jewish settlement but the result of criminals or nomads not representative of majority Arab sentiment. Many Zionist Americans were so accustomed to an image of Jews as a civilizing force in "the Orient" that they could not imagine Arabs rejecting either Jewish benevolence or Jewish rights to the land. Jewish counterviolence after 1929 thus appeared acceptable and even righteous because it enforced this earlier view: Arabs were not qualified for democratic freedoms, and so ingrained was their backward worldview that the only way Jews could enlighten the region was through forcefully imposing their democratic values.[48] However, the *NP* did not print journalistic photos of the unfolding events in Jerusalem. Photography was not yet the trusted source of journalism it would become during and especially after World War II.[49] Absent journalistic visual culture, however, the only imaginable visions of the Western Wall or the Temple were the idealized images of Orientalist arthouse photography and romanticized artistic renderings. These played an important role in other areas of Jewish visual culture, such as those discussed in chapter 4 on the *Jewish Encyclopedia*.

Depiction of this violent fanaticism walked a line between rationality and irrationality, and Arabs were portrayed as easily duped or misled, particularly by their own manipulative leaders. Adeed Dawisha, for example, describes the gap between government and popular Arab interests from the 1920s to mid-1930s and the extent to which Arab leaders may have misled their populace until the 1930s.[50] Further, Zionists often collapsed Arab and Muslim identities, applying Muslim religious motives (as imagined by Zionists) to all Arabs and demonizing Islamic traditions in general. Finally, responses to the incidents of 1928 and 1929 in the *NP* characterized Jewish rights to the Western Wall as immemorial, even though, as stated earlier, the Wall had only been a pilgrimage destination since the sixteenth century and a typical religious symbol since the nineteenth century. For example, a full-page image printed in the issue responding to the 1929 riots showed a man praying at the Wall while a woman leaned forward against it, perhaps kissing the Wall. The caption read, "The Wailing Wall, whose uncertain status, despite the immemorial right of the Jewish people to worship before it, has caused immeasurable grief."[51] This image along with the verbal text that framed it created a distinction between Muslims and Jews, delegitimizing Muslim claims. While Zionists were adamant that the Wall had no true religious significance for Muslims, representing the Jewish claim suggested that for Muslims the Wall was simply a recently developed political tool, while for Jews it offered religious experience.

Chalutzim as Objects of Orientalism

After the Arab riots of 1929, Orientalist images of proximate Jewish others tended to disappear from the pages of the *NP*. In their place, the magazine focused on images of the new Jewish society and the new Jew, typically represented as hypermasculine farmers and soldiers. Though most Jews could not or did not choose to farm in Europe or in the United States, "a vocal minority among Western Jewry did identify, however vicariously, with agriculture as a means of transformation through Zionism."[52] Images of Jews as soldiers did not appear for the first time with Zionism. Depictions of Jewish soldiers became iconographic in German bourgeois culture through mass reproduction as items designed for the home. For example, Hermann Junker created works such as *Jom Kippur vor Metz* (ca. 1870) that "celebrated civility and proud self-identity" and accordingly were mass-reproduced for postcards. Visual culture from newspapers and magazines to postcards could offer an argument for or vision of becoming images of Jews, even if the content of that visual culture did not reflect the daily or even occasional life of most Jews.[53] In transnational Zionist visual culture, "the mythical image of the Zionist pioneer in national Hebrew culture portrays him as holding a plow in one arm and a gun in the other."[54] As with images of East European and Mizrahi Jews, Jewish Americans continued to construct a sense of their own heritage through envisioning Jews in "the Orient," though increasingly those Jews were portrayed as pioneers able to work the land and defend themselves, fulfilling romanticized characteristics of Jewish Americans who longed to be seen as "normal" according to gender norms that valued physical might and connection as aspects of masculinity to territory. Pioneers did not serve as the same type of visual foil to Jewish Americans as East European and Mizrahi proximate others did, but images of East Europeans, Mizrahim, and Arabs, as well as pioneers, existed in an imaginary panorama in which they all related to each other. The ZOA linked these figures to imagine an "Orient" through which they saw themselves, even as they never saw themselves living in the East.

The earliest publications of the FAZ/ZOA included images of *shomrim* (guards) who protected the Jewish community, which developed many of the basic characteristics of chalutzim that would appear more and more regularly during the latter part of the pre-state period. Even Hasidim could be transformed into physical and healthy pioneers in the land of Israel. The *NP*'s verbal text attempted to direct how visual culture should be interpreted, such as being "most astonished" by a group of Polish Hasidim who persisted as pioneers, despite their "personal, physical and financial" difficulties (fig. 2.16). However, "in transforming their lay habits so completely they have not departed an iota from their former religious life." This persistence in Hasidism nevertheless fit the image of the new Zionist ideals: "Their children are taught not in a stuffy Cheder, but under the open sky, yet the boys and girls are kept strictly separate."[55] A large photo spread of Hasidim turned pioneers asserted that "these Chassidim, foreign to all the arts of agriculture, unused to continuous stay in the outdoors, have learned to work all day, digging canals, building roads and ploughing fields—all because of their zeal for the speedy re-establishment of the National Homeland." Despite these long days of work, "they are never too fatigued, however, to spend an hour or two in the Beth Hamidrash [synagogue]." Images showed Hasidim hard at work, retaining characteristics such as their beards and head coverings even as they began to pose for photos similarly to other chalutzim, such as one man who stood upright with his tools slung over his shoulder (fig. 2.16).[56] These images presented Zionist American fantasies of East European Jews and children as immi-

Figure 2.16a. "Images of Chassidism."

Figure 2.16b. "Scenes of Palestine Life."

grants who had no complaints about how Zionists sought to integrate them into a vision of present-day success in "the Orient" and the implied potential this success pictured for Jewish unity in a future state. The fantasy of Jewish unity constitutes an important difference between the image of "the Orient" and Jewish life in Palestine, where many different ideologies, languages, and cultures existed. Photographs quieted those differences to create an idealized "Orient," that in this case combined visions of Hasidim from East Europe with hypermasculine Zionist ideals. Though the FAZ/ZOA's visual culture often feminized East European life, the persistence of Hasidic life could appear as a success rather than a failure of Zionist vision to mold "the Orient" through visual and verbal text that suggested the transformation of Hasidim from feminine to masculine. This depicted a visual argument for the power of Zionism to remake the appearance of Jewish bodies and in so doing remake Jews and "the Orient" at once.

These examples "rehabilitated" the image of Jewish bodies, particularly of halakhically observant Jews, implicitly addressing internal Jewish and external non-Jewish stereotypes of Jews, especially men. Anita Shapira presents three ways of categorizing visions of the "New Jew" as imagined by European-born architects of Zionist thought. One, the "Jewish gentleman," who would be normalized in the eyes of non-Jews vis-à-vis forging a connection to land and nature and developing muscular, bodily ability. She points to Herzl, Nordau, and Jabotinsky as three primary examples. Two, might be called "Jewish self-identity," which is less focused on the body than categories one and three. With Ahad Ha-am as the primary example, this vision sees Zionism supplanting Judaism as the religion and way of life of Jews. It includes a rejection of rigidification of Jewishness to be replaced by a vibrant moral life in the land of Palestine specifically, where Jews could "return" to an idealized state of rationalism and self-definition. Three, "transvaluation," a complete rejection of Jewish ancestors as strong models for determining a healthy way of life. Transvaluation shared much in a vision and focus on Jewish men's bodies with category one and in a focus on the power of the land of Palestine specifically with category two. This vision saw Palestine as essential because it rejected diaspora and therefore assimilation. Fighting off Arab antagonists specifically was a key piece of the vision of Jewish physical ability and existential necessity.[57] Life in Palestine of course saw those who held these visions of "the New Jew" sometimes at odds but often working together to fight for Jewish national rights and to oppose the habits of new Jewish immigrants to the land of Palestine. Shapira labels the umbrella philosophy encompassing all three visions "Palestinianism," one that insisted on Hebrew and new lifestyles for Jews. Shapira opposes Palestinianism to the customs of new immigrants, particularly those arriving in the second half of the 1920s, who were not ideologically committed to Zionism in the same ways. In other words, Zionists in Palestine had to confront actual Jewish life in Palestine to reconcile their understanding of Jews as a group and their Zionist philosophies. The differences between how most Jews in Palestine lived and wanted to live and how a few Zionist ideologues longed to transform Jews created stumbling blocks to be confronted. We see these new populations pictured in the pages of the *NP*, but the distance between the United States and Palestine meant that the same stumbling blocks did not exist for Jewish Americans. Zionist ideologues could project their ideal visions to the United States in the pages of the ZOA, even if East European immigrants loathed those ideologies and the discriminations against new immigrants that resulted from them. "They did not wish to be 'new Jews,' but merely everyday Jews living in Palestine." The *NP* presents pictures of immigrants who happily left their degraded life in the East European diaspora behind and who conformed to "Palestinianism." This presented an imagined "Orient" to Jewish Americans and even perpetuated the fantasies of some Zionist ideologues who had moved to Palestine but found themselves disappointed in its realities. The *NP* does not relay these disappointments, only the fantasies.[58]

From the 1920s through the 1930s, images abounded of chalutzim as workers of the land as well as brave soldiers, though the ZOA purported they preferred peacefully pouring their strength into the land rather than into war. Images of "typical" chalutzim or pioneers depicted men with tools in hand. For example, one image shows a man seated on top of a man-made structure, surveying the land.[59] The photograph foregrounds his body, implicitly emphasizing the ideology of the "New Jew" who transforms the land and in turn is transformed by his mastery and physical labor. This image embodies stereotypically ideal physicality popular in Europe and the United States, paradoxically rejecting those locations and fulfilling their constructs of body and desire at once. These images abandon earlier images of Jews dressed in attire indigenous to Arab Jews, Muslims, Christians, and others, such as the kaffiyeh. This chalutz sits atop a building he and his fellow pioneers may have constructed, staring across the land. The bird's-eye view suggests both power and possession. We see a rolling landscape with hills in the background, but we also see its modern transformation: a railroad. Regardless of whether this chalutz constructed the built landscape, the image implies the chalutz's power and possession. As a metaphor for the emerging Jewish nation, the FAZ/ZOA's imagination of "the Orient" subsumed the hypermasculine vision of the chalutz as representative not only of Zionism but the nature of Jewish men's bodes all over the globe, especially in the United States.

Chalutzim became the hypersymbolized, overdetermined vision of all the ideals of the new nation. Alongside images of Zionists erecting government buildings, sinking wells, and laying railroad tracks, captions proclaimed that chalutzim were "blazing the trail" in the move to "a new colony," and "it is the chalutz-immigrant that builds the country."[60] The verbal text complicates the vision of the chalutz: he is both the "native" who has "returned" to his long-lost land to make it anew, and he is also an immigrant. Zionist vision required this paradox to mold the reality of Jewish immigration in the shape of Orientalist idealism, but also to emphasize that the chalutz is distinct from the land and the indigenous inhabitants frequently linking them to a supposedly unmodern, unproductive existence. The FAZ/ZOA's visual culture argued for transforming images of Jews from negative stereotypes to seeing Jews as modern world citizens. The images made room for both Hasidism and Zionism in Jewish Americans' view, linking both in a panorama that offered Jewish Americans the possibility to imagine themselves through envisioning "the Orient." This powerful new visual imagination distanced Hasidism from eighteenth- and nineteenth-century kabbalistic and halakhic practices, linking Jewishness to new images and practices. Those images created a visual basis of Jewish American heritage that connected to the Jewish past but reconfigured how that past related to the present and future.

Sacrifice, Spectacle, and State-Building

The NP represented chalutzim as willing to enter battle only for self-defense. This drew on hegemonic Labor Zionist narratives to critique supposed bloodthirsty Arabs and Bedouins as well as the excessively aggressive Revisionist Party and created a narrative of sacrifice of Jewish bodies for the Zionist state.[61] Mark Raider has noted the striking similarity between stories of *shomrim* and American westerns in Labor Zionist materials in the United States.[62] The trope of a Jewish soldier was transferred from the early *shomer* to the increasingly pervasive image of the chalutz. Images of the chalutz combine new visions of Jewish power with rhetoric of

Jewish intelligence and constraint. The chalutz or "New Jew" mastered not only the land and military ability, but also physicality itself. The chalutz as a symbol of the state synthesized myths of strength, control, and self-sacrifice through both strength and control for the nation. Jodi Eichler-Levine argues, "Sacrifice functions as a spectacle. That is why the visual iconography . . . is so powerful." The visuality of sacrifice is central due to "a logic in which sacrifice must be viewed in order for it to be real."[63] Stories of chalutzim would not have contributed to consolidating a conception of a new Zionist Jewish community—in Palestine or in the United States—without pictures, particularly photography. Stories such as Louis Golding's "Olive-Tree and Windy Hill: Pioneers Who Made the Supreme Sacrifice," and other images and tales of Jews who lost their lives as a sacrifice for the Jewish homeland, molded a significant new Jewish type, valiant Jewish heroes who served to contest a long-standing antisemitic stereotype that Jews were incapable of death with honor.[64] The *NP* proclaimed that chalutzim created the not-yet-existing state through work in the land. However much it was true that Jews turned the land of Palestine into the future State of Israel, the photographs of chalutzim performed imaginative work as well, projecting the appearance of legitimacy and power. Before the state existed politically, it existed visually in the photographs and visual culture of Zionism, in the land of Palestine but especially in the diaspora.

Through this visual spectacle, the *NP* showed chalutzim not just building but protecting the fragile national structure coming into being. Verbal text accompanying photographs and the communal nature of chalutzim's symbolism heightened the spectacle, which "proved" not only chalutzim's sacrifice but the nation's power *and* justness. As symbols of the modern military state, chalutzim "carry rifles and shotguns in their hands." However, "in their hearts is the firm conviction that the cause of their people is just, that of building up peacefully and progressively a barren and neglected land which the evil-minded would throw back into its original sloth." The righteousness of chalutzim—and therefore Zionism at large—was thus cut against the villainy of Arabs: "If the Arab assassin and sniper feels that there is no law in the land, then the defender must become the law." Chalutzim were not extrajudicial vigilantes in this picture, but, in their transformation, embodied law and order. Chalutzim emerged in these images and stories, operating in tandem, as the archetype of modern military and classical honor: "There is no duty too dangerous, no enterprise too hazardous, which the Jewish watchmen will not undertake."[65]

Emphasizing the extent to which Zionist Americans sought to recast their images and become new Jews in future American generations, American youth groups—many of which were branches of groups originally established in Poland—were named for the *shomrim* and for other groups and values associated with chalutzim, such as Avukah (Torch), Habonim (The Builders), Hapoel Hamizrachi (The Eastern Worker), Hashomer Hadath (The Religious Guard), Hashomer Hatzair (The Youth Guard), Junior Hadassah, Masada, and Young Judaea.[66] These groups in the United States became visions and practices of what it means to be Jewish American.

It did not matter that Jewish Americans might never set foot in "the Orient." What mattered was the way that imagining "the Orient" allowed Jewish Americans to envision their heritage and how they would pass it on to their children. These groups suggest that Jewish Americans created a heritage that looked to "the Orient"—both Palestine and Poland—to envision life in the United States. Jewish American culture suggested that Jews could internalize the good parts of life in "the Orient" as a means of being Jewish in the United States. Jewish success, in other words, took place in the United States and used the images of Eastern Europe and Palestine to construct a narrative of Jewish heritage that implied the acceptability of being Jewish in the United States. This addressed anxieties over the true "place" of the Jewish future as well as the rights of Jews as American citizens. The ubiquity of camps in the range of Jewish American denominations and ideologies confirms how diffuse Zionism's influence on Jewishness in America was, even if not all Americans joined the ZOA and never intended to move to a Jewish State in Palestine.[67]

Conclusion

Though Zionist American visual culture did not require Jewish Americans to immigrate to Palestine—and most did not, images of a few Americans who did move to Palestine appeared in the *NP*. Including images of Jewish Americans in "the Orient" helped to authenticate the link Jewish Americans could see between themselves and those living in "the Orient." For example, on November 4, 1938, the *NP* included the image "An American Chalutz at Ain Ha'shofat," picturing a Jewish American who carries a load on his back to build the new Jewish homeland.[71] Less than 5 percent of those in the Yishuv worked on agricultural settlements, but their image still served as the symbol of Palestinian Zionist heritage.[72] Paradoxically, this image

Figure 2.17a. "Bringing Health to Palestine."

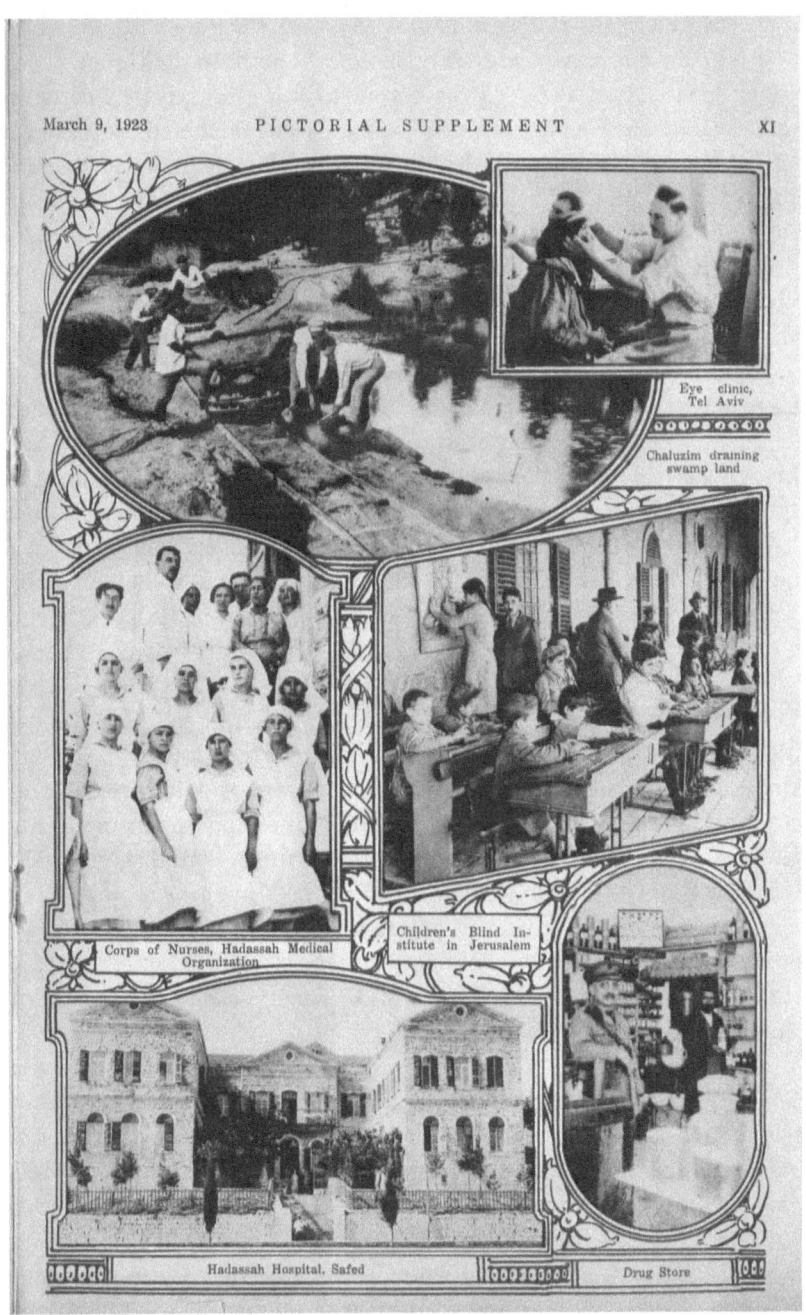

Figure 2.17b. "Corps of Nurses, Hadassah Medical Organization."

of Jewish Americans in Palestine created a visual culture through which most Jewish Americans could see themselves at home in the United States. Not all Jewish Americans may have gone to Palestine, but they certainly were capable. Their ability to move to "the Orient" mattered less than the new image created of Jews in Jewish American imagination. By claiming "the Orient" as part of Jewish American heritage, Zionist American visual culture envisioned Jewish Americans, especially men but also women, as powerful nation builders. Jewish Americans were represented as physically capable, as able to bond to the land as anyone else. They thus no longer needed to see themselves or be seen as weak.

The appearance of any Jews on the land of "the Orient" affirms Jewish Americans' normalcy and capabilities. Zionist American visual culture offers a view of "the Orient" that aspires to envision Jews as nation builders: this transfers to the United States, even as the visual culture represents "the Orient." Zionist American visual culture, along with the verbal text that interacted with and accompanied images in outlets such as the *NP*, upheld a tension between envisioning Jewish American belonging in the United States and Jewish reconstruction of a "homeland" in "the Orient." For example, the *NP* explicitly pointed to the shared skills between agrarian colonies in the United States and those in the Yishuv. One photograph of twenty-two "American Chalutzim" sailing for Palestine noted, "Although this was to be their first trip to Palestine where they intend to join the American colony in Kinnereth, their work as farmers on the Hachsharah Farm at Highstown, N.J., seemed to have imbued them with the feeling that they were returning to a land that was already familiar ground."[73] Although Zionists envisioned Jewish life in Palestine in ways that it had never been practiced before, this newness was linked to the idea of Jewish heritage and the past. Jews could not be seen as creating something from whole cloth, else their participation in American or Zionist nationalism could be seen as illegitimate.

Through images of East Europeans, Mizrahim, Arabs, and chalutzim, Zionist American visual culture created a unique form of Orientalism that allowed Jewish Americans to construct simultaneously an American and Jewish heritage. Like much other American visual culture, Zionist American visual culture looked toward "the Orient" as Jewish Americans experienced social change in the United States. This visual culture offered a way to balance the sometimes-contradictory ways that Jewish Americans constructed their heritage and to contain a multifaceted Jewish American heritage. Zionist Americans also sought to create, participate in, and influence a world Zionist movement and a Jewish commonwealth in the land of Palestine. As much as these publications were a performance of a particular American heritage, they also contributed to the construction of a Jewish state in Palestine.

By 1938, the ZOA's visual culture offered a rich panorama of "the Orient" through which Jewish Americans could imagine Palestine. The proliferation of magazines and support of the circulation of artwork, photographs, travel narratives, and public performances extended that vision well beyond the small circle of Zionist Americans who supported the movement ideologically or joined as full members of the organization. The vision or visions that the ZOA promulgated depended on both old and new forms of Orientalism. On the one hand, the ZOA used established tropes imagining Jews connected to "the Orient" and antiquity. But the ZOA attempted to dislodge the association of this conception of Jews as being an immutable quality of all Jews. Rather, the ZOA focused associations of Orientalism on East European Orthodox Jews and Mizrahi Jews as well as Muslims, Arabs, and other non-Jewish people living in the Middle East and occasionally the Far East. This suggested that to the extent Jews were "Orientals," it could be a positive aspect: Jews were not a people without heritage. East European Jews represented tradition, and Mizrahi Jews represented territorial ties to the land of Israel. The ZOA claimed each group not as a contemporary group with differences but as contemporaneous aspects of Jewish American heritage. Finally, that Jewish heritage from "the Orient" was potentially negative was mitigated by the ZOA categorizing Jewish Orientalism as cultural rather than racial and by offering the "modernizing," "civilizing" guidance of Jewish Americans, Jews from Western Europe, and the ideology of Zionism in contrast to the entrenched vision of Arabs as indelibly different from Jewish Americans.

Chapter 3

Reviewing the Past

Jewish Art Calendars of the National Federation of Temple Sisterhoods

Need I assure you that the women form no inconsiderable part of these forces?

—Mrs. Israel Simons, Address of Welcome,
Proceedings of the First Biennial Meeting of the National Federation of Temple Sisterhoods, Chicago 1915

To ape our Christian neighbors on an occasion which is fraught with religious significance for them and which means absolutely nothing to us, seems inexcusable.

—Berthe Born, December 3, 1923

For the Hebrew months of Sivan–Tamuz 5674 (May 1913–July 1914), the art calendar of the National Federation of Temple Sisterhoods (NFTS) depicts Michelangelo's sculpture of *Moses*, a work of art that is housed in the Church of St. Peter in Chains in Rome as part of the tomb of Julius II (fig. 3.1). The calendar explains, "Michelangelo's heroic figure of Moses and the Tablets brings out the chief thought of Shabuoth—the giving of the law." Sketches of Mount Sinai and a modern pulpit and ark surrounded the photograph of Michelangelo's sculpture.[1] The inclusion of Michelangelo's *Moses* exemplifies the NFTS art calendars' production of a narrative of Jewish heritage through visual culture that relies on images

Figure 3.1. *Michelangelo's Moses.*

of biblical life and "the Orient" that implicitly argued not only for the place of Jewish Americans in "Western" culture but for Jewish Americans' ability to correctly model and interpret "Western" civilization. Like their Christian-American counterparts, NFTS members—the auxiliary organization for Reform Jewish women in the United States—valued visual culture that included "high art," including images crafted by Christians that explicitly appeared in Christian contexts such as a Catholic church. Indeed, a viewership that included non-Catholics who appreciated visual culture for reasons other than a production of a Catholic sense of self is precisely what created and maintained a category such as "high art." Many such viewers were not only Protestants, but also Jews and even Catholics themselves. The art calendar is an example of how the NFTS simultaneously shared visual culture with non-Jews and offered a reviewing of or counterhistory to non-Jewish, especially Christian, theological understandings of and through visual culture. Christians value the Hebrew Bible as the Old Testament, especially the figure of Moses and the reception of the Ten Commandments. But the calendar asserts—as indicated by the association of the sculpture with the celebration of Shavuot—that Moses belongs in the tradition of Judaism, not Christianity. The calendar makes one other change to the representation of Moses: the horns that emerge from Moses's head on the sculpture in Rome were removed for the Jewish art calendar. These horns appear in Michelangelo's *Moses* due to a Christian tradition dating back to Jerome's translation of the Vulgate, the Latin translation of the Old Testament, in which Jerome drew on Greek and Hebrew renderings of the canon in the fifth century. Jews and Christians alike had traditionally translated the Hebrew word to suggest that Moses was radiating or glowing after his encounter with God. However, Jerome selected a dehumanizing translation that fit an anti-Jewish view of Moses as part of the "old" covenant, a horned Jew. It was linguistically possible to render the text this way, but Jerome knowingly rendered Moses in an ekphratic form of anti-Judaism. Later Christians invoked the trope against Jews, and whether Michelangelo was aware of this history or not, the image of Moses as a Jew with horns does not appear to have fit the image the women of the NFTS sought for themselves. By reviewing Jewish history, the NFTS assembled Jewish art calendars that recontextualized images created by Jews and non-Jews and that reframed what moments of the past mattered, and how.

The NFTS calendars offer counterhistories to Christian Orientalism and to Zionism. The calendars use many images produced by Christian and Zionist artists, but the calendars refute the conclusions of Christian Orientalists and Zionists about Jewish heritage. In this sense, the calendars are excellent examples of how cultural exchange, including the sharing of images, can subvert rather than reify the meanings of visual culture. Early NFTS calendars especially focus on biblical scenes and figures. When the NFTS calendars use Christian artists' work, the calendars do not use

Christian artists whose works were some of the more egregiously racist examples of European Christian Orientalism. Instead, the calendars imply there is more than one European Christian visual heritage. The Christian images that link the NFTS calendars to European "high culture" implicitly play against antisemitic Christian Orientalist heritage. This detaches Jewish heritage from a negative image of "the Orient" as backward or antimodern while linking Jewish Americans with the image of Palestine in very different ways from the ZOA as discussed in chapter 2. Even so, the early NFTS calendars' use of anachronistic nostalgia to construct a vision of ancestral heritage in Palestine for world history, American history, and Jewish history parallels similar constructions of Zionist American heritage.

Over time, the calendars turn to images produced by Jewish artists, mainly men and women who had lived in East Europe, Palestine, or both. Much of their artwork pictures an imaginative "Orient" in the twentieth century, but not all. Through both the biographies of the artists and the content of their work, the NFTS art calendars produced a visual culture that remained dependent on "the Orient" but not necessarily the biblical past. Turning to a contemporaneous imagination of "the Orient" created a vision of the continual production of Jewish heritage, countering Christian assumptions that Judaism was not dynamic or that Jews could not produce art. These new images did not depend on imagining the biblical past to assert the validity of Jewish heritage over Christian claims on the Bible. Nor did they use the recontextualization of Christian images. Turning to Jewish artists to envision the Orient, these later calendars often used images made possible by Zionism or circulated by the Zionist movement. Artists' immigration to Palestine from Europe, especially following World War I, was not just the result of a refugee crisis, but the ideological decision of artists to live in Palestine over the United States or other parts of the diaspora. By contextualizing these artists' work in the art calendars, the NFTS calendar committee could offer a counterhistory to the Zionism that may have underlay the artists' lives and visions while using those artists' images at the same time. As with Christian artwork, it was precisely the use of Zionists' artwork that allowed the NFTS to offer a counterhistory to Zionism. For example, the NFTS maintained a special relationship with the Bezalel art school in Palestine, which became a pillar of Zionist claims for the vibrant Jewish life possible only in Palestine. The NFTS art calendars used these images, combined with verbal text such as artist biographies, that obscured Zionist views to present an American Reform vision of "the Orient" that saw a place for Jewish life and citizenship (not necessarily in a Jewish state) in Palestine but did not eclipse the exceptional role of the United States in Jewish heritage.

Seeing Jewish heritage through the frame of a counterhistory opened up the ability of the NFTS calendars to critique narratives of history that bolstered Christian supersessionism, argued against conceptualizing the diaspora as meaningless exile, or implied Jewish heritage in "Oriental" antiquity trapped Judaism in outdated practices. Additionally, selling these art calendars created a role for the NFTS in Reform Judaism, which did not yet allow women to assume leadership roles, such as serving as rabbis or cantors in the early twentieth century. The NFTS saw multiple dimensions in the calendars, as stated in the *Proceedings of the Third Biennial Meeting*: "Even if this Calendar be not a financial success, its wide circulation may prove an educational and a religious power for good." NFTS women created supposedly auxiliary roles for themselves in American Reform Judaism, but their calendars became a tool that allowed Jewish American Reform women to take a lead role in shaping Reform visual culture, religious education, and the financial stability of Reform's institutions such as the rabbinate.

The role of women in Jewish life had very long traditions, often associated with the home, but Jewish American women created new forms of institutional life in the late nineteenth and early twentieth centuries that used language about the "home" and "motherhood" to take leadership roles in Jewish communal life. At the start of the nineteenth century, European and American Jews interpreted the public nature of synagogue services and communal Jewish life as limited to men. Although Reform's reconceptualization of the authority of Jewish law sought to remove barriers to women's full participation in Jewish public life, men and women continued to struggle to envision new roles for women in Judaism. Moreover, social norms constrained the roles for women across religious traditions in America. Therefore, it is not surprising that women were largely "invisible" in early Reform institutional life.[2] Generally, Jewish women continued to be unable to take lay or rabbinic leadership roles and were often denied membership in synagogues throughout the nineteenth century, despite reforms in specific Jewish laws and more importantly the restriction of the authority of halakha to determine normative practice. These limits on women's membership and lay leadership in Jewish communities went beyond what was typical for Christian American women, indicating that Jews were not just copying Christians in order to acculturate. However, like their Christian counterparts, Jewish women became increasingly present in congregational life. Reform Jewish women who organized themselves into local sisterhoods and then NFTS challenged the institutions of Reform, pushing all Reform Jews to see new places for women and rethink what Judaism could mean in the twentieth century.[3] Jewish women used the same rhetoric of domesticity that Christian women used, but they faced a different set of challenges. Jewish tradition conceptualized synagogues as public, setting up a clear tension between the rhetoric of domesticity and the efforts of Jewish women to play a greater role in Jewish communal life.

Like other Jewish American movements and organizations, members of the NFTS sought to understand Judaism as a tradition with geographical heritage in "the Orient." NFTS art calendars produced prior to the creation of the State of Israel articulate a narrative of Jewish history that begins in "the Orient" in antiquity, runs through Europe, and culminates in the United States. The NFTS continued to print calendars throughout the twentieth and into the twenty-first century. I have confined this study to the pre-state period, but I conclude with one example of the legacy of the pre-state calendars after the creation of the State of Israel. Even as Jewish culture flourished in Palestine in the early twentieth century, Reform Jews valued "the Orient" more for its "pastness" than as a contemporary political entity, which would have rivaled American exceptionalism. In that way, the NFTS art calendars countered hegemonic world Zionism, which valued some type of Jewish political autonomy in Palestine as the culmination of contemporary Jewish civilization, as exemplified by the ZOA in chapter 2 and Hadassah in chapter 6. The NFTS art calendars present "the Orient" in a way that confers value on the Holy Land within the larger frame of Reform Judaism and American citizenship. This emphasis on Reform critiqued the tendency of some Jewish American Zionists to see Zionism as a superior substitute for synagogue life. Henrietta Szold, a figurehead of Hadassah, argued that Zionism was the very means by which Jews could be their best American selves (discussed at length in chapter 6); for many Reform Jewish Americans, "Zionism infringed upon the good Americanism of the Jew."[4] Throughout the nineteenth century, Reform Judaism passed institutional rejections of Zionism or the creation of a Jewish state, and the NFTS art calendars offer an embodiment of how Reform Jews could reject the tenets of Zionism while sharing visual culture with Zionists. As with the NFTS calendars' use of Christian images such as Michelangelo's *Moses*, the NFTS calendars' use of images circulated by Zionists created an opportunity to subvert Zionist narratives about those images.

At the same time, both Reform and Zionist Jewish Americans saw their movements as superior to Orthodoxy as defined by strict interpretations of halakha. Orthodoxy was not unchanging in the United States or elsewhere, but many Jewish Americans represented it as ossified to bolster their own conceptions of what Jewish heritage should be instead. Members of Reform Judaism, the ZOA, and Hadassah considered that interpretations of halakha as the sole arbiter of heritage constricted what Jewish life had been at its best and could be in the future. Shifting heritage from halakha to history allowed Reform Jewish women, as well as members of other Jewish American movements, to "release themselves" from what they considered the internal problems of Jewish life while also attending to the public perception of Jews as good American citizens. The calendars present Jewish history as a precursor to American history, culture, and politics. That the visual culture of NFTS calendars articulate a counternarrative to European and Zionist visual cultures by use of images drawn from both speaks to the very production of heritage—a process that "adds value to the outmoded by making it into an exhibition of itself."[5] By exhibiting images originally produced in European and Zionist contexts, NFTS art calendars recontextualize those images. In doing so, they make two simultaneous implications: that those European and Zionist meanings are outmoded *and* that a new layer of American Reform meaning exists on top of them.

Aestheticism and Space for Women

In 1913, women from congregations within the Union of American Hebrew Congregations formed the NFTS (today known as Women of Reform Judaism). This united many sisterhoods that predated the federation and that would at times express skepticism about the benefits of a national organization. American Reform Jewish women and men who created NFTS saw its constituent sisterhoods and members' acts of caring for the synagogue community as part of feminine norms of spirituality. Such practices included purchasing and using ritual objects, raising funds for Hebrew Union College (HUC), supporting religious education, celebrating new traditions such as Mother's Day as a fulfillment of Jewish values, contributing to and patronizing a Reform Union Museum, and producing Jewish art calendars. These are the practices I focus on in this study to see the creative ways women reworked their roles in Reform Judaism to construct new spaces in which they could be authoritative.

The art calendars are just one example of the roles that NFTS work and committees created for Jewish women. The NFTS's National Committee on Religion chose the images, oversaw the printing, and distributed the calendars for sale. The Committee on Religion sold calendars to individual sisterhoods at wholesale cost (ten cents in 1915), and each sisterhood was responsible for selling its calendars at a requested price (twenty-five cents in 1915). The sale of the calendars for two and a half times the wholesale price allowed each sisterhood to use the calendars as a fundraiser. While local sisterhoods could decide how to use the money, NFTS's National Committee on Hebrew Union Scholarships tried to direct how funds could be used: for local sisterhoods' discretionary needs but also as "an additional source of revenue to make up for the 25 cents per capita abstracted for the Scholarship Fund"—the minimum required.[6] By raising funds for the seminary, NFTS members showed their commitment to men's training and the rabbinate; at the same time, they established a position of power for themselves by being in charge of every aspect of the calendars. Advertisements for the calendars emphasized their importance in marking domestic space as Jewish and as the specific realm of Jewish mothers. But although the calendars raised funds for contemporary American rabbis, images of rabbis are conspicuously absent in the stories told through the artwork of the calendars.

The images of the calendars published during the first half of the twentieth century present a pictorial message about Jewish American heritage vis-à-vis "the Orient." "The Orient" featured centrally as a site of Jewish heritage in NFTS Jewish art calendars. The vast majority of the extant calendars from 1913 to 1938 depict Jewish life in "the Orient," from the subjects of the images in the calendars to the biographies of the artists. These pictures give an account of ancient Jewish life in Palestine as a chapter of Jewish heritage. The visual narrative culminates in a claim that America would serve as the future community of Judaism, which also frames the end of the European Diaspora. These new images created tension with their emphasis on American exceptionalism—an emphasis that had reached a peak during World War II. The tension lay between a visual focus on Palestine but a goal of visually narrating American exceptionalism in such a way that it included Reform Jewish American values. The NFTS art calendars' emphasis on American exceptionalism contradicted international Zionist nationalist narratives that saw Palestine as a or the Jewish state. Instead, Reform Jewish American exceptionalism emphasized Palestine as a source of heritage, but not as a politically Jewish entity. The appearance of images of the State of Israel after its creation in 1948 would have seemed to be in visual continuity with earlier representations of "the Orient," even though images of a Jewish nation-state outside of the United States marked a shift in ideology and heritage for the NFTS.

In addition to signifying developments in American Reform and the role of Palestine in the NFTS's vision of Jewish heritage and the future of Judaism, the NFTS art calendars also were on trend regarding aestheticism at the turn of the twentieth century. For many Jewish Americans and their children, the value of aestheticism centered around the home. Jenna Joselit demonstrates that by the early twentieth century, Jewish Americans—especially women—expressed a "powerful interrelationship between décor and identity." I argue that seeing material and visual culture as objects producing heritage explains *why* they marked a home as Jewish. These materials—however new—placed relics of Jewish memory in the home, tying Reform Jews to a vision of a long lineage of heritage. Artists, objects, and images of Palestine played a key role in the creation of this Jewish American material aesthetic.[7] Jewish Americans desired objects that displayed their good taste and American style. Home observance was part of the founding mission of the NFTS, and leaders sought to include among these materials not only Judaica but "Judaica *plus* the knowledge of how and when to use it." The NFTS Executive Committee noted that this was an important goal for sisterhoods and Jewish women because so many Jewish holidays were home celebrations. To cultivate this observance, NFTS members focused on material goods, such as Passover plates, candlesticks, and the Jewish art calendar. The calendar sought to help cultivate and assist home observance by displaying "a beautiful reminder" of holidays in every home. In this context, sisterhoods sought to "solidify the bridge" between synagogue and home.[8] The art calendar offered the possibility of displaying Judaica that boasted the style that middle-class Jewish American homemakers sought, it introduced Jewish artists to an American audience, and it offered the dates of holidays as well as Bible readings for Shabbat that touted Judaism as "religion" not "nation." Positioning halakha as heritage rather than law or commandment, Reform Jews re-signified how Jewish material, ritual, and canonical texts mattered.[9]

Reclaiming Biblical Heritage through Visual Culture

The NFTS established a visual culture that signified the organization's Jewish heritage by presenting scenes of the Bible and Jewish holidays. The first calendar, 5674/1913–1914, Orientalized Jewish, European, and American heritage. The calendar engages European artists, Jewish and Christian, who imagined Jewish antiquity through modern European models for clothing and material culture. This anachronism links Jewish visual culture with the "high art" of modern Europe while nostalgically remaking Jewish history over in the image of the "modern West." Though the calendar features images of antiquity, the style and iconography of the images authorizes seeing the biblical past through changing interpretations. Each page included two calendar months, showing dates for both the Jewish and Gregorian calendars; later calendars continued the trend of naming the year according to the Jewish calendar, but only included Gregorian months. Each page features a central black-and-white depiction of Jewish life surrounded by embellishments that invoked Jewish ritual objects and practices. The first image from 5674/1913–1914 depicted life *In the Synagog*, showing men wearing *tallitot* and surrounding the Torah in the foreground, while women look on in the background (fig. 3.2). As the calendar explains, the page border includes symbols of the holidays that fall during these months: a *shofar* to evoke the High Holy Days and a *lulav* and *etrog* to represent Sukkoth. Although it is not noted in the calendar, this image was also displayed at the Fifth Zionist Congress in 1901. Originally titled *Jews Praying in the Synagogue on Yom Kippur*, by Maurycy (Moshe David) Gottlieb, the painting was exhibited in 1878 in the Vienna Künstlerhaus, in Warsaw, by 1898 in the Dresden Gemäldegalerie, and a photograph of the work was exhibited at the Fifth Zionist Congress.[10] In *Jews Praying in the Synagogue on Yom Kippur*, Gottlieb depicted personal and family trials over his Polish and Jewish identities.[11] By including Gottlieb's piece in the calendar, the NFTS contributed to the development of a visual culture that crossed geographic and ideological lines. Gottlieb painted the piece before the Zionist movement, but the Zionist movement's co-opting the image made it easier for Jewish Americans such as the NFTS to access his artwork. The NFTS calendar then shared the image with circles of high art and the Zionist movement while subverting both. The calendar itself made "high art" accessible, reprinting it using the new technology of mass production.

On one level, this page simply offers a depiction of Yom Kippur, bolstering the NFTS's sense that synagogue and ritual life should remain a key part of Jewish heritage and therefore a vision of how best to be Jewish in the future. Gottlieb's personal struggle over how to retain a foot both in Jewish and emerging national camps might have appealed to NFTS members as well. Neither the brocade coats nor the *tzitzit* depicted by Gottlieb would have reflected daily life for the NFTS. Gottlieb's image does not depict Palestine, but diasporic life in Poland as "the Orient." As discussed in chapter 2, prior to the nineteenth century, Jewish conceptions

Figure 3.2. *In the Synagog.*

of heritage typically separated antiquity—exemplified by the Temple—as a golden age distinct from life in exile, even in places where Jews flourished for centuries, such as Poland. The ZOA accepted that periodization of Jewish history, romanticizing Temple life as a golden age while rejecting life in Poland as a stifling corruption of true Jewish heritage. Unlike the ZOA's visual culture, the NFTS art calendars present both antiquity and Poland as significant moments in Jewish heritage, but decidedly part of the past. Placing Gottlieb's image of a Polish synagogue in the same calendar as images of Palestine (discussed later) links the images as pieces of Jewish heritage but suggests there may be little difference in how the NFTS incorporates them into a narrative of Jewish history. In eschewing a representation of biblical texts that relate to Yom Kippur, the NFTS calendar avoided associating the holiday of Yom Kippur with the ancient Temple in Jerusalem, though plenty of images existed that might have been used to show the high priest or the Holy of Holies. I discuss the importance of imagery of the Temple and visual reconstructions of the Holy of Holies in the following chapter on the *Jewish Encyclopedia*. By excluding such images, the NFTS calendar does not associate the practice of the Jewish high holidays with historical national life. In contrast, the calendar does use images depicting biblical scenes throughout the rest of the calendar, though not to emphasize national life as a model for contemporary Jewish practice.

The rest of the 5674/1913–194 calendar featured scenes illustrating biblical stories rather than postbiblical life in the synagogue. The calendar included the Swiss Italian painter Antonio Ciseri's 1863 *Martyrdom of the Seven Maccabees* from the Church of Santa Felicita in Florence and eighteenth-century French Neoclassical painter Jean-François de Troy's design for one of several tapestries depicting *The Story of Esther*. Ciseri's work is retitled simply *The Maccabees*. De Troy is cited as "G. F. de Troy" and the calendar features only one of the tapestries, *The Crowning of Esther* (fig. 3.3). In *The Maccabees*, we see Hannah, whose sons are being killed for refusal to renounce their religion, with Judah the Maccabee in the background. The story of Esther is surrounded by symbols of ancient and modern celebrations of Purim, and it represents another victory of the Jewish people. Beginning in the eleventh century, many Christian artists used an identifiable and Orientalist iconography of Jews in illuminated manuscripts and other depictions of the Bible. These included images based on Persian dress with some additions based on neoclassical imagination of Greco-Roman dress in antiquity. These signaled the link between Jews and Old Testament prophecy as antiquated and superseded by the contemporary dress symbolic of the revelation of the New Testament and its relevance to the ongoing world after the life of Jesus.[12] By the eighteenth to twentieth centuries, artists sometimes turned to various cultures such as Mesopotamia, Assyria, Babylon, Egypt, Rome, Greece, and the Arab world to depict biblical Jews or Israelites. This created an image of historical Jews otherwise lost to the past—like a visual midrash—and Orientalized not just Palestine but the entire Mediterranean and Middle East. In contrast to these cultures, de Troy turned to eighteenth-century

Figure 3.3. *The Crowning of Esther.*

France to envision biblical royalty. The NFTS calendar's selection of his work does not Orientalize the image of Jews but instead made Jews over in the image of European royalty. Though de Troy designed his *Crowning of Esther* for a Christian audience, the NFTS calendar recontextualizes the image for a twentieth-century Jewish American audience who might have recognized the continuity of this portrayal of Esther with other images of extravagant European royalty, trendsetters for "high culture."

Whether or not such images are examples of Orientalism depends on how we understand what Orientalism means and does. By a conventional definition of Orientalism, images such as de Troy's *Esther* are an alternative to the "Oriental" iconography that represents ancient Jews as looking like Arabs, Persians, other Muslim cultures, or people from the Middle East. Representing Jews in the dress of people from the East has the double value for Christians of arguing that Jews are stuck in antiquity and that this is obvious because Jews look like Muslims and others from the Middle East, whom many European Christians considered backward and enemies of the Church. This way of seeing and thinking emerged with the Crusades and persisted in much Christian culture through colonialism and modernity, when encounters with Muslims took on new political import and such images layered on new visual valences.

However, my definition of Orientalism as any means of producing and understanding "the West" by imagining the East reveals something about Christian art and its reception among Jews and reuse here in the NFTS art calendar. For one, Jews were not the only ones who imagined a "West" whose origins were rooted in ancient Palestine. Christian artists such as de Troy who depicted Esther as looking like French royalty, for example, linked ancient life in the land of Palestine with contemporary European life. The NFTS calendar borrowed this theory of history by sharing the image. Yet, by using a "Christian image" in a Jewish context, the NFTS calendar argues that Esther should be seen as a predecessor of ongoing Jewish life, not an ancient Israelite predecessor of Christianity. Through this view, images are not inherently Christian or Jewish, regardless of the artist's identification or intentions. Context shapes the meaning or argument of visual culture. Moreover, the image does not represent ancient Jewish life as it has ever looked, in modernity or antiquity. The calendars present biblical scenes through the lens of "nostalgia," which inherently includes anachronism. Nostalgia is a longing or looking to the past that suggests the present can never be quite like the past. Though colloquially imagined to be a pleasurable trip down memory lane, nostalgia is fraught with ambivalence and often "failure" to remember the past accurately. This anachronism is not actually failure, though, as the remaking of the past in the vision of the present is a crucial part of the construction of heritage. Nostalgia's ultimate distancing of the past serves the construction of individual or group narratives as having moved beyond the past even if memory of the past continues to remain constitutive of heritage.

Ancient Jewish life is a canvas for Christian and Jewish imaginative vision: it is a fictional yet meaningful "Orient" for those who envision it.

Though this image does not depict Esther looking like Arabs or Persians, for example, it still uses the structures of Orientalism. It could even be odd that Esther would not be in Persian dress, given that the plot of the book of Esther takes place during the reign of the ancient Persian Empire. The fiction is indeed what makes the image more meaningful: this tendency in visual culture makes the Bible appear relevant to contemporary life by imagining the past as looking like the present, and in so doing asserts a link between a moment in the past and contemporary heritage. It is unimportant to the power of the image to project "the Orient" as a constitutive piece of Jewish or Christian heritage that the book of Esther is a work of fiction. That the book is fiction frequently read by Jews and Christians as nonfiction emphasizes the imaginative work done in literary and visual interpretations of the past.

Arnold Eisen argues that images of Jewish ancestors evoke memories of Jewish national life, but not enough to change behavior to base contemporary practice on reinstalling the priesthood at a third Temple, the monarchy, or other aspects of ancient Israelite national life. Instead, reflection on Jewish history functioned as a reason for rejection of certain laws and for observance of others along with maintenance of Jewish heritage.[13] This understanding of nostalgia is a key part of Orientalism as heritage. Eisen argues that beginning in the nineteenth century, Reform Jews "selectively remembered" Jewish heritage in ways that "conferred [Jewish ancestors'] blessing upon change."[14] Selective remembrance is not unique to Reform Jews in Germany and the United States. Selecting what aspects of history and previous practices resonate in the present is the nature of heritage. This selective process sometimes romanticizes and sometimes demonizes the past, but the construction of heritage necessarily molds the past according to perceived needs in the present and hopes for the future. Cultural exchange with Christians of such contested material as the Hebrew Bible was not new or unique to Reform Jews in the United States.

Instead, there is a long history of Jews using but recontextualizing Christian images. For example, Jewish publications of the Bible in translation became possible in mass production by the seventeenth century, and the illustrations accompanying the *Tsene-Urene* provide a useful example of premodern exchange between Christian and Jewish visual culture. Jacob ben Isaac Ashkenazi of Janow wrote the *Tsene-Urene*, a Yiddish "translation" and interpretation of the Torah, with an earliest known publication date of 1622. There was a tradition of Jewish illuminated manuscripts, however, Milly Heyd argues that it was not influential for the illustration of the mass-printed *Tsene-Urene* and instead Christian presses and publications were quite influential. Jewish illuminated manuscripts would have been rare and expensive, whereas Christian presses and publications would have been much more readily available. In many cases, Jews used Christian presses to publish editions of the *Tsene-Urene* because of their affordability and due to limitations on Jewish printing.[15] In multiple editions of the *Tsene-Urene*, Jews borrowed images from Christian texts, evidence at once of cultural exchange yet also of the financial and social constraints on Jewish life. Yet, this borrowing did not mean a wholesale important of Christian concepts. In some instances, identical or nearly identical images are printed alongside the *Tsene-Urene*'s text as in Christian Bibles. Various editions of the *Tsene-Urene*, for example, borrowed identical images but recontextualized them alongside different passages or made slight alterations of the images, either through cropping or copying. Even small changes reflect Jewish awareness of the meaning of the images in Christian contexts and an interest to reclaim texts and shift the meaning of images toward Jewish concepts and worldviews.

The 5674/1913–1914 calendar romanticizes Jewish antiquity in "the Orient," highlighting Jewish triumphs like those of Esther and the Maccabees. Yet the calendar also ends with Eduard Bendemann's *The Destruction of Jerusalem* (fig. 3.4). Like Gottlieb's, Bendemann's work was also shown at the Fifth Zionist Congress, though this piece was not. Bendemann was a Jewish German who ultimately converted to Christianity, as did several other nineteenth-century Jewish artists living in Germany. He produced works that depicted scenes from the Hebrew Bible offering interpretations or representations that were heavily influenced by the Nazarene movement. Richard Cohen argues that most depictions of the Hebrew Bible from the nineteenth century were similarly influenced by Christian readings of the Old Testament rather than by Jewish tradition or midrash.[16] But this assertion does not account for the ways that Jews could recontextualize images created by Christians or by Jews influenced by Christian artists to shift the argument of the images to reflect concepts that are influenced by Jewish views of heritage. Iconography alone does not reveal how visual culture has developed.

The context of images reveals subtle ways that influences or shared images are also opportunities for polemics. That these images were used in the NFTS art calendar indicates the cultural exchange with Christian visual culture. But at the same time, the recontextualization of these images in the NFTS art calendars spoke back to their source and added news layers of meaning. Presented in the NFTS art calendar, there is a clear assertion that these images tell a Jewish story. Bendemann's status as Jewish or as a Christian convert becomes either irrelevant or polemicized,

Figure 3.4. *The Destruction of Jerusalem.*

especially considering the use of Michelangelo's work discussed earlier. These images did not have a Christian meaning for Reform Jews, and gained an alternative meaning for Reform Jews through their recontextualization in the art calendar. The NFTS's use of these works asserts that viewing images created by Christians is not dangerous to Jews. This makes an argument for the possibility of living in a plural society at the same time that the calendars make claims for the ability of Jewish Americans to change, reclaim, or assert new Jewish meanings for these images. The central picture depicts the destruction of the First Temple, while Romans erected the Arch of Titus pictured in the border to commemorate the destruction of the Second Temple.

The 5676/1915–1916 calendar continued to use images of biblical figures created by a Christian artist, namely, Michelangelo. Featuring the theme "The Prophets of Israel" as portrayed by Michelangelo in the Sistine Chapel, the cover and calendar pages from that issue depict paintings of Isaiah, Joel, Ezekiel, Jeremiah, and Zachariah (fig. 3.5). These images of

Figure 3.5. *Ezechiel.*

ancestral national life in ancient Israel demonstrate the NFTS's comfort in borrowing visual culture from Christians, even so far as such central and celebrated artists as Michelangelo. For biblical illustration or other Jewish visual culture, Jews have considered artists, even Christian artists, "as functional and instrumental." That Jews have been willing and able to turn to Christians for the production of their visual culture and have exchanged artistic influences with Christian communities across medieval and early modern Europe indicates complex exchange rather than simplistic polemic. Jews have looked at Christians to understand themselves for two thousand years, and vice versa, and members of the NFTS were no different.[17] In the case of the images of the Sistine Chapel, even though the artwork was European and Christian in its original context, the combined images in NFTS visual culture as well as the interest in making that culture available for mass consumption were American impulses, shared between Jews and non-Jews. As their Christian American neighbors produced visual culture that reflected their constructions of heritage, NFTS art calendars helped create a visual Judaism that drew on "European impulses that spread to America": sentimentalism and romanticism, which "understand faith as an element of feeling rather than rationality"; devotional emotionalism at home, where the calendars would mark space as "Jewish"; and industrialization, which facilitated the inexpensive availability of material goods.[18] The NFTS art calendars appropriated European and Christian history and visual culture for Jewish American heritage, transforming sites so powerful as the Vatican from an overtly dangerous site to a more complicated visual text that could be safe for Jewish viewing. As a category, "art" reframed many examples of Catholic or European images into visual culture "safe" for American aesthetic encounter.

Using Michelangelo's artwork established a cultural realm for NFTS members vis-à-vis their Christian American neighbors in two distinct ways: (1) it demonstrated commonality through their shared values of art and consumption, and (2) it and maintained boundaries by making polemical claims about the function of prophets in Jewish tradition and theology. The images of the prophets are not themes nor figures from Christian art that have been reworked by Jewish artists; they are exact reproductions of explicitly Christian artwork that indicate an exchange of symbols and meanings on a Jewish-Christian American middle ground. But printing images of the Sistine Chapel in the Jewish art calendar suggests these images rightly belong to Jewish tradition. They did not even need to be reworked to be properly Jewish; the original images assert the centrality of the prophets in both Jewish history and in Jewish understandings of prophecy over Christianity's claims. Much Christian visual culture has depicted prophets in ways linked to New Testament apostles, visually reading the Hebrew Bible as a typological prophecy of the New Testament to come.[19] Dressed in neoclassical style, Michelangelo's prophets appear like figures in Greco-Roman style, locating them in the Roman context of the New Testament. But by borrowing and recontextualizing Michelangelo's Renaissance sculptures, the NFTS calendar undermines the power of the prophets' dress and appearance to make claims on the Hebrew Bible that construct it as merely foreshadowing the New Testament and the truth of Christianity.

Similarly, the 5674/1913–1914 calendar suggests such a reclamation of Moses as well. One of its pages features Michelangelo's sculpture of *Moses* from the Church of Saint Peter in Chains in Rome (as discussed in the opening of this chapter) with the explanation that the artwork is "illustrative of Shabuoth."[20] While both Jews and Christians understood Moses to have received the law on Mount Sinai, Michelangelo or his Christian viewers would not have had the Jewish holiday of Shavuot in mind. This altered the meanings of both Jewish and Christian culture. The very means of acculturating—of becoming like their surrounding neighbors—was also a means of speaking back to that culture and of creating boundaries between Jews and Christians. Ivan Marcus argues that cultural exchange, shared customs, and polemics were critical aspects of premodern inward acculturation, but they disappeared with the greater tendency to assimilate in modern contexts when Jews were granted full citizenship. However, the visual culture of NFTS suggests that these complex modes of acculturation characterize both premodern and modern Jewish practice.[21] Instead of concluding that polemics as an aspect of cultural exchange disappeared after the premodern period, we can see the NFTS calendars as an example of "counterhistory," a genre of narrative that subverts hegemonic Christian narratives of "the West" and thereby the world. Though Susannah Heschel locates this radical political effort more among Jews in Europe than in the United States, the revision of the meaning of Michelangelo offers a counterhistory that dethrones Christianity at the same time that the NFTS calendar shares Michelangelo's explicitly Christian images. This counterhistory responds to Christian repression of Judaism through its construction of "Judaism." Heschel places Judaism in quotes at times to signal the comparison of Christian imaginations of Jewish life to the construction of Orientalism, even as she questions many of the methods and implications of Said. The calendar implicitly overthrows Christian power to define not just the events but the structures of history, and "the subaltern Jewish voice [insinuates] itself as necessary to [the] Christian, even while claiming that the Christian is not necessary to the Jewish."²² In the case of this NFTS calendar, Jewish Americans can engage Michelangelo's art as such—the calendar uses the images as "art" and not pieces of Christian visual culture. If secularism has frequently applied the structures of Christianity to a supposedly egalitarian plural society, this calendar takes the opportunity of access to Michelangelo to offer a counterhistory as to the place of the prophets in "Western" heritage to claim them for Judaism. Though many Jews may have sought to "question or even overthrow the standard portrayal of Western history" as Susannah Heschel argues of nascent nineteenth-century Jewish studies in Europe, many Jews did not seek to overthrow the concept of "the West" but instead to write themselves into it. Rather than looking to the New Testament and Greek civilization, Jews placed the Hebrew Bible at the origin of "Western civilization."²³

Jewish Heritage through Jewish Artwork in the NFTS Calendars

Beyond subverting the meaning and therefore import of Christian visual culture to Jewish and more generally "Western" heritage, the NFTS calendars presented figures such as Moses's mother Jochebed (fig. 3.6) in an effort to counter assimilation. Whereas Christianity connected Jesus's mother Mary to the idealization of motherhood, NFTS found a Jewish alternative in Jochebed to depict maternal love. The importance of establishing such a Jewish symbol is illustrated by Johanna Kohler's "Report of the National Committee on Union Museum"—a vehicle for requesting sisterhoods to donate funds—in which she directly invokes the intentions to commission artwork from Boris Schatz's Bezalel school in Palestine for display in the Union Museum and synagogues:

> Mr. Schatz has had in mind for a long time an idea for a piece of sculpture which will portray Jewish Motherhood with all the depth of maternal love which is characteristic of the Jewish woman. This work would, in a measure, offset the popular conception of ideal Motherhood as depicted by Christian artists in the representation of Mary, the Mother of Jesus.
>
> The artist believes that maternal love might be typified in the person of "Jochebed," the mother of Moses, and that the group of sculptures might show Jochebed at the moment of supreme sacrifice, when she is bidding farewell to the infant Moses.²⁴

Figure 3.6. *Jochebed*.

By supporting Schatz, Kohler supported the representation of the values of motherhood that had been foundational for NFTS. Kohler and Schatz asserted through Jochebed that motherhood was at least as central to Judaism as it was to Christianity. Like the prophets and Moses himself, Jochebed was a figure that Judaism and Christianity share. The place of Jochebed in traditional Judaism serves to emphasize her as a symbol for Jewish women. But the prominence in American national consciousness of the Exodus story in general and Moses specifically, whose story begins with Jochebed's resistance against the orders of Pharaoh, may also have helped to elevate Jochebed as a symbol for Kohler and Schatz.[25] If Jochebed was revered as an excellent mother and a symbol of Jewish women, then Jewish American women could see their potential as virtuous mothers as rooted biblically and equal to their Christian neighbors. Further, although Schatz and Kohler selected Jochebed as an alternative to Christian symbols of motherhood, Kohler's suggestion that Schatz's artwork would depict Jochebed at a moment of "supreme sacrifice" of her child for the good of Israel seems to draw polemically on language typically used by Christians to portray Jesus, Mary, or God the Father.

The substitution of Jochebed for Mary does more than solely adapt Christian symbols by Judaizing them; it inserts Jewish symbols into American culture. In their embrace by NFTS, Jochebed and Moses became a part of American sensitivity designed as a corollary and alternative to Jesus and Mary. Jochebed and Moses were always a part of the symbolic repertoire of Jewish tradition, but Jochebed, especially, was a more marginalized figure in the past. Moses and Jochebed's significance was heightened beyond tradition through this injection into American culture insofar as Moses became a kind of Jewish Jesus and Jochebed, a Jewish Mary. This wrote out Jesus from NFTS members' view of history, positing a heritage of Judaism that dated farther back than Christianity, suggested that commandments were not an "Old" Testament, and drew a line from Jochebed's imagined maternalism to the NFTS members. The NFTS calendar made Jewish women more visible in antiquity to create space for contemporary women in Reform Judaism.

A decade later, in 5685/1924–1925, the calendar focused solely on the story of Jeremiah, through the work of German artist Eduard Bendemann. Bendemann, who converted from Judaism to Christianity, had his work exhibited at the Fifth Zionist Congress in 1901. He produced *The Mourning Jews in Exile* in 1831, before his conversion (fig. 3.7), and *Jeremiah on the Ruins of Jerusalem* later that decade, after his conversion (fig. 3.8). His work thus predated Zionism and did not articulate a

Figure 3.7. *Jews Taken Captive into Babylon.*

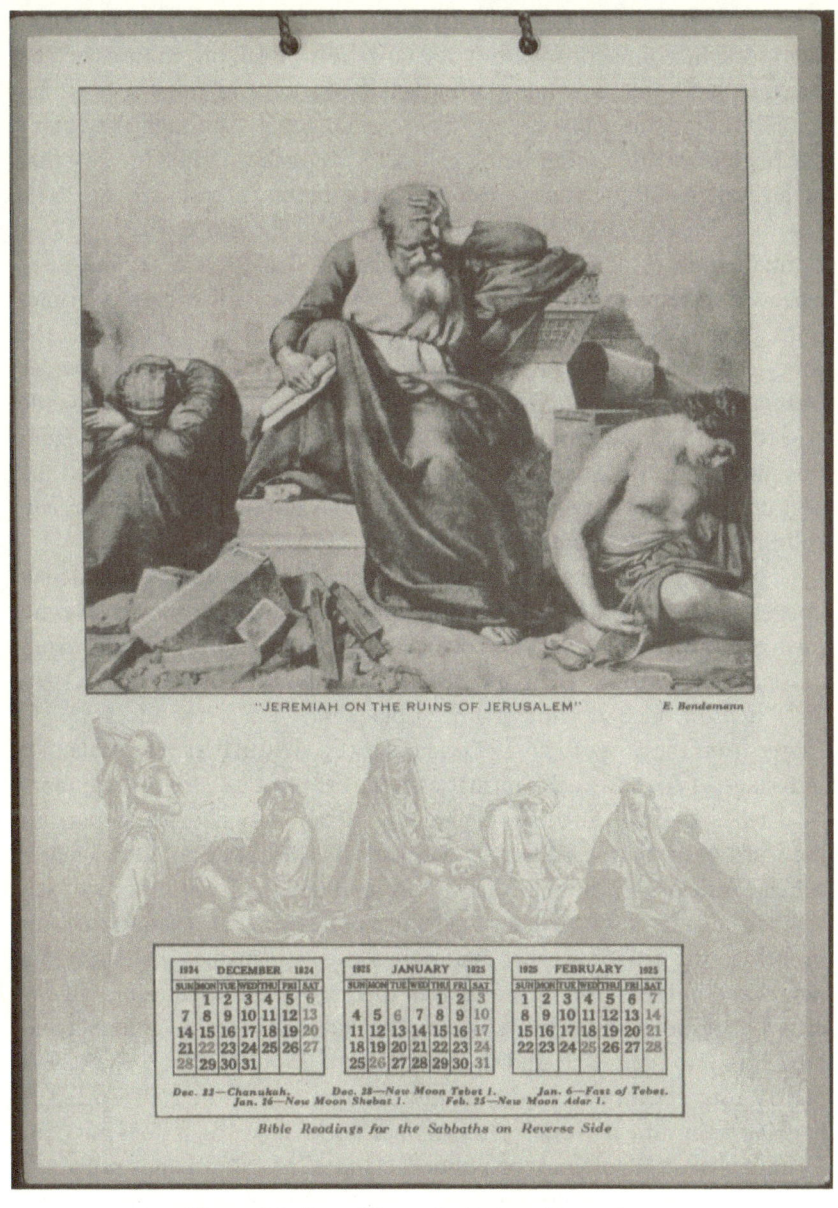

Figure 3.8. *Jeremiah on the Ruins of Jerusalem.*

hope for a Jewish return to the land that the Zionist movement would later seek in connection with a revitalization of Jewish culture. Yet he struggled with the same questions of emancipation and equality to which the NFTS and the Zionist movement responded.[26] Although the calendar begins with Jeremiah being called to prophecy, a later image—that of Jerusalem's destruction—becomes even more central (see fig. 3.8). The final image actually takes place outside of Palestine. Psalm 137 in German frames the image: "By the waters of Babylon we sat and wept when we remembered Zion"[27] (fig. 3.9). Marked by Bendemann's German translation rather than the quote in Hebrew, this image subtly links the American Reform Jewish community to German heritage and invokes Germany as a place of high culture. It reminds viewers of Zion while also referencing the progress that the Jewish community has made from this moment in time, suggesting American Reform Jews internalized the best of Jewish heritage, from antiquity to the European Enlightenment, culminating with the Reform movement.

Not all of the calendars produced during the pre-state period depict images of Palestine, though Palestine played a new role for artists who traveled, studied, and occasionally relocated there. Biblical stories from outside of the land were portrayed, as well as other images associated with Judaism, such as photographs of plaques of *The Scribe* and *Midnight Prayer* from the 5690/1929–1930 calendar (fig. 3.10). That year's calendar introduces a change in the format as well. Previous calendars were more than twice the size of this one and most likely designed for display on the walls of the home. This calendar, with its cork backing, seems better suited for desk use, though I have not found any firsthand reports of sisterhood members on their own calendar use. Along with the differences in format and artistic subject matter, this calendar invokes Palestine in a new way—not obvious in the images themselves but in the lives of the artists. It presents the artwork of Schatz, who was born in Lithuania and moved to Jerusalem to found the Bezalel art school (fig. 3.11). The school played a significant role in the Zionist movement, but the NFTS presents his biography and artwork within its own worldview, which does not conform to Zionist ideological or political claims. Though it is not explained in the calendar, Schatz also designed plaques for HUC and several Reform synagogues, thus establishing a tie among contemporary Palestine, Jewish American communities, and a developing visual culture outside of the calendar that would have been familiar to the women of NFTS.

Over the next five years, the calendars continued a similar pattern. They maintained a smaller format and eventually became similar to today's

Figure 3.9. *By the Waters of Babylon.*

planners, a format that the NFTS continued to use through the end of the twentieth century. Members could carry their calendars wherever they went, marking all of their organizational duties—at home and away—at once as Jewish and as contemporary. In these later calendars, as in the Schatz

Figure 3.10. *Midnight Prayer.*

Figure 3.11. *Boris Schatz.*

calendar, the NFTS selected artists born in Central or Eastern Europe, and their biographies describe immigration or travel to Palestine, along with art exhibitions there, as arguments for their excellence. Sometimes these calendars included images of Palestine-as-"Orient" (fig. 3.12). For

Figure 3.12. *The Boy David.*

example, the 1933 calendar included a sketch of *The Boy David* (March–April 1933/5693). The image draws on a long history of interpretation of David, which includes many possible visions of both his body and activities. As a boy, David is pictured herding sheep and playing music. This image of David is canonical, though it eschews David as a warrior or king, other central aspects of David's life in biblical narration, along with extensive visual and verbal interpretive traditions. Through David, Palestine is romanticized as a peaceful place, associated with communion with God, especially through the symbol of David's lyre. Jews have long connected David's musical abilities with his ability to know God's will, rooted in biblical prooftexts such as I Samuel: 16 and II Samuel: 1, 17–18, and 25–27, in addition to the tradition that David wrote or inspired many of the Psalms.

Other images show contemporaneous Palestine (fig. 3.13). Images of *Mystic Safed* and *Gypsy Arabs in Sephardic Quarter—Jerusalem* depict the architecture of fabled cities in Palestine, filled with robed and faceless inhabitants. In *Mystic Safed* from June–August 1934/5694, we see three Jews, closer to God by mere virtue of their presence in not only the land of Israel but specifically the space of Safed as indicated by the description of the city as "mystic" in the image title. Safed symbolizes kabbalistic connection to God in two ways. It has been populated by many who seek to practice kabbalah since the medieval period and the explosion of the practice of kabbalah in Judaism. This very population of Jews throughout history, not only during the Zionist period, is owed to traditions that the place is holy, somehow more likely to result in an experience of God. Moreover, many who practiced kabbalah believed that the messiah might return first to Safed before traveling to Jerusalem. Many Reform Jews eschewed this type of messianic heritage and the specific practices of kabbalah as anachronistic, and therein lies the power of this image of Safed in an NFTS art calendar. Safed and thereby Palestine appear not as instructional for such practices. The image of Safed suggests a kind of timeless dress and architecture, depicting "the Orient" as a place connected to the Jewish past—the medieval period at least, but potentially an unchanged presence of God and appearance of inhabitants that date to the biblical period. The generic nature of the robes and dress cannot be linked to any single time period, or even certainty that these are Jews who walk the romanticized streets of Safed. The image is contemporaneous because it does not offer a depiction of the specificity of Jewish life in Safed, Palestine, in the early twentieth century. Instead these timeless streets and inhabitants are converted to a link to a rich Jewish heritage as seen and understood through the lens of Jewish American

Figure 3.13. *Mystic Safed*.

Reform values. Reform can extract the spiritual connection to God that such an image or symbol offers, yet the NFTS calendar's inclusion of this image indicates that the symbol can only by properly understood through Reform's ideology of progress.

Figure 3.14. *Gypsy Arabs in Sephardic Quarter—Jerusalem.*

The NFTS oriented and Orientalized the view of such scenes in Palestine, including the image of Gypsy Arabs who are located in the Sephardic Quarter of Jerusalem (July–August 1935/5695) (fig. 3.14). Labeling the Arabs as "Gypsy," the image and calendar depict Arabs as homeless and wandering, as opposed to Jews whose history may be rooted in Palestine and who find themselves at home in the United States and perhaps in Palestine. "Gypsy," "Arab," and "Sephardic" all mark the space of this scene as "Oriental" Jerusalem. These homeless Arabs are not progressive contemporaries of the Jewish Americans who own and view the NFTS art calendar. Rather, they are contemporaneous, linking Jerusalem to an othered and romanticized "the Orient" that contrasts with the workaday lives of Jewish Americans. These Arabs, like Jewish "mystics" in Safed, are more human relics that demonstrate the link of Jerusalem and "the Orient" to Jewish heritage than they are contemporary participants in dynamic politics. As with the image of David, these Arabs are depicted playing music, again suggesting the link to generic spirituality rather than specific halakhic practices or Christian or Muslim practices, as might more likely be the case. The depiction of Safed and the Sephardic Quarter and their inhabitants as contemporaneous transforms them into relics of Jewish heritage, biblical and medieval "the Orient," than as individuals or members of contemporary social groups.

The pattern of invoking Palestine through images in the calendars, the biography of artists, or both, along with the birth and travel of artists in Eastern Europe, suggests a simultaneous connection to and distance from Eastern Europe and Palestine that may subtly indicate the supersession of America as the future of Judaism. Scenes of the destruction of Jerusalem and the exile to Babylon argue for the progress of Jewish Americans after the end of Jewish national life. The romantic and Orientalist nature of these later calendars evoke both Palestine and Eastern Europe as claims of grand Jewish pasts that had come to an end. Just as Jewish artists and their artwork moved from Eastern Europe and Palestine to America, the calendars imply, so did the center of Jewish religious practice.

This sense of "Americanness" that the NFTS art calendars constructed was formally similar to that created by the prolific examples of Protestant American visual culture that represented Catholic European life as Protestant American religious and national heritage. Artwork and photos of Europe as well as travel and travel literature became popular in nineteenth-century Protestant American visual culture. As Protestants viewed this visual culture, they othered Catholicism by experiencing it through images of Europe that treated Catholic sites as museums and tourist attractions—relics of Protestant Christianity's past rather than dynamic spaces and practices of contemporary American or European Catholic life. By internalizing these images, Protestants learned about Christianity by gleaning the best of Catholic culture while avoiding what they considered to be Catholic idolatry and discarding any negative aspects of the culture through their construction of distance.[28] Additionally, Protestant Americans also portrayed "the Orient" in travel literature, photographs, postcards, and replicas. As Protestant Americans saw themselves drawing from the best of the Christian past, they also used representations of "the Orient" to extract the best of ancient Israelite culture to form ideal contemporary Protestant selves.[29] The Jewish women of the NFTS, then, followed a similar path in representing their Americanness, by predominantly viewing Palestine and Europe as communities and cultures eclipsed by American progress. NFTS calendars authorized a construction of Reform Jewish selves juxtaposed to Jewish life in Palestine and Europe as the Jewish past, i.e., "the Orient." While some positive essence of Judaism might be extracted from those communities, NFTS art calendars represented a key aspect of Reform Jewish Americans' heritage as their ability to discard the anachronism of their "Oriental" and

European Jewish counterparts while importing the best of this heritage into their American lives.

Later calendars did not focus on biblical scenes at all, though they did continue to include narratives about "the Orient" as the less progressive past compared to the United States, articulating an argument for American exceptionalism. The rise of Nazism further entrenched the representation of Jewish life in Europe as surpassed by Jewish vitality in the United States. The 5697/1936–1937 calendar features the artwork of Hella Arensen. The calendar includes a brief biography of Arensen, and the March–April 1936 NFTS newsletter explained that Arensen was "a young German-Jewish artist who is now residing in the United States." Encouraging NFTS members to purchase a calendar of Arensen's drawings of European cities as a gift for weddings and other occasions, the newsletter also notes that purchase of the calendar would give Arensen "encouragement and necessary practical assistance" as a refugee in the United States.[30] In addition to several overt statements of the security Arensen could find in the United States, the image titled *Old Jewish Quarter* could be taken as a pun: Not only is the Jewish Quarter "old," as in well established for centuries in Germany and other European nations, but it was also already in the past (fig. 3.15). Though

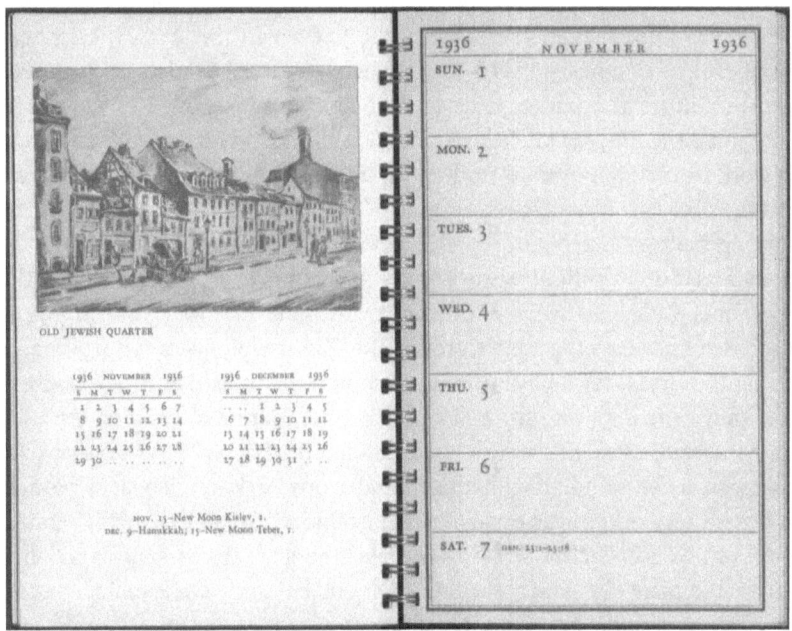

Figure 3.15. *Old Jewish Quarter.*

Arensen painted images of Jewish life from her own experiences, the presentation of these images in the art calendar, along with their description in the newsletter, suggests that Jewish culture in Europe had been eclipsed by Jewish American culture. The calendar simultaneously reminds users of the success of Jews in America by embodying American values of good taste in material consumption *and* commenting on the struggles of European Jews. Of course Jews struggled in "contemporaneous" Europe: only the "contemporary" United States was safe in this view. This turned space—Palestine, Europe, and the United States—into time. These were not three dynamic places, but two pasts and one progressive present/future. Unlike previous calendars, this calendar did not draw on Palestine, but similar viewing practices—treating Europe, like Palestine, as a land of heritage and thus imposing a sense of its anachronism—were applied here as well.

The Debate over Zionism

Although the NFTS calendars feature many images of the biblical "Orient" and later bibliographical and visual representations of a contemporaneous "Orient," none of the images discussed so far endorse Zionist ideology. One exception exists in the calendars, but even in this case, the strategy of carefully selecting words and images shapes the NFTS's inclusion of Zionist culture as an attempt to leave the organization open to those who may not have embraced Zionism. The 5698/1937–1938 calendar features artwork from Max Pollak, including several etchings that use similar subject matter to earlier calendars, such as *David's Tower in Jerusalem* (fig. 3.16), harking back to a staple of representation of "the Orient" as a relic of the Israelite nation in antique history, but also an image of a *haluzah* (fig. 3.17), or "pioneer." Chalutzim were central to pre-state Zionist visual culture as discussed in chapter 2, representing the Zionist pioneers who prepared the land of Israel for Jewish immigration and the imagined future national life. They remained a continuous part of Israeli national imagination even after the state came to fruition, as discussed in chapter 2. A viewer would not have to be familiar with this visual trope to know it was a pioneer in Palestine, as the reverse page of the calendar explains that this pioneer girl lived in a collectivist colony in Palestine and was known as a Sabra, the cactus plant for which children born in Palestine were nicknamed.

Even though the NFTS calendar invokes the pioneer, a shared icon with Zionist culture, it does not represent Jewish pioneers either visually or verbally in similar ways to the ZOA. The term "Zionism" is never

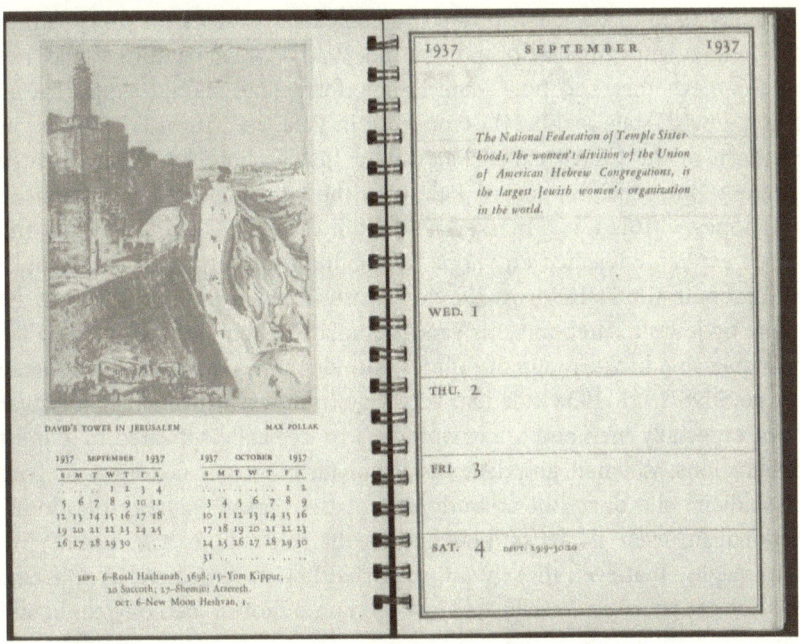

Figure 3.16. *David's Tower in Jerusalem*.

Figure 3.17. *Haluzah*.

explicitly used in the description. This reflects a strategy for unity within the Reform movement throughout the 1930s, when factions could not agree on whether and how American Reform Jews should support a an ethnic Jewish state or liberal democracy in Palestine. The 1937 Columbus Platform of the CCAR called Palestine a "Jewish homeland," one created through "the rehabilitation of Palestine, the land hallowed by memories and hopes."[31] This was a marked shift from the 1885 Pittsburgh Platform, which explicitly rejected any hope for rebuilding Palestine or the Temple. But even in 1937, Reform did not institutionally endorse Zionism by name or Jewish statehood. Instead, it emphasizes culture and spirituality, palatable to a broad range of politics and ideologies. Further, the *haluzah* in the 5698/1937-1938 calendar looks quite different from the muscular Jews, especially men and a few women, who typically appeared in Zionist publications. A small girl detached from farm scenes, factories, or lives of soldiers, she does not embody any of the typical imagery of Zionist nationalism even as she is linked to life in Palestine as a *haluzah*.[32] We can imagine that even those who supported Jewish settlement in Palestine but not necessarily a Jewish state or hegemonic Zionist ideology could still connect to the image of the *haluzah*. The careful representation of the girl suggests that while NFTS members were certainly aware of the debates and divisions over Zionism, they also sought ways to hold their movement together and to find images and language that allowed them to maintain a sense of unity despite disagreements. Even though the calendar did not emphasize a robust Zionist vision, the images in the 5698/1937-1938 calendar are still different from earlier images that suggested a fraught Jewish life in contemporary Palestine, Orientalized as contemporaneous or ossified.

After 1938: Explicit Nationalisms

Though this book focuses on visual culture through 1938, a quick view of a few NFTS calendars published after 1938 heightens the difference between postwar nationalism and prewar experiments with various ways to represent Palestine, Europe, and the United States. Two images serve as exemplars. The first shows how the NFTS focused on icons of American nationalism during World War II, and a final image shows the State of Israel as connected to a vision for Reform life. These are transformations in the iconography of the NFTS, but not of the underlying argument of the NFTS art calendars that Jews are American and can see Palestine—even turned Jewish state—as a place of heritage. Seeing Palestine as an ancient biblical homeland influenced how the NFTS articulated a narrative of a national life of citizenship rooted clearly in the United States in the twentieth century but with unthreatening connections of heritage in the "Orient." Presenting "the Orient" as heritage shows Reform Jews having no citizenship connections to the new Jewish state. The NFTS makes no ambiguous claims about their citizenship and political loyalties: these lie only with the United States. Other Jewish visual cultures in the United States equally argued for loyalty to the United States even while expressing interest in a future, or recently created, Jewish state, but none included imagery as explicitly focused on American nationalism as the NFTS.

During World War II as they had during World War I, Jewish Americans used numerous expressions—from public performances of massive pageants to poetry to military service—to show their loyalty and optimism in American values while simultaneously articulating their sense of the relevance of Jewish history.[33] But nearing the end of World War II, artistic assertions of America's exceptionalism and the NFTS's commitment to the American nation became even more explicit. No longer implying American triumphalism through the visions of "the Orient" and Europe, a

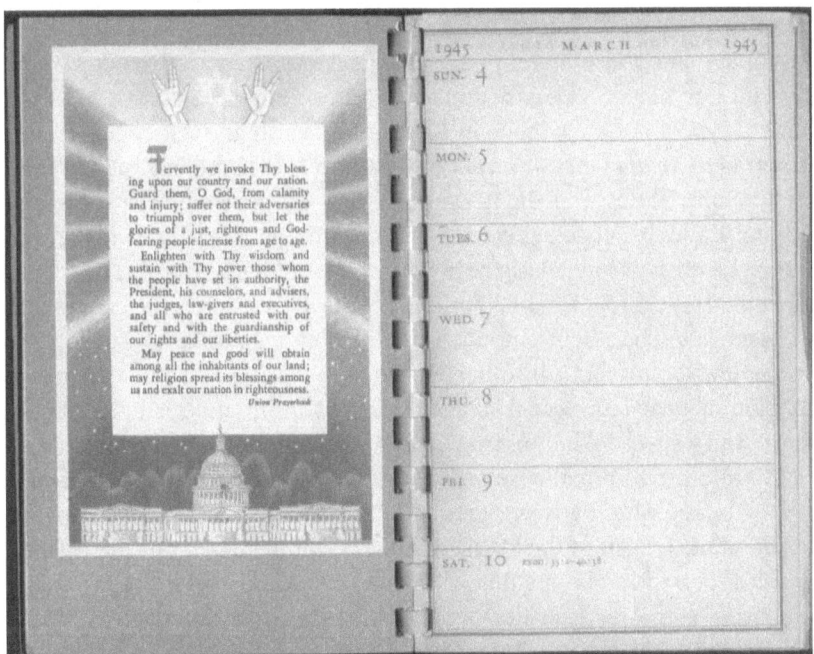

Figure 3.18. *Fervently We Invoke Thy Blessing.*

5705/1944–1945 image explicitly invokes a prayer from the *Union Prayer Book* over America, as represented by the United States Capitol Building (fig. 3.18). The prayer reads:

> Fervently we invoke Thy blessing upon our country and our nation. Guard them, O God, from calamity and injury; suffer not their adversaries to triumph over them, but let the glories of a just, righteous and God-fearing people increase from age to age.
>
> Enlighten with Thy wisdom and sustain with Thy power those whom the people have set in authority, the President, his counselors, and advisers, the judges, law-givers and executives, and all who are entrusted with our safety and with the guardianship of our rights and our liberties.
>
> May peace and good will obtain among all the inhabitants of our land; may religion spread its blessings among us and exalt our nation in righteousness.

This prayer dates to the fourteenth century, and various Jewish communities have altered it to suit their context, such as changing the focus of the prayer from a monarchy to a presidency.[34] Taken together, this image and prayer assert that, from the NFTS's perspective, "our country and our nation" refers definitively to the United States, not a Jewish nation. It portrays a complete integration of Jewish and American values, ushering in an era when Jews felt more securely at home in America than ever before. The rays of light exuding from the Star of David onto the Capitol Building suggest not only a connection between the two but that the righteousness of Jewish heritage would influence the future of the United States as well. Channeling Isaiah, the calendar projects a sense that Judaism would be a light unto the United States, suggesting a reconception of the Jewish covenant. In other words, here "chosenness," or the Jewish mission, appears connected to Jews' ability to join and lead the United States and a special relationship between Jews and other Americans rather than a more traditional conception of the observation of halakha and a special relationship between Jews and God. This image can be compared to the ZOA's reprint of the Statue of Liberty shining down on "the Orient" that I discussed in the opening of chapter 2. Both images place the visual architecture of American democracy at the center of an image of Jewish American life. Unlike the ZOA's magazine's cover, this NFTS art calendar does not include "the Orient" alongside a picture of American democracy, though both the NFTS and the ZOA's images are imaginative depictions of symbols of the United States. Here, Jewish heritage shines down on the United States from the Star of David. In the ZOA's cover, the United States shines down on "the Orient." Both picture a connection between Jewishness and Americanness, but the NFTS art calendar pictures the United States as the land of its primary focus. Perhaps influenced by the start of World War II and the increased patriotism throughout the United States, the art calendar focuses on American nationalism while presenting an image that includes a sense that Jewish heritage will guide the United States' governance toward peace.

After World War II ended, a totally new context for understanding Jewish experience emerged in the United States. By 1951, the Holocaust was well known, the State of Israel had been established, and the United States permitted a number of immigrants to enter, though most refugees from Europe had moved to Israel. Perhaps due to these changes and the new atmosphere, the 5711/1950–1951 calendar linked the significance of Israel for Jewish American heritage more strongly than in the past. The biography of the artist, Elinor Mintz, described her visit to Israel from 1947 until her return to the United States shortly after the establishment of the State of Israel as "the most potent influence on her life to date." Mintz's *The Workers' Village* (fig. 3.19) included the caption, "With Immigrant Camps In the Distance: And the legend becomes a reality, after the camps they are building their settlements." Contrary to the depiction of Israel in the calendars of the early twentieth century, by 1950 the NFTS had chosen to closely define itself through images of Jewish settlement in the land of Israel. NFTS members from 1950 might have been able to look back and see how this alignment came out of the patterns and practices throughout the first half of the twentieth century, when calendar images drew on Jewish life in "the Orient" in various ways, frequently left open the interpretation of images of the land, and always indicated the importance of American patriotism and Jewish American life throughout shifting iconography of "the Orient."

Conclusion

Three major changes catapulted visual culture into more central importance for the construction of Reform Jewish American women's heritage: technology, shifting roles of halakha and Jewish tradition in American Reform Judaism, and the development of new women's organizations.

Figure 3.19. *The Workers' Village.*

Images may always have been a part of Jewish culture,[35] but technological developments in photography and the ability to cheaply reproduce images en masse created a new possibility for the production and circulation of visual culture. Reform's deauthorization of halakha as *the* practice of Judaism opened up space for alternative ways of embodying and marking one's Jewish life, especially for women. This, along with broader social changes in the United States, influenced the innovations of NFTS in the organization of Reform Jewish communal life. Using new technologies and visualizing a new place for Judaism in American and "Western" heritage, much of the NFTS visual culture displayed cultural exchange with Christians. Including Christian images produced in the Renaissance and modern European art movements, the NFTS art calendars recontextualized these images and thereby created new arguments for the images' meaning and the place of Jewish heritage in understanding the roots of democracy and the unfolding of world history. Reprinting Christian images did not merely "ape" or copy Christians, but offered a counterhistory not only to Christian interpretations of the Bible but to Orientalism and the place of Jews in a binary conception of "the West" vis-à-vis "the Orient."

By using images of "the Orient," the NFTS created an overt connection to Jewish heritage while also practicing a form of Jewishness not structured by halakha. Through distributing and viewing those images, NFTS women could assert their own vision for American Judaism and create roles for themselves within it, at once drawing from and speaking back to Jewish tradition, American culture, and Zionism. NFTS art calendars were thus part of a process in which sisterhood members inscribed themselves as American and part of broader American narratives without compromising their connection to Jewish history. The production of a visual culture in the United States through materials such as the art calendars thus proved innovative for Jewish culture and American culture by combining the two. The calendars were visual arguments that one could be both Jewish *and* American. The increasing centrality of American exceptionalism indicates the comfort that NFTS members felt in asserting that their participation in Judaism not only did not conflict with American citizenship but was, in fact, an affirmation of American values.

Aside from serving as a space to debate and construct how NFTS members understood Palestine, Europe, and the United States, the calendars reveal various other concerns with which Palestine and politics were always in tension. Women created sisterhoods as spaces for leadership that did not overtly challenge either halakhic or cultural structures within Reform Jewish institutions. Women worked in ways that helped them define themselves as Jewish subjects, even if many aspects of Jewish tradition were unavailable to them. Their ascension to leadership went hand-in-hand with their turn toward new forms of visual culture that relied on Palestine as a motif. This constructed Palestine not only as a political question or as a space for women in the NFTS to inhabit but also as an ideal with which to synthesize their many commitments as Jewish Americans.

Chapter 4

Reconstructing History

The Jewish Encyclopedia

> Fundamentally one as are the manifestations of the Jewish spirit, they are distractingly variegated when viewed without a clue. Scattered through all lands, and passing through all the historic periods, the Jewish people have been connected with every phase of the western-Asiatic and European culture which is called civilization.
>
> —Joseph Jacobs, *The Jewish Encyclopedia: A Guide to Its Contents*, 1906

Alongside an article on "Temple, Plan of the Second" in the *Jewish Encyclopedia* (*JE*), Charles Chipiez's reconstruction of "The Court of Priests" imagines what the Second Temple would have looked like in late antiquity (fig. 4.1).[1] French archaeologist Chipiez worked with Georges Perrot to envision the Second Temple and turning to the biblical books of Ezekiel, 1 Kings, Chronicles for a description and then filling in the missing gaps based on architecture common in Phoenicia and Mesopotamia. Chipiez's work offered a studied attempt to reconstruct the historic Temple, implicitly acknowledging the impossibility of understanding the Second Temple's appearance with certainty. Chipiez's reconstructions were not produced for the purpose of the *JE*, but reprinted. Archaeologists had only recently extensively uncovered Mesopotamian architecture and relics, and many French archaeologists were drawn to its possibilities to reveal aesthetics common in ancient Assyria and Babylon. These new archaeological discoveries sparked Christian and Jewish scholars' imaginations in their

Figure 4.1. "Court of Priests."

reconstructions of the past, and they valued Assyria in particular for its "authentic" link back farther in time than the Greek or Roman Empires.[2] Scholars eventually dismissed Chipiez's reconstructions as unreliable, but at the time the *JE* was published, they were considered reliable work. Yet the methods Chipiez used to reconstruct the plan of the Temple indicate the ways that even historicized, scholarly work is always imaginative and potentially imbued with Orientalism. Faced with the need to fill in the gaps of archaeological ruins and verbal descriptions such as in the Bible and the Talmud, scholars selected other sources such as Assyrian archaeology to suit their imagination and values. Turning to Assyria over Greece or Rome to fill in the gaps, even the impulse to visually reconstruct the Temple in drawings rather than to work from ruins alone, indicated a desire to see ancient Israel as whole again and to imbue it with authority. The use of Assyrian style to imagine the Temple placed this icon farther back in history than Rome or Greece, implicitly authenticating a narrative of history that saw ancient Israel as the oldest origin of "Western" heritage. The *JE*'s use borrowed that visual "authenticity." Chipiez was not a Jewish scholar, and precisely because of that, his images lend greater significance in positioning Jewish history at the core of "civilized" world history.

Recontextualizing Chipiez's images in the *JE* located the Temple and its antiquity in a trajectory of explicitly Jewish rather than Christian history. The *JE*, like the NFTS art calendars, presented some Christian images in new contexts that altered the implications of those texts. However, the *JE* used different types of images, scholarly work rather than "high art," which shaped a narrative of Jewish heritage quite differently. The *JE*'s use of Chipiez's reconstructions alongside verbal articles on the Temple may appear to offer access to the past that is less mediated than Renaissance or modern art, engaging methodologies such as history, archaeology, and literary criticism. But this scholarly work represents Jewish heritage through Orientalism, valuing certain visions of "the Orient" over others to make claims about the roots of the contemporary "West."

The *JE* was the first successfully completed Jewish encyclopedia, and visual culture representing "the Orient" played a central role in creating the *JE* as a landmark in "Western" Jewish scholarship and its over fifteen thousand entries. Alongside textual narrative, images played an important role in this historical project. In addition to Chipiez's reconstructions, other articles on the Temple included less historically oriented images of the structure, such as images of the Temple as imagined in early modern Haggadahs. The *JE*'s editors also reprinted photographs of archaeological sites, sketches or maps drawn by encyclopedia entry authors, and photographs of Jews and Jewish communities at the turn of the twentieth century. These came from all kinds of sources, from arthouse photographers to archaeological ventures. Jews and Christians produced images, as well as wrote entries and sat on the board of editors. Though less overtly political than Jewish organizations such as the ZOA, the *JE* could not be separated from politics given the nature of some of its contributors and sources as well as the choice to include Christian and Jewish but not Arab and Muslim contributions, even though Palestine remained under the control of the Ottoman Empire and many similar research projects were under way under the auspices of the Ottoman Empire. In his 1906 guide to the contents of the *JE*, Joseph Jacobs discussed the variety of over two thousand illustrations in the encyclopedia.[3] Jacobs indicated the vibrancy of Jewish life throughout the diaspora as depicted by the *JE*'s images. His emphasis on synagogues, for example, heightened the significance of Jewish life that did not center around the physical Temple.[4] "The Orient" as an imaginative panorama plays an outsized role in the landscape of Jewish heritage, however, by its very nature as an encyclopedia, the *JE* covers many different landscapes.

My focus on "the Orient" in the *JE* creates the opportunity to see how turn-of-the-century scholars struggled to make sense of highly interpretive verbal and visual traditions about the land of biblical heritage. This has included seeing Jerusalem as an earthly space but also as a mystified space that tells Jews about the structure of the heavens, the messianic era, or the world to come (the afterlife). No such mystification weighs on descriptions of sites such as Venice or Vienna, that is, sites that became important for Jewish life after the biblical era ended. Additionally, to reconstruct Jewish heritage, there is a struggle of evidence: there was little in 1901–1906 to corroborate the Bible and Talmud's narratives of antiquity. These texts remained reliable sources at the turn of the century as they would not in later scholarship, as archaeologists unearthed new findings from the Code of Hammurabi to the Dead Sea Scrolls. But there is also a struggle of vision: scholars worked to dissociate the visions they had of Palestine, its buildings, and its inhabitants that offered truth about heritage from scholarly work that offered truth about public history—accessible to and directed toward not only Jews but at least theoretically non-Jews as well, especially Christian Americans. In this broader aspiration for audience, the *JE* shared an aspirational vision of the relevance of Jewish history to non-Jews with the exhibitions at the World's Fair in the following chapter but differed from Jewish organizations such as the ZOA, NFTS, and Hadassah, although those organizations' visual culture also engaged in cultural exchange with Christians and sought to revise how Jews understood themselves in comparison to Christian images of Jews.

The *JE* was edited by Isidore Singer (1859–1939) and published in twelve volumes from 1901 to 1906 in the United States by Funk and Wagnalls. Responding to the significance of social and cultural changes of fin de siècle Europe and the United States for Jewish life, Isidore Singer pursued the *JE*. He initially sought to establish himself in France but moved on to New York in 1895, where he launched the project in hopes that its outline of the contributions of Jews to civilization would dampen antisemitism and ignite pride in Jewish culture. Even though he relocated to the United States, Singer sought the approval and cooperation of scholars in Europe. His prospectus proposed that the encyclopedia would turn to the scientific method to eschew religious bias, producing a work beneficial to scholars as well as to the Jewish and non-Jewish public. The *JE* board of editors included a large number of prestigious Jewish scholars. To balance the Jewish nature of this group and aspire toward the Enlightenment ideal "universal" scholarship, the Christian scholar George Foot Moore was added as editor of Biblical Archaeology, History of Biblical Exegesis, Hebrew Philology, and Hellenistic Literature, though Moore had to leave the project and was replaced by Crawford Toy.⁵

Encyclopedias typically appear at moments of self-conscious social and cultural changes, thus providing a window into a community's perception of its past, present, and future in attempts to shape and respond to those changes.⁶ Diderot's *Encyclopédie* and then the *Encyclopaedia Britannica* set the early standard for encyclopedic works in Europe, but a variety of groups did not wish to allow the *Britannica* to have the final word on their histories and heritages, Jews included. Not simply consolidations of knowledge, encyclopedias forge heritage both by remembering a "proud past" and anticipating a "bright future." By presenting many different aspects, figures, and moments of Jewish heritage, the *JE* argued for the place of Jews as citizens in the United States and also the whole world. Additionally, encyclopedias were part of a "profoundly transnational context" aimed at the gentrification of the nonscholarly middle class. But despite their transnational character and interest in disseminating "universal" knowledge, they were a site for heritage-building, each nation or subculture presenting its contributions and interpretations of the "universal" through the lens of its own worldview.⁷ The *JE* sought to further the work of the *Wissenschaft des Judentums* or Science of Judaism. This movement began in Europe in the nineteenth century and crossed the Atlantic as the foundation for Jewish American academic scholarship. Participants in the *Wissenschaft des Judentums* believed Judaism must be a complete culture, encompassing not just compartmentalized religious belief but all aspects of life, characteristics they shared with many forms of Zionism that would emerge in the late-nineteenth and early twentieth centuries.⁸ The *Wissenschaft des Judentums* also sought to respond to both antisemitism and assimilation. The methodologies that Jewish scholars at the turn of the twentieth century worked to incorporate into studies of Jews, Jewishness, and Judaism were many: history, sociology, anthropology, art history, literature, philosophy, and more. Using these methods, Jews who participated in the Science of Judaism also participated in the ongoing project of "Enlightenment" and brought Enlightenment values to bear on their understanding of Jews. These values included, for example, a view of history as linear and progressive, valuing the new over the old from ideology to technology; the assertion of the dignity of all humans as individuals, including a set of rights such as citizenship and autonomy; and the possibility for all humans to live together under a set of universal truths that could be discovered rationally. Encyclopedias appeared at the onset of the Enlightenment and became a key part of all scholarship, not just Jewish studies, that presented the work of numerous scholars in one place and appealed to a broad audience. As such, encyclopedias cannot be reduced to a single goal or effect.

Reconstructing the Temple

As discussed at the beginning of the chapter, alongside Judah David Eisenstein's entry on "Temple, Plan of the Second," the *JE* includes images of "The Temple Area," "Court of Priests," and "Holy of Holies of the Temple at Jerusalem," all reconstructed by Chipiez (fig. 4.2).[9] Twelve articles in the *JE* cite "reconstructed" images attributed to Chipiez. During the late-nineteenth-century search for "pure" or "authentic" forms of Jewish architecture to contrast with non-Jewish regional and ethnonational architectures, French scholars Charles Chipiez and Georges Perrot published *Histoire de l'art dans l'Antiquité, Égypte, Assyrie, Perse, Asie mineure, Grèce, Etrurie, Rome, vol. 4: Judée, Sardaigne, Syrie, Cappadoce* in Paris in 1887; I. Gonino published an English translation in London in 1890. The section directly addressing the Temple, which included a section on the House of Lebanon, was additionally published separately.[10] The reconstruction of the Temple by Chipiez and Perrot took Ezekiel's vision in chapters 40–42 as inspiration, so that their images offered "'a blending of idealism and reality,' but not an actual edifice" verifiable in any historical period. Given that Ezekiel lacks full details of the architectural edifice, Chipiez and Perrot filled in the details by turning to alternative sources: first, they used examples of Phoenician architecture, arguing that the Temple architect Hiram of Tyre was stylistically influenced by his native Phoenicia. They then turned to the entire Mediterranean basin and Mesopotamia, on the logic that Hiram of Tyre and other Phoenician architects engaged in cultural exchange. Further, they applied their own sense of aesthetics in determining proportions, given the lack of exact measurements in Ezekiel and discrepancies between 1 Kings: 6–7 and 2 Chronicles: 3–4.[11] Chipiez and Perrot's work initially enjoyed critical acclaim, but shortly after the publication of the *JE*, their reconstruction fell out favor with scholars of the Temple. In 1911, the *Encyclopedia Britannica* rejected their work as a source for the appearance of the Temple as "probably untrustworthy." Contemporary Jewish architecture was influenced by reconstructions of Solomon's Temple in turn, such as Joseph Barksy's plan for the Herzliya

Figure 4.2. "Holy of Holies."

Gymnasium (a building that has since been replaced). Barsky's famous sketch published in *Ost und West* of the gymnasium identified Barsky as a student of Boris Schatz and the Bezalel art school. Although Bezalel influenced him and his ties to the school contributed to the Zionist nation-building project, Barsky was trained in the Russian Empire and graduated from the Architectural College in Odessa in 1900. Józef Awin, an architect and artist from Lvov, joined the Herzliya Gymnasium project and altered some of Barsky's initial plans, but from 1910 to 1962, the building stood under the influence of Chipiez and Perrot. Construction on the building began on the tenth of Av in 1909, symbolically emphasizing the rebuilding of the Temple. The day before, ninth of Av or Tisha B'Av, is the liturgical date of mourning the destruction of both the First and Second Temples. In 1962, it was destroyed and a new building was constructed on a separate site that did not include references to Chipiez and Perrot's reconstruction.[12]

Joseph Jacobs's guide to the *JE*'s contents, which came with the encyclopedia set, claimed that images would facilitate "empirical" knowledge. The *JE* approaches historical time as linear, characteristic of Enlightenment scholarship and differing from Jewish tradition, which saw time as cyclical and Jewish life "in exile" after the destruction of the Temple as unimportant or a waiting period before the coming of the messiah. The encyclopedia's entry headings and narratives indicate that the Temple changed in appearance as various dynasties controlled and altered its architecture and decoration. About five pages of the *JE* are allotted to an entry on "Temple, Administration and Service of," another five pages to "Temple of Herod," four pages to "Temple, Plan of Second," three to "Temple in Rabbinical Literature," two to "Temple, the Second," and four to "Temple of Solomon." These entry headings suggest several ways that the *JE* has organized study of the Temple and incorporated multiple methods of attempting to historicize its use and meaning in Jewish life.[13]

Alongside the entry on "Temple, Administration of," the *JE* printed images of "The Temple at Jerusalem" from the Passover Haggadah printed in Amsterdam in 1695, "Utensils of the Temple" from an illustrated Hebrew manuscript of the thirteenth century in the Bibliothèque Nationale in Paris, and a "Greek Inscription, Found on Site of the Temple Area, Forbidding Gentiles to Enter within the Inner Temple Walls" from a museum in Constantinople.[14] In the image of the Temple from the Amsterdam Haggadah (an oft-cited source of Jewish images outside of the *JE*, including in the visual culture of the ZOA), the sun rises over the intact Temple Mount, surrounded by domes and towers that pierce the sky (fig. 4.3). The image of the Temple is here idealized rather than historical. The *JE* does not address the basis for the visual outlines of utensils used in the Temple from the thirteenth-century illuminated manuscript, though it could not

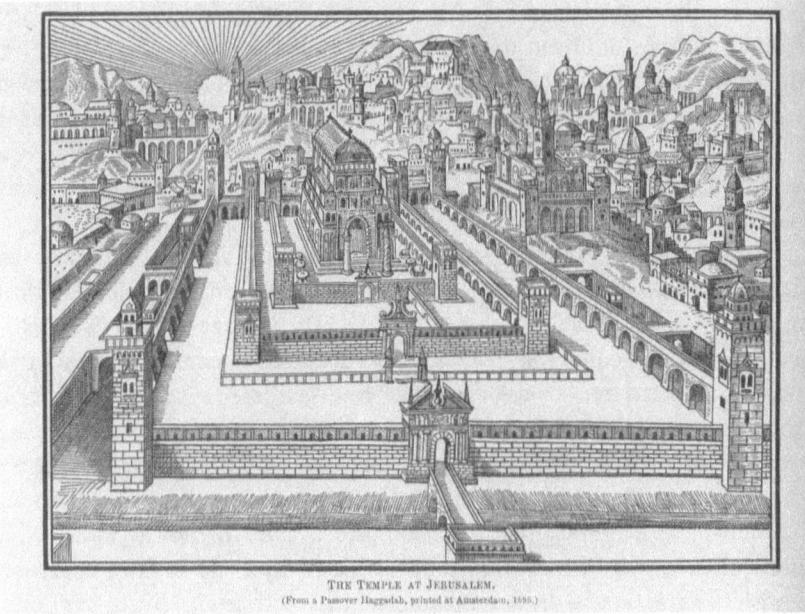

Figure 4.3. "The Temple at Jerusalem."

be architectural as was possible to some extent at the turn of the twentieth century. The photography of the Greek inscription on the Temple is an example of an archaeological artifact, though it had not remained in situ in Jerusalem but had been relocated to Constantinople. Four pages prior to the placement of the photograph of the Greek inscription, the verbal text of the entry explained that "Israelites when ritually unclean and Gentiles were not allowed to pass beyond the 'soreg,' a fence which surrounded the courts."[15] Little archaeological evidence existed that demonstrated the contours of the physical space of the Temple. This inscription did not do that, though it served as definitive evidence of the Jewish administration of the Second Temple. The exclusion of gentiles plays a very small role in the discussion of the administration of the Temple; however, the vivid image of the inscription—in Greek and thus accessible to Greek-speaking gentiles and Jews in the Second Temple period—conjures the importance of boundary and the Temple. The representation of this stone inscription makes at least as strong an argument about the place of the Temple and Israelite history in Jewish heritage as it does about Israelite history. The relocation of the stone to a museum in Constantinople implies a link between the Temple and the Byzantine Christian kingdom, of which Constantinople had been the capital. By recontextualizing the inscription in the *JE*, the encyclopedia asserted its importance for Jewish heritage at least as much as Christian heritage. Like NFTS art calendars with their polemicized recontextualizations of Christian images, the *JE* offered a vision of Israelite heritage that located the Temple in a Jewish "Orient" rather than a Christian one.

The use of these three images to visualize the administration of the Temple creates an imaginative "Orient" that relies on multiple historical moments to construct a vision of the Jewish heritage in the twentieth-century *JE*. The goal of the *JE* to assemble historicized empirical knowledge was complicated by the editors' ahistorical use of medieval, early modern, and contemporary images alongside an entry such as "Temple, Administration of." Without acknowledging the limits of a seventeenth-century image from an Amsterdam Passover Haggadah to reveal something about antiquity, for example, the visual culture of the *JE* moved away from presenting Jewish history according to linear time and instead collapsed Jewish imagination in the seventeenth century with Jewish life in antiquity. This collapse produces a view of the Temple as "Oriental" Jewish heritage. The presence of the image asserts that the visions of later time periods are necessarily connected to antiquity in an unmediated way. This use of an image from a Haggadah pulls together several time periods at once.

The Second Temple itself is a reconstruction in Jewish tradition, and the First Temple or Solomon's Temple remembered as the apex of Israelite history according to biblical text and its interpretation in the rabbinic period. Eisenstein notes that in rabbinic literature, the Second Temple is not as holy as Solomon's because there was no Ark and *kapporet* (the "mercy seat" and cover to the Ark, where God would appear) in the Holy of Holies and because the divine presence did not inhabit Herod's Temple as had been the case with Solomon's Temple. This is noted in the Talmud, in Yoma 21b.[16] The rabbinic period was after the destruction of the Temple, characterized by nostalgic memories of the Second Temple period. During (or shortly) after the Rabbinic period, the most detailed writings about the Temple's appearance were recorded in the Talmud and other texts. Though the Talmud includes no drawings, rabbinic text is highly visual. Ekphrasis, or highly visually descriptive verbal text that encourages readers to visualize what is written verbally as part of the reading process, plays an important role throughout the Talmud as it did in a variety of verbal texts in antiquity, especially in Rome and Greece. Rabbinic text itself thereby transmits "a theory about how language was intertwined with, and could invoke, vision and other senses and sensations."[17] The image from the Haggadah is an example of not only reading rabbinic text and mentally visualizing the Temple, but of realizing that visualization in an image. However, the image shows us more about the production of visual culture in Amsterdam in the seventeenth century as an aspect of Jewish life than it does about what the historical Temple looked like. Finally, the image is mediated again by the recontextualization of the Haggadah image in the *JE*. The image's role in an encyclopedia is different from its place in a Haggadah, the first "historical" and the second liturgical. However, the imaginative role of visualizing the Temple and its meaning for Jewish heritage in the diaspora is not lost in its recontextualized place in the *JE*. Forms of meaning embedded in the liturgical contact leak into or remain visible in the "historical," if not fully operative, blurring the distinctions between the two contexts." Each reprint re-mediates the knowledge any image might produce. Even if the image dated to antiquity when the Second Temple still stood, it would be mediated by the choices of the artist and the recontextualization in the *JE*. However, this is not to say the image offers no knowledge. Though it remediates the past several times over, carrying with it several different pasts, it also produces a new argument. It is not merely a copy that accompanies the verbal text of the *JE*. It interacts with that verbal text and offers its own internal argument that presents a vision of the Temple that centers an imagined "Temple" as a key location of Jewish heritage in "the Orient." The image's multiple layers of meaning and multiple removes from antiquity create the gap between the Temple in ancient Palestine and a vision of "the Orient" in the twelfth volume of the *JE* printed in 1906.

Medieval and early modern images from all over the globe became authoritative for a representation of antiquity, manifesting an ahistorical conception of heritage and transforming historical Palestine into "the Orient." The lapses of historicity when pairing visual culture with verbal text, in other words, created an Orientalist view that allowed contemporary Jewish imagination to influence how the Temple appeared. The Jewish communities who created images such as those from Haggadahs had engaged in imaginative construction of heritage through a vision of the Temple, and the *JE* editors also did so when they selected images such as those illustrating Haggadahs and placed them alongside verbal narratives of antiquity. Whether the editors were aware of the dissonance between the historical goals of the verbal text and the resulting ahistorical representation of the juxtaposition of these verbal and visual texts, the *JE* presented an imaginative vision of "the Orient." In this "Orient," Jewish heritage is constituted by the memory of antiquity, and the encyclopedia opened this conception of Jewishness to Jews and non-Jews, one role the *JE* editors saw for the encyclopedia. Presenting visual memory of the Temple and opening the memory of the Temple to Jews and non-Jews as scholars or as readers, the *JE* claimed authority over Jewishness and Jewish history. This subverted the power of Christians to present Jews as exotic through Orientalism, as frequently embodied in Christian scholarship. Instead the *JE* used Orientalism to imagine a glorified Jewish past that could be proudly remembered in the present and symbolize the significant place of Jews in the "modern West," an imagined community that now included Jews and Christians rather than distancing Jews as relics of the Christian past.

Instead of images of representations made by earlier Jewish communities, images alongside the entry on "Temple of Herod" did not construct Orientalism in the same way as the ahistorical use of traditional Jewish images. For example, two contemporary photographs and two contemporary drawings imagining the Temple as it stood in the past depicted the "Temple of Herod." It is useful to see how the verbal text of the entry took care to lay bare the complicated historiography of the Temple of Herod in contrast to what images revealed. The verbal text of the entry was written by the Christian scholar George A. Barton (1859–1942), a Canadian-born minister in the Religious Society of Friends and Professor of Biblical Literature and Semitic Languages at Bryn Mawr College with a BA and MA from Haverford and a PhD from Harvard.[18] Alongside the verbal text, the *JE* printed "Substructure of Temple of Herod, Now Called 'Solomon's Stables'" (fig. 4.4), from a photograph by the American Colony at Jerusalem; "Column from the Temple of Herod," from a Palestine Exploration Fund photograph; a pen and ink sketch of a "Sectional View of the Temple of Herod, Looking South"; and a reconstructed model by Conrad Schick, titled "View of the Temple of Solomon" (fig. 4.5).[19] Frederick Bohrer has shown that archaeology cannot be separated from photography. Both are mediated re-presentations rather than direct access to the past, though they are each often viewed otherwise.

Photography is the means by which the vast majority of people are familiar with archaeology, such as in the case of the *JE*, wherein the encyclopedia's editors assembled photographs as evidence. Not only did photography make views of archaeological sites more widely accessible, but the increase in public and governmental funding for archaeological projects, such as from the American Colony at Jerusalem and the Pal-

Figure 4.4. "Substructure of Temple of Herod, Now Called 'Solomon's Stables.'"

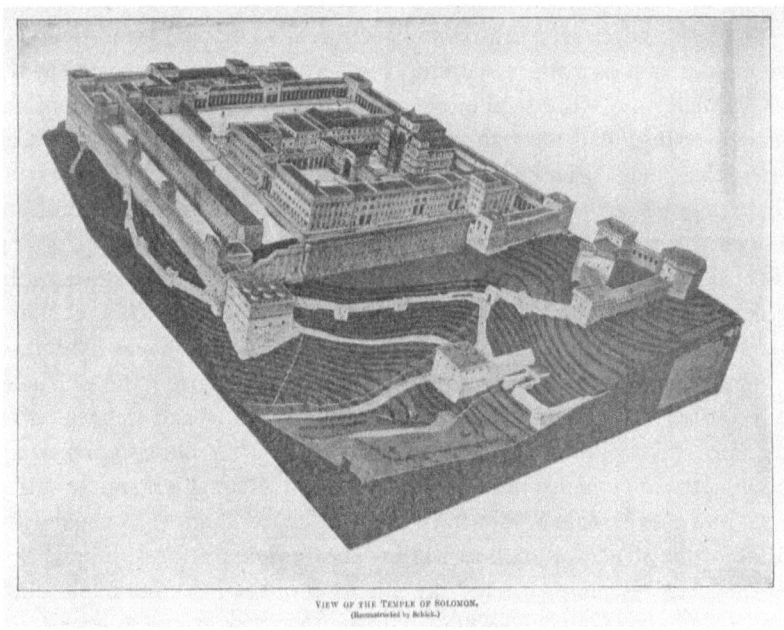

Figure 4.5. "View of the Temple of Solomon."

estine Exploration Fund, determined a greater need to show the people how their money had been used.[20] Photography mediates the representation of archaeological discoveries, which are already mediated heavily by scholars' motivations to seek archaeological relics and viewpoints of what they find. Archaeological photographers, in their quest to represent an "objective" view of physical artifacts, relics, and ruins, tend to avoid picturing humans. The only humans who could be pictured are from the present, and their careful erasure helps present photography as an unmediated experience of the past. This obscures the role of contemporary humans in framing an image and also gestures to the absence of historical populations from archaeological photographs. The objects in archaeological photographs were at some point used by people, those people being the imagined subjects of such photographs. But those people remain invisible, no matter the archaeological discovery.[21] Both the fields of photography and archaeology do not present direct access to the life of Israelites, as much as archaeologists and the scholars who cite them, such as the editorial board of the *JE*, may have wished to access that past. Instead, the past is re-presented, imaginatively constructed and viewed, producing an Orientalist visual culture that integrates these photographs of archaeological discoveries and reconstructions such as those by Schick and, as discussed earlier, Chipiez and Perrot.

These images represented archaeological advances in knowledge of the area as well as scholarly attempts at reconstructing the past. But the mediation through the methodology of archaeology and the lens of the camera, re-mediated through contextualization in the *JE*, constructed an Orientalist view distanced from the historical past several times over. Photographs and drawn reconstructions both engage historical questions and yet cover over the choices made by the scholars, photographers, and editors. Conrad Schick's reconstruction was based on explorations he undertook of the Temple area between 1873 and 1875. Schick explored and built his model for the 1873 Turkish pavilion at the Great Exhibition in Vienna. Like Chipiez and Perrot, Schick necessarily had to take liberties to reconstruct the Temple, no matter how much textual and archaeological research he did. Although Schick sought to produce a scholastic representation of the Temple, his model also engaged in imagination and deviation from how the Temple would have looked, taking liberties to expand his vision of the structure, such as tripling the Temple platform in height on the east. His research garnered the attention of the Palestine Exploration

Fund, which was looking for a pretext to explore below the platform. As Schick explored the area, Ottoman authorities began repairs on the Temple area, and arches in the parapet were discovered in the process. Some of the expansions to the Temple in Schick's model were based on previous models and research, but others were his own imagination. In adding many flourishes, Schick may have hoped that he would be commissioned as architect for a reconstruction in 1896.[22]

Unlike Barton's article that discussed the conflicting evidence and gaps in what was knowable, the image presents a set of choices made. These choices reflect scholarship on the one hand, but also imaginative selections on the other. Schick contributed drawn images such as those used by the editors of the *JE*, but he also sought to help influence the physical architecture and landscape of Jerusalem and the Temple area itself. His reconstruction efforts reveal the national and ethnoreligious competitions to control representation and even exploration of the Temple area itself. Though Schick cooperated with Ottomans for the pavilion in the 1873 world exhibition, he and other groups later competed with the Ottoman Empire for rights to the physical territory of the Temple and implicitly symbolic control over the narrative of the Temple area in Christian, Jewish, and Muslim worldviews. Orientalism emerged in the Crusade era and became entrenched when Christian Europe failed to permanently conquer the medieval Muslim empire. Scholarship ultimately reenacted similar competition over the Temple area in the nineteenth and twentieth centuries. The power to undertake archaeological explorations and produce reconstructions, whether on paper or on the Temple area itself, represented the power to locate the Temple in not just an academic but a theological or cosmological view of the space of the Temple. The *JE* included no images from Muslim reconstructions or Ottoman explorations, belying the practical and symbolic political allegiances present in scholarship. The absence or breakdown of exchange of ideas between European and American scholars with Ottoman scholars structurally reified differences that had long informed Orientalism and produced a perception of difference between "the West" and "the Orient." The Ottoman Empire became aligned with antiquity, a territory to be controlled and organized by "Western" thinking.

A variety of projects with alternative interests in Palestine produced images of the Temple and frequently borrowed each other's images almost immediately. Charles Chipiez, Conrad Schick, the Palestine Exploration

Fund, the Ottoman authorities, and the *JE* all had separate reasons for exploring the Temple area and producing reconstructions of its appearance, which sometimes (but not always) directly conflicted. Images and research even bounced between different groups: Schick explored Palestine and produced a model of the Temple with the support of Zionists and Ottomans. Then the *JE* printed the image, which circulated the Temple in Jewish and non-Jewish circles in the United States and internationally. The *JE*'s publication of images of the Temple contributed to a secular community of scholars of Jewish history, though the narratives of Jewish history produced in scholarship did not conform to those of Zionists or Ottomans. Yet scholastic history helped construct the place of the Temple in Jewish visual culture. At the publication of the *JE*, Zionism was not widespread in the United States nor was the Temple central to Zionist American visual culture. But in later years, the *JE* was among the sources to which Zionist Americans could selectively turn as they sought to augment the place of the Temple in Jewish visual culture and to anchor that place within Jewish memory. In other words, non-Zionist initiatives inaugurated the production of many images of the Temple; Zionist activity in Europe (whence many archaeologists and their funding came) and in Palestine helped produce and circulate those images; scholars whose primary motivations were not overtly linked to Zionism incorporated these images in their own worldviews and histories and further circulated images of the Temple in the United States. Zionist Americans then participated in cultural exchange wherein Jewish and non-Jewish conceptions of the Temple played an important role as Jews and non-Jews added their own narrative, multiplying images of the Temple and their meanings. Though the *JE* included such images from a broad panorama or reservoir of early twentieth-century visual culture, the tendency to present the Temple as a timeless center of Jewish life complicated the very goal of historicity. The *JE* presented a visual and verbal narrative of Jewish history that shifted between new and developing academic methodologies and constructions of Jewish heritage. In that way, it helped popularize a new narrative of the Jewish past that met its own historical goals to some extent by differing from Jewish textual tradition as well as contemporary movements—including Zionism, British and Ottoman authorities, and the popular practice of Judaism and Christianity in America—even as it borrowed from those movements. Yet in its uneven historicity, the *JE* shared in the construction of Jewish heritage.

Mapping Jerusalem:
Above and Below, Ancient and Modern

The verbal and visual text accompanying entries on Jerusalem demonstrate a greater sense of connection between the two types of text and to the symbolic as well as historical significance of the city in comparison to the entries on the Temple. The entry on "Jerusalem—ancient" explained that only small numbers of Jews were able to physically reside in Jerusalem throughout most of the common era, but the article emphasized the significance of the city as a powerful Jewish symbol, an image through which Jews have imagined themselves even while living in the diaspora. The entry reported that the Talmud says little about the city of ancient Jerusalem outside of the Temple, but a third-century colored glass (see "Archives de L'Orient Latin" 2: 439) from the Jewish catacombs depicted the Temple and Jerusalem as the center of the world, a view held by both the rabbis and later adopted by medieval Christendom. "The earthly Jerusalem (*Yerushalayim shel matah*) was believed to be paralleled by the Jerusalem above (*Yerushalayim shel malah*), which had been prepared before the creation of the world (Apoc. Brach, iv. 3)." After the destruction of the Temple in 70 CE and subsequent expulsion of Jews from Jerusalem, the Temple and Jerusalem were mystified. In rabbinic rendering, the city became "an idealized center of rabbinic geography."

Yet this geography of heritage was temporal rather than spatial, tied in later generations to messianic hopes, such as from Kabbalists to Maimonides. Arnold Eisen argues that Jerusalem and the Land of Israel were demystified in modernity, seen again as a physical territory that stripped Jerusalem of particular mystical qualities projected onto the idealized future Jerusalem above or Jerusalem-as-redemption. Eisen's concept of "demystification" means that modern Jews paid attention not only to the imaginative space of Jerusalem but also to its physical territory and political status unlike most of their medieval Jewish progenitors. Zionists preserved Jerusalem as a powerful symbol and drew on the history of idealizing Jerusalem in order to make present-day claims on the physical space of earthly Jerusalem, as shown in chapter 2. The *JE* is not overtly interested in the political status of Jerusalem, but including Jewish verbal narrative and Christian visual narrative constructed a "West" against the unpictured Muslim "Orient." Eisen points to the "demystification" of Jerusalem to demonstrate how Zionists deployed traditional Jewish images in new ways to make claims on the physical political territory. However, the *JE* presented a demystified Jerusalem while mustering Christian visual culture in such a way that presented an argument for Jews and Christians constituting the heritage of "the West" versus an Orientalized Muslim East. The *JE* represented a different set of stakes than Zionists and different narratives of the Jewish past, but nevertheless sought to position Jews positively in "the West" by assembling a select range of sources that mediated how Jerusalem could be seen and asserted the need for Jewish control over Jerusalem's symbolic and physical space. In the case of the *JE*, Jewish heritage is more explicitly linked with Christian heritage to produce an image of "the Orient." Additionally, the stakes of the physical claim are archaeological not national, though it is obvious in retrospect that archaeological rights and interpretation of ruins and relics have determined political status.

The *JE* does verbally describe the history of Muslim rule over Jerusalem, but the editors' choice to leave out images that portray Muslim imaginations of Jerusalem in favor of a Christian image of the medieval period constructs an Orientalist view. Including an imaginative Christian map of Jerusalem, the Hereford Mappa Mundi, instead of engaging Ottoman sources privileges an Orientalist "Western" structure for representing Jerusalem.[23] Alongside verbal text describing rabbinic imagination in Jewish antiquity and the history of Jerusalem after the fall of the Temple, the *JE* printed a medieval Christian image of Jerusalem, the Hereford Mappa Mundi (fig. 4.6).[24] The Hereford Mappa Mundi is perhaps the most famous Christian map of the world with Jerusalem at the center. Christian mapping of the world with Jerusalem at the center emerged as a part of Christian visual culture in the eleventh century and became more popular as a way of seeing the world at the end of the Crusades.[25] This practice in mapping, in other words, emerged at the exact moment that the Christian Empire became violently obsessed with regaining control over the territory of Jerusalem. Barring that territorial success, Christians mapped a world in which Jerusalem remained central but Europe appeared in "the West." The Hereford Mappa Mundi therefore presented a map with Jerusalem at the center of a sphere of holiness that also encircled Western Europe. This map, therefore, had long played a role in seeing a "West" that could literally be mapped around Jerusalem and that mapped the Muslim world as an "Orient" separate from "the West." This subverted the political reality that Jerusalem was not a part of Christian territory

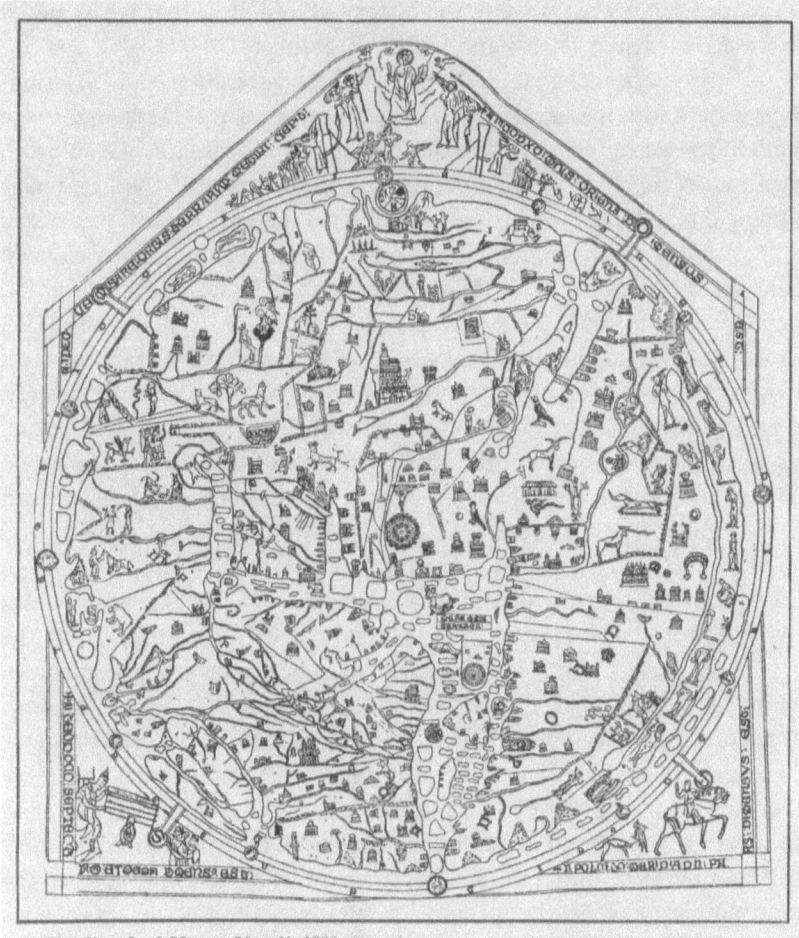

Figure 4.6. "The Hereford Mappa Mundi, 1280, Showing Jerusalem in the Center of the World."

but the Muslim Empire. Even if the editors of the *JE* wished they could include Ottoman and Muslim scholarly sources, that they did not creates a narrow view of the history of Jerusalem that reproduces the structure of Orientalism in the *JE*. This structural Orientalism, making Jewish and Christian imagination visible over the narratives and sources of the Muslim world, produced a narrative of the history of Jerusalem that positioned it as a piece of shared Jewish and Christian heritage.

This view of ancient Jerusalem—which conflates antique Jewish visions of Jerusalem with medieval Christian perspectives, is in contrast to maps of modern Jerusalem that used very different spatial and visual styles, although even the "modern" retained a connection to the ancient. The first image accompanying Martin Meyer's article on "Jerusalem—Modern" was a map of the "modern" city (fig. 4.7). Yet much labeled on the map is ancient: Gate of Abdul Hamid, Damascus Gate, Herod's Gate, Stork's Tower, St. Stephen's Gate, Golden Gate, Dung Gate, Zion Gate, Citadel, Jaffa Gate, Pool of Hezekiah, Church of Sepulchre, Haramesh Sherif, Omar's Mosque, Mosque el-Aksa, Wailing Place, Robinson's Arch, Armenian Monastery, Tower of David, Tomb of David, Tombs of Jehoshaphat and Absalom, Jeremiah's Grotto, Tombs of the Kings. The line of the aqueduct is dotted throughout the city. The Colony of Yemen Jews is on the southeast corner. A few modern points are on the map, mostly outside the old city and many hospitals: a railway station in the south, Montefiore Hospice, Russian Colony, several Jewish colonies, Spanish Jewish Hospice, German Jewish Hospice, Rothschild Hospital.[26] Similarly, the rest of the images in the modern Jerusalem entry depict ancient sets and characters. For example, the image of Jaffa Gate shows the ancient wall and gate, swarming with Arabs dressed in headdresses and robes, whose camels and donkeys carry their items.[27] The Damascus Gate, Golden Gate, Zion Gate, and Site of the Temple similarly offer little that might be perceived as modern, depicting Jerusalem as a place unmarked by the passing of time.[28] Though the entry claimed to present "modern" Jerusalem, the visual culture transformed the contemporary city on the ground in Palestine into a contemporaneous object and space of heritage in "the Orient."

The photographs of the Golden Gate within the City of Jerusalem, the Zion Gate, and the Haram Area around the Temple Mount are reproductions of the photographic work of Bonfils, a French photography firm founded in 1867 by Félix Bonfils when he and his wife Lydie moved from France to Beirut. The majority of the images produced by the firm were attributed to Félix, though Lydie and later their son Adrien contributed photographs as well. Certainty in photo authorship is nevertheless nearly impossible to determine, though social conventions in many communities they photographed indicate Lydie quite likely captured any images of female subjects. Sometime after 1907, Abraham Guirafossian, a photographer from Palestine, acquired the firm and continued to use the Bonfils name until

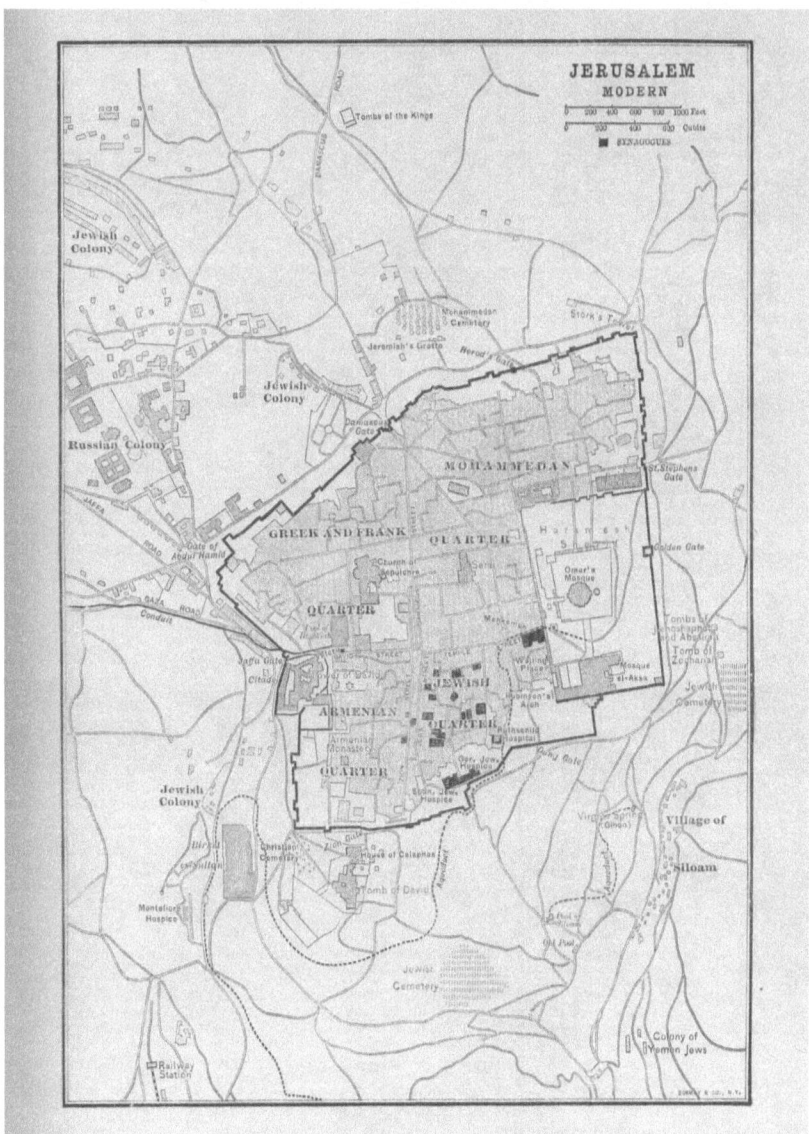

Figure 4.7. "Jerusalem—Modern."

at least 1932 (fig. 4.8).[29] The Bonfils firm produced tens of thousands of images—contributing to the "prolixity of the Oriental dream" not only of the Holy Land, but also Egypt, Syria, Constantinople, and Greece, and the costumes and ethnographic types to be found in each of these Oriental

Zion Gate, Jerusalem.
(From a photograph by Bonfils.)

Figure 4.8. "Zion Gate."

regions. The photographs are archetypes of the images that characterized nineteenth-century romantic Orientalism: "They are *picaresque* since they are images of travel and souvenirs of distant locales meant to instruct and entertain. They are *picturesque* in that they depict the exotic as well as the natural in order to pictorially delight." A sense that the images depict the picaresque and the picturesque expands the number of categories at play in these images: the mundane and the exotic, time and space, past and future, earthly and heavenly, instruction and fantasy. Sobieszek and

Gavin emphasize the didactic nature of Bonfils's images as to the nature of "the Orient," calling the Bonfils portfolio a "veritable photographic chrestomathy," equivalent in importance to Arabic texts compiled in the nineteenth century for the purposes in language instruction.[30] To label them didactic is not to determine *what* they teach: I argue that more than instruction about the Temple past or present or life in the land of Israel past or present, these images produced "Western" viewers' knowledge of themselves as such.

Including images from the Bonfils portfolio turned to an imaginative Christian art project for sources for the visual culture of the *JE*. The *JE* used many images from many sources throughout its pages, and it is was not new for Jews to use Christian images in new contexts or for their own purposes, as discussed at length in chapter 3. But the production of these artistic, romantic photographs was quite different from the framing, printing, and reprinting of photographs taken as part of archaeological research. As discussed earlier, archaeological photographs offered imaginative representations of Jewish heritage in the *JE*. So much more so the work of photographers who sought to frame their images of "the Orient" through a romantic lens rather than a scholarly one. In contrast to archaeological photography, arthouse photography had freer dictates for seeing "the Orient," although arthouse photography certainly had its conventions. Arthouse photography did not necessarily look below the surface or back in time to find the past. One of the conventions of European arthouse photography firms such as Bonfils in the Middle East was to assume that what stood above ground somehow illumined not just contemporary life but the past of "the Orient" and its place in the eyes and hearts of "Westerners." But arthouse photography's conventions were not as separable from the invention of archaeological photography as they may seem, and indeed archaeology was one of the most cited justifications for the importance of photography in the nineteenth century. The first major testimony about the advances in photography made possible by the daguerreotype already suggested the power of the European lens to counter the destruction of the Arab world and to preserve if not recover "the Orient." François Arago reported to the French Chamber of Deputies that if Europeans had had Daguerre's invention sooner, they "would possess today faithful pictorial records of that which the learned world is forever deprived of by the greed of the Arabs and the vandalism of certain travelers."[31]

The changelessness of time in "the Orient" is underscored by the interchangeability of the streets, walls, and buildings in the old city of modern Jerusalem. One image depicts a "Typical Street in Jerusalem,"

Figure 4.9. "A Typical Street in Jerusalem."

showing unidentified figures along an unnamed set of stairs leading to an unnamed tower (fig. 4.9).[32] The interchangeability of any ancient wall or street for another created a visually identifiable panorama for Orientalism. Through this stereotyping, these streets became sets for "Western" imagination. In the entry on modern Jerusalem, Meyer vividly painted the scene for his readers, describing "narrow, crooked, and steep streets" where "sunlight never enters" and sanitary conditions are poor. But "outside the walls the streets are wider and better cared for, and the houses are more European in appearance."[33] Spatially and symbolically, the "modern" physically surrounded the ancient, giving the *JE*'s historical mode power over Palestine. Jerusalem may not have been empty, but it was primitive and neglected. Even so, these places do double duty: if the encyclopedia seemed to assert power over the ancient, the physical spatial centrality of the old city suggests that ancient Jerusalem continued to anchor the heritage of the "modern" as its heart or core. The earthly ancient Jerusalem is in this way served a similar role in the early twentieth-century scholarship as the role the mystified Jerusalem above played in medieval cosmology.

Jews from "the Orient": Eastern Europe and the Middle East

The *JE* also included visual culture representing ongoing Jewish communities from the medieval period to the turn of the twentieth century, using these studies to show a rich Jewish heritage that pointed to possibilities for a dynamic Jewish future. In addition to "contemporary" Jewish civilizations, that is, communities shown to be "modernizing" and part of "the West," the *JE* showed exoticized, "contemporaneous" groups, that is, communities whose appearance signaled the Jewish past but not models for the present or future. For example, the representation of East European Jewish life in the *JE* was complex. In a significant departure from typical *Wissenschaft des Judentums* scholarship, the *JE* included classical Yiddish literature. Rather than idealizing the shtetl as model for insular Jewish life, entries on Eastern Europe tended to emphasize openness and harmony between Jews and non-Jews in Eastern Europe. The *JE* often critiqued traditional ways of life of Hasidim and orthodox Jews in Eastern Europe. Yet this cannot be taken as a simple East/West divide, as these critiques of Hasidim and orthodox Judaism grew out of the perspective of Maskilim, participants in the Jewish Enlightenment or *Haskalah* in Eastern Europe. East European Maskilim considered their orthodox and Hasidic Jewish neighbors ignorant, narrow, and superstitious.[34] It is significant, though, that this allegiance to enlightenment values undergirded the sense that the pitfalls of traditional East European life were cultural and not racial. East Europeans were not an immutable race of primitives, but only needed to subscribe to enlightenment to transform themselves into viable contemporary citizens, whether in Russia, the United States, or Palestine.

The *JE* devoted a substantial amount of space to Jewish life in Eastern Europe: the entries pertaining to "Russia" took up fifty-seven pages, despite the fact that the *JE* began by noting that much of the history of Jews in Russia appeared elsewhere in the encyclopedia. The presence of images helped signal what the *JE* considered most significant and often most contemporary, though some images emphasized the "exotic" nature of a Jewish community in contrast to the life of Jewish scholars in "the West." Like the ZOA's periodicals, the *JE* presented images of Jews in "the Orient" to demonstrate difference. The demonstration itself constituted the construction of difference. The difference did not pre-exist its presentation: seeing difference is not natural but selective and dynamically made over as needed. The use of images of Jews from "the Orient" to show their exotic nature is one piece of the way that the *JE*'s editors deployed Orientalism in their collation of Jewish heritage. Despite the substantial amount of space given to relating Jewish Russian history, the *JE* included few images alongside Rosenthal's narrative of that history. Only a "Map of Western Russia Showing the Jewish Pale of Settlement" was included; no artwork or photographs.[35] In Rosenthal's entry on "Russia—Poland," two images showed "Polish Coins with Jewish Inscriptions."[36] Unlike the visual culture of the ZOA that heavily represented East European Jews in photographs, sketches, and artwork, the *JE* narrative of Russian history did not rely on visual representation of East European Jews. As I argued of the lack of representation of Muslim life in the history of Jerusalem, the lack of visual depiction seems to signify a deemphasis on a site, person, or group as part of contemporary Jewish heritage.

In contrast to the lack of visual representation of Jewish life in Eastern Europe, several images of contemporary Palestine appeared alongside entries such as "Agricultural Colonies in Palestine." Images of this very specific area of life in Palestine included a map of Palestine by Judah David Eisenstein, four photographs of farm landscapes, and one of an administrative building (fig. 4.10).[37] The "General View of Rehoboth Colony, Palestine" shows two men speaking in the left foreground, though they are not actively farming. For the most part, the *JE*'s depiction of agriculture colonies in Palestine included no pictures focused on pioneers, instead focusing on overviews of the land. Each view of the landscape similarly depicted one or two men, not identifiable by any of the visual tropes of pioneers that would develop in later Zionist visual culture. These images focused on the colonies as developed land, not as communal spaces or sites that included the transformed bodies of Zionists.

Pictures of historical agriculture utilized a photograph of modern Palestine from a wide lens and drawings of farming methods, but to different ends than the views of contemporary colonies. Accompanying the

Figure 4.10. "General View of Rehoboth Colony, Palestine."

entry on "Agriculture—Historical Aspects," there is a bird's-eye view of the "Division of Fields in Modern Palestine," chronologically incongruous with verbal text sections on "Agriculture Learned from the Canaanites," "Estimation of Agriculture in the Bible," and "In Post-Exilic Times" (fig. 4.11). These verbal texts cite the books of the Hebrew Bible as historical sources while the visual culture depends on a contemporary image of agriculture in Palestine. The verbal text does not emphasize methods of agriculture, but instead the normality of agriculture as part of Jewish life: "The love for Agriculture became so ingrained in the Jew that he contemptuously gave the trader the name of 'Canaanite' (Zech. Xiv.21: compare Hosea, xii.8 [A.V. 7])." This responded to antisemitic tropes of Jews as alienated from any territory and all land—and thus contemporary citizenship or belonging. To counter antisemitic stereotypes, the interaction of visual and verbal text implies the collapse in time or at least uniformity across time of Jews in agriculture. The verbal text acknowledges the role of non-Jews teaching Jews agriculture in history not only in Palestine but in Europe, such as the claim that "in Spain, in the early Middle Ages, the Jew were the chief agriculturists, and remained such," citing Grätz's *History*

Figure 4.11. "Division of Fields in Modern Palestine."

of the Jews at the same time that verbal and visual text work together to suggest that Jews are natural farmers linked to the land, not the weak or alienated rootless parasites of antisemitic stereotypes. In addition to use of the bird's-eye view as in entries on contemporary colonies, the historical entry on agriculture used images from a range of Jewish and non-Jewish sources to illustrate methods of plowing in times past. One image shows "Plowing and Hoeing" in ancient Egypt and another shows "Plowing in Palestine," an image that appears to be of contemporary farming methods, although it accompanies verbal text on agriculture "In Rabbinical Literature" (fig. 4.12). This section of the article cites verse after verse "culled from rabbinical literature" to demonstrate "the estimation in which Agriculture was held in the latter days of Jewish national life." The implication, of course, is that the practice of farming the land of Palestine both continues the relationship between Jews and working the land that has been sustained even in the diaspora at the same time that agriculture in Palestine serves as a key restoration of Jewish national life.[38] Though the *JE* appeals to tropes linking Jews and working the land, especially the land of Palestine, the visual culture does not look like the image of the chalutzim that became distilled in Zionist visual culture later in the twentieth century, as discussed in chapter 2. Nevertheless, the visual culture of the *JE* works with the verbal text of the encyclopedia articles to normalize Jewish agricultural life.

Figure 4.12. "Plowing in Palestine."

The encyclopedia also devoted entries to agricultural colonies in Argentina, Canada, Russia, and the United States. Several images of colonists in Argentina and the United States were included, along with photographs of the administrative, housing, and school buildings of those colonies.[39] The implications of images of Jewish agriculture were complex in their representation of Jews as "Oriental" or "Western," primitive or modern. The narrative and visual representation of Jewish agriculture indicated that Jews worked the land throughout history and the globe, not only in modern Palestine. This implicitly contradicted the stereotype that Jews were alienated from the land and unable to work with their hands. Yet images Orientalized agriculturalists in Palestine through dress and depicted farming techniques as old-fashioned. Adding to the complexity, images of Russian colonists did not appear in the encyclopedia, though pictures of East European immigrant colonies in the Americas indicated that these orthodox Jews would soon be transformed by their life in the new world, away from the backward rituals and political life in Russia.

Depictions of Arabs and Bedouins, when they do appear throughout the *JE*, Orientalize Arabs in contrast to Jews by associating them with biblical antiquity rather than contemporary life. This is not to say that images of Arabs were unimportant to constructing an imagination of Jewish heritage. Rather, Arabs consistently appear in contrast to "modern" Jews and constitute the vision of the Jewish past. This may be a response to or inversion of Muslim views of Jews (and Christians) as people who received but corrupted God's revelation, necessitating the appearance of Prophet Muhammad and his recitations to supersede backwards Jews and Christians. Arabs and Muslims do appear, but not as a part of narratives of historicized space such as the Temple or Jerusalem. Instead, sprinkled throughout the *JE*, Arabs and Bedouins seem a living approximation of biblical ancient Israel. For example, a photograph of a "Bedouin Tent" with Bedouins squatting in the foreground appears in a general article on the word "tent," subtitled "ohel," the Hebrew word for tent (fig. 4.13). In a similar vein, an image of "Village Wells in Use in Palestine" from a photograph by the American colony at Jerusalem illustrates the entry for "well," which cites the Hebrew Bible and New Testament. Images of Bedouins, Arabs, and Mizrahi Jews throughout the *JE* suggested that life for those living continuously in Palestine had not changed since the biblical period.[40] East European Jews similarly appeared throughout the encyclopedia in articles on ritual practice and Jewish life, such as in a full-page image of a "Tashlik Ceremony in Galicia," a ritual of casting sins into a stream on Rosh Hashanah from a painting by Wilhelm August Stryowski.[41] Mizrahim (Middle Eastern or Arab Jews) appeared as well, such as in an image of the "Interior of the Great Synagogue at Teheran," which showed two men and a young boy seated in the synagogue, in the entry on "Teheran"; an image of the "Interior of a Bet Ha-Midrash [a synagogue] at Tripoli," which showed several men struggling to study by candlelight; or a photograph of men, women, and children who constituted a "Group of Yemenite Jews."[42] These images indicated a continuity in if not the identical nature of Jewish ritual practice prior to the "modernizing" interventions of West European and American Ashkenazi Jews in the late nineteenth and early twentieth centuries.

Aside from these images, the *JE* extensively catalogued Jewish "types" throughout "the Orient." Along with a full two-page color depiction of the costumes of late medieval and early modern Jews throughout Europe and the East, the encyclopedia preserved Jews throughout history by cultural "costume," including images of the costumes of Jews in Germany, the Rhineland, Swabia, England (an antisemitic caricature), Tunisia, Algiers, Turkey, the French rabbinate, Jerusalem, Constantinople, the Orient, Kolomea (Austrian Galicia), the Caucasus, Poland, Warsaw, and Hasidic dress. A two-page, full-color insert showed Ashkenazi Jews from the thirteenth

Figure 4.13a. "Bedouin Tent."

Figure 4.13b. "Jews of Tunis in Native Costume."

to nineteenth centuries from England to Russia. While images of Western regions tended to depict drawings of dynamic changes in medieval and early modern European Jewish "costumes," images of "the Orient" presented photographs of contemporaneous "Oriental figures," suggesting the progression of "Western" Jews beyond the static and exotic dress in "the Orient," linked to persistence in outmoded lifestyle.[43] The very use of the term "costume" exoticizes those living in "the Orient" and distinguishes images of "Westerners" whose clothing would not be labeled costume. "Western" clothing was usually not marked at all, implying its "normality." For example, in a detailed study of Tunisian Jews, the *JE* printed two images of a "Tunisian Jewess," as well as "Jewish Girls of Tunis," "Jews of Tunis in Native Costume," and "Jewish Cemetery at Tunis," which shows Jews seated in mourning at the cemetery (fig. 4.14).[44] Tunisian Jews, in other words, were produced as representative types, and Jewish "Westernness" was produced in the projection of difference onto the bodies of Tunisian Jews and other representative types. The *JE* does not label these Jews "Oriental," unlike tendencies in the ZOA and Hadassah's visual culture, but a similar worldview is evident in the representation and subtler language about Tunisian Jews in the *JE*.

As the guide to the encyclopedia explains, "Western" Jewish types also appeared in the *JE*. Images of Jews were not included in the entries on America, not even in the entry on Judaism in America, but the article on "Types, Anthropological" defined types as the "correlated norms of racial qualities," especially facial features, hair, and eye color. The encyclopedia thereby presents race as a body of knowledge significant for contemporary scholarship, ordering the world, and categorizing Jews. The verbal text sought to guide interpretation of such visual texts: "What is popularly known as 'the Jewish type' is not a correlation of definite anthropological measures or characteristics, but consists principally in a peculiar expression of face, which is immediately and unmistakably recognized as 'Jewish' in a large number of cases of persons of the Jewish race," the article asserted. While Jews as a group were supposed to be a racial type, the article explained, "the Jews have not maintained their type in as pure a state as has been generally supposed." Language of purity frequently characterizes white supremacist language, wherein impurity would signify a lower place in a hierarchy of races. But here the language of "impurity" of Jewish race offers a payoff of making race mutable and distinguishing among Jewish groups, implicitly and explicitly leaving room between Jews in Europe and the United States and "Oriental Jews."

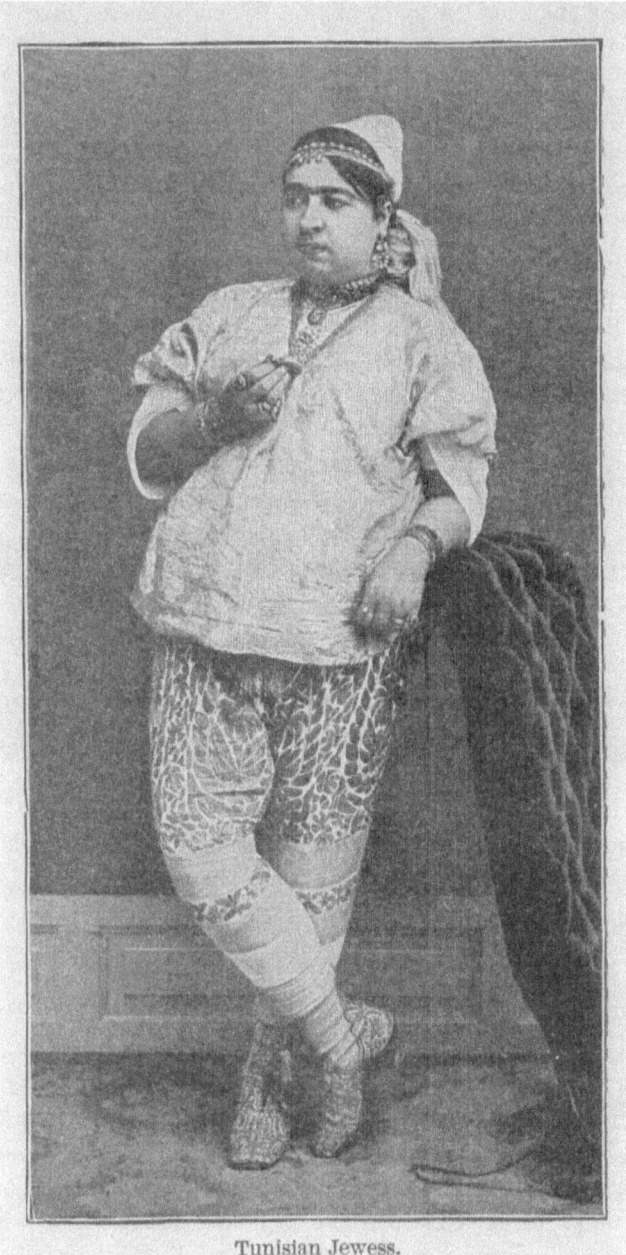

Figure 4.14. "Tunisian Jewess."

Charts depicted the pigmentation (blond, brunette, mixed) of Jews in Eastern and Western Europe as well as the United States, but only young Jewish boys in New York and London were represented pictorially indicating the emphasis on Jewish boys and men's bodies to counter antisemitic claims that Jewish men were weak and effeminate. "What could be worse than being femme?" this logic went. The *JE* did not challenge the conceptual binary of masculine/feminine as contemporary/contemporaneous. The *JE* only shifted the place of Jews, from effeminate to normal masculine "Westerners." This sustained the binary in gender and the insult to "Oriental" men as like women, which depended on a foundation of misogyny. These images showed "Composite Portraits." Reprinted from the *Journal of the Anthropological Institute*, for example, Portraits A and B composite five boys each into a single portrait, and Portrait C is a composite of A and B.[45] A full-page illustration showed composites of ten boys in New York, including the individual images of the boys, then composites of five, then a composite of the ten (fig. 4.15).[46] Images of western Jewish types affirmed and authorized the depiction of Jewish types throughout the world. However, although the article treated anthropological or racial types as a category of genetics, these images of Jewish types in New York and London constructed the ideal image of Jews more culturally than biologically. And more importantly, the verbal text claimed, "a considerable proportion of Jews fail to betray their racial provenience . . . about 53% of the subjects can be more or less certainly identified as Jews by their facial expression, the remaining 47 percent fail to show any distinctive feature which would definitely mark them as Semites, though if compared with Gentiles of the same class they could probably be differentiated."[47]

Conclusion

In 1926, the Sephardic Jew Jose Estrugo wrote in *The American Israelite* that the *JE* was "one of the greatest achievements of American Judaism." Even so, he considered that its history was incomplete, noting that it did not "give a place to all the men who have had some influence on Jewish life." To fill in the gaps, Estrugo offered names of Sephardim who might be included in a future reprint of the encyclopedia.[48] Estrugo's frustration with the *JE* indicates the seriousness with which some responded to the encyclopedia's publication for making Jews visible, but also the particular

Figure 4.15. "The Jewish Type Composite Portraits of Ten Jewish Boys, New York."

viewpoint that the encyclopedia presented of Jewish heritage and history. The *JE* focuses on a vision of Jewish heritage for Ashkenazi Jews, many in the United States but also for those still living in Europe. However, the *JE* did not look at Sephardic and Mizrahi histories in the same ways as Sephardim and Mizrahim did. When the *JE* did look at those communities' heritages, they generally served a picture of Ashkenazi heritage. The *JE* contained entries about Jewish life all over the world, but a disproportionate number of images represented Jewish life in "the Orient" and the images that the *JE*'s editors chose to accompany verbal text describing Jewish life in "the Orient," whether in the past or the present, represented "the Orient" imaginatively rather than offering an unmediated window into history. Objectifying and speaking for Sephardim and Mizrahim, The *JE* Orientalized them.

The use of images as part of the *JE*'s scholarship indicates the extent to which visual culture is always a re-presentation. Photography itself places many layers of interpretation between an object and its viewer, although we are often unable to easily detect those layers. The photographer is, generally, invisible. No trace of photographers' bodies, identities, or choices regarding subject matter, framing, distance, or other decisions are visible in the visual culture of the *JE*. Though photography may have appeared to capture its subjects, from the physical world, to built landscapes, to people "as they were," photography does not offer an unmediated "truth." The history of photography itself is tied up with European colonialism and Orientalism. The specific photographs used in the *JE* were not first produced for the encyclopedia but by many different organizations and photographers. Though the *JE* cites its sources, these citations rarely explore the relationship between the *JE*, its editors, and the sources. At times, the *JE* offers a counterhistory of the visual culture of others, especially Christians, similar to the NFTS as discussed in chapter 3. Sometimes the *JE*'s editors co-opted photographers' projects for their own scholarly project. The *JE*'s representation of "the Orient" did not include any analysis of the different sources of photographs or the methodologies of different types of photographers. Some photographs came from archaeological projects. Like photography, archaeology also has a history, and one frequently linked to Christian Orientalism and European empire. Also, like photography, archaeology may appear to offer direct access to the past while the nature of the methodology covers over the many imaginative decisions that archaeologists must make, not limited to the photographs they take. Scholars of archaeology must fill in the absence of people in archaeological artifacts and sites, and archaeologists along with historians and others who turn to archaeology for evidence create narratives of the place of archaeological discoveries in heritage and how that heritage relates to the past. By choosing Jewish and Christian sources of photographs, the editors of the *JE* made a variety of views of "the Orient" visible at the same time that the *JE* gathered those visions under the umbrella of Jewish heritage. By leaving out Ottoman and other sources of excavation projects, the *JE* also excluded certain views of "the Orient" and its place in heritage. This contributed to the construction of a vision of Jewish heritage that reproduced "the West" and located Jews within it. In addition to archaeological photographs, the *JE* also printed images produced by Christian arthouse firms. Sources such as the Bonfils firms set out to produce a romantic picture of "the Orient," and the *JE* represented that vision. This suggested that imaginative visions of "the Orient" were as relevant to scholarship as archaeological ones. Artistic and archaeological photographic projects influenced each other and shared overlapping connections with the history of photography, and the *JE*'s use of both types of images created new ways of seeing both photographic styles together.

Much of the visual culture of the *JE* imaginatively filled out visual interpretations of "the Orient," whether or not that process of imagination was visible, and the *JE* turned to many more images than photographs. The use of maps, woodcuts, drawings, and other visual culture informed the *JE*'s view of Jewish heritage. The editors' use of visual culture from different moments and places in Jewish history, including medieval illuminated manuscripts and early modern Jewish texts, suggested a connection between these visions of "the Orient" and the *JE*'s project. However, these images produced an ahistorical picture of "the Orient" rather than a historicized view of Jewish antiquity. The *JE* represented earlier reconstructions of "the Orient," layering interpretive contexts on top of each other. Sites such as the Second Temple could not be accurately pictured, whether in scholarly reproductions, artistic renderings, or contemporary photographs. The Second Temple itself was a reproduction of the First, suggesting an even greater distance from the Jewish national past in antiquity. The space of "the Orient" was not the only image of Jewish heritage that the *JE* presented. The *JE* also included images of Jews from "Oriental" communities, such as Turkey, which contrasted with images of Jews in "the West," especially the United States. The *JE* sought to offer a unified account of all of Jewish life, struggling to make sense of Jews as a people. The *JE* tried to produce this imagined unity through multivocality and a variety of views. Even as an imagination of Jewish unity played an important role and the *JE* offered "the Orient" as a place and time to tie together Jewish heritage, differences were a key part of envisioning the authors and editors of the *JE* as "Western" compared to "the Orient" that appeared in the fissures and fragments of the *JE*'s vision of Jewishness.

Chapter 5

Envisioning Citizenship

The Jewish Exhibit and Jewish Day at the 1933 World's Fair

Since Jews are primarily a religious community (an indisputable fact which certain Jews still fail to appreciate) there is no earthly reason why Jews should have a building of their own at the Century of Progress International Exposition, particularly when no other religious group even thought of anything of the kind. Others in our midst suggested the erection of a Palestine building for the demonstration of Jewish progress in Eretz Israel under the British Mandate. This idea was an excellent one, but unfortunately financial difficulties prevented its being carried into effect.

—Rabbi Felix S. Mendelsohn, *Sentinel*, Chicago, June 29, 1933

This day will long be remembered. The portrayal of the Romance is itself woven into the Romance. Here we are more than one hundred thousand Jews, the largest Jewish assemblage since Temple days. Here are thousands of Christian friends, brothers in spirit, witnessing with us our trials, our triumphs, our misery, but also our never-ceasing hope.

—Solomon Goldman, *The Romance of a People* souvenir book

While a disembodied voice read the annals of Jewish history from the Torah, the Temple served as the stage for all of Jewish heritage. These events took place not on the Temple Mount in Jerusalem, but in the center of Soldier Field in Chicago in 1933, where Jewish history was performed by thousands of Jewish Americans for a mixed crowd of over a hundred thousand Jews and non-Jews in the Jewish Day pageant *The Romance of a People*. The Zionist Organization of America constructed a massive replica of the Temple, influenced by architecture of the recently constructed Hebrew University in Jerusalem, which was itself influenced by models and reconstructions of the ancient Temple as discussed in the previous chapter (fig. 5.1). A cast of thousands of Jewish Americans depicted Jewish history-cum-heritage from the creation of the world to its culmination, namely, the liberty of America and the establishment of a new Jewish homeland in Palestine. At the culmination of the performance on July 3, 1933, massive banners with the red, white, and blue of the United States as well as the six-pointed Star of David and blue and white representing Palestine adorned the 350-foot-tall Temple with its four tiers and thirty-two flagstaffs. The culmination in two nations, presented as possible without conflict, was possible on the temporary stage of the Temple in "the Orient" more so than in Palestine. However, the producers designed the spectacle to elide the gap between "emotional" connections to "the Orient" and immigration and territorial policies on the ground in Palestine *and* the United States.

Figure 5.1. Stage as pictured in Chicago World's Fair guidebook.

Distinctions between diaspora Jewish heritage and the national myths that developed in Jewish settlements in Palestine later inherited by the Israeli State were in tension in the representations of "the Orient" at the World's Fair. Two different spaces staged Jewishness at the 1933 fair. Separately from *The Romance of a People*, the Synagogue Council of America (SCA) controlled the Jewish Exhibit in the Hall of Religion, designed to articulate the place of Jewish practices in and contributions to American society. The Hall of Religion was a rival vision for the nature of Jewishness and therefore how to understand Jewish heritage, from how the past shapes the present to visions for the future. Accordingly, the Jewish Exhibit in the Hall of Religion did not represent Palestine in the frame of nation-building. Even so, the SCA displayed activities in Palestine alongside images of Jews in the United States and Europe as evidence of Jewish contributions to civilization and participation in pluralism. At the same fair, the ZOA offered an alternative vision of Jewishness. As part of "Jewish Day," held on July 3, 1933, Isaac Van Grove and Meyer Weisgal directed and produced the pageant *The Romance of a People*, which told the story of Jewish history beginning with creation and culminating with Jewish immigration to America and the construction of a new Palestine. Though sponsored by the ZOA, Weisgal recalled that his intention was not to produce a narrowly Zionist narrative but a spectacle that "would have something for everybody, Zionists, non-Zionists, the religious, the nationalists, everybody."[1] This pageant took place on a stage featuring a four-level replica of the Temple of Solomon, included no fewer than 3,500 performers, was viewed by 180,000 people in two performances in Chicago, and traveled to other major American cities including New York, Philadelphia, and Los Angeles to be experienced by tens of thousands more. The pageant presented a vision of Jewish history that overlapped with the SCA in many ways, but also diverged in ideology, collective memory, and approach to presentation.

Moreover, Rabbi Felix Mendelsohn's assertion that "since Jews are primarily a religious community (an indisputable fact which certain Jews still fail to appreciate) there is no earthly reason why Jews should have a building of their own" alludes to the internal and external disputes about the nature and place of Jewishness.[2] Nations were eligible to construct a building to display their heritage and hopes for the future: the 1933 World's Fair planners did not deem Jewishness to be sufficiently "national" to warrant a building or pavilion. But Jewish Day paralleled the many nation days held throughout the fair, suggesting the slippage between Jewishness and a growing national life in the eyes of the fair planners and observers alike. Mendelsohn's very frustration at the lack of "appreciation" displayed by many Jews for the status of Judaism as a religion and no other category of heritage demonstrates the dispute over what mattered in Jews' past, how it would shape their future, and the role of Palestine as a site and sight for envisioning Jewish citizenship in the United States and "the Orient."

In chapter 4, I argued that the *Jewish Encyclopedia* constructed Jewish heritage through images of "the Orient" due to the mediated nature of all visual culture and especially when images accompanying text inadvertently undermined the goal of historicization and instead created a timeless sense of the significance of the Temple. Like the *JE*, the World's Fair was a unique opportunity for Jews to speak to multiple communities at once about the significance of Jewish heritage for all Americans and to reclaim "the Orient" from narratives of Christian heritage. Through either Jewish Day or the Jewish exhibit in the Hall of Religion, Jewish Americans could speak to fellow religious and ethnic Jews in the United States, to the nation of the United States as a whole, to the transnational Jewish community, and to the world to say that Jews were modern. Jewish Day and the Jewish exhibit demonstrate that Jewish Americans in the early twentieth century disagreed about what it means to be Jewish and that they turned to visual culture to argue what Jewishness should be in the future. This meant selectively choosing from the past to assemble a vision of Jewish heritage. "The Orient" did not serve as the central stage for the Jewish exhibit, but the visual presence of "the Orient" emphasized the claim that Palestine was one of many international Jewish communities deserving a place in national citizenships and worldwide respect. In contrast, Jewish Day literally made "the Orient" the stage for the Jewish Day pageant *The Romance of a People*, and it visually asserted that American heritage would be incomplete without the history of "the Orient" and that Jewish Americans' heritage bridged "the Orient" and the United States.

At the 1933 Century of Progress World's Fair in Chicago, Jewish Americans created two representations of Jews, Jewishness, and Palestine during the Jewish Day pageant described earlier and in the separate Jewish exhibit in the Hall of Religion, one of the permanent exhibits of the fair that included Judaism alongside many other American religious groups. To evaluate the displays and their reception, I consider repositories of memory such as guidebooks and photographs, as well as reports in the press. In addition to using the media to reconstruct the displays at the fair, I compare coverage in major newspapers such as the *Chicago Daily Tribune* and the *New York Times* with reactions in Jewish newspapers such as the *Sentinel* and Yiddish newspapers such as *Forverts* [The Forward], and *Der Tog* [The Day]. I end by examining the legacy of the 1933 fair and *The Romance of a People*, in particular in its transformation into *The Epic of a Nation* for the 1934 fair and the role of the pageant in the construction of Jewish heritage throughout the twentieth century. These displays were "prime site[s] for transforming the Holy Land into the Jewish homeland," but they offered more than one vision of what the Jewish homeland could be and intimately linked the development of a Jewish homeland with Jewish American heritage and practice.[3] Though a Jewish state did not yet exist in Palestine—and no one could know with certainty that a Jewish state there would ever exist, such is the contingency of history—Jewish Day organizers used the fair to argue that such a state should exist. By creating and performing a particular Jewish heritage at the World's Fair, Zionist Americans created the idea of a Jewish state before its existence. The stage of the World's Fair was "both a setting for performances . . . and a performance in its own right."[4] These performances had implications for Jewish citizenship in the Middle East: they helped materialize a Jewish state in the Middle East through its simulacrum in the United States. But in addition to the influence of the fair on the construction of Israel and its heritage and politics, the World's Fair had goals and consequences for American heritage and culture, both Jewish and non-Jewish.

There is a two-part struggle evident in the performances at the 1933 World's Fair. There was an external struggle regarding Jewish heritage within American society broadly concerning the model of the melting pot and the alternative possibility offered by cultural pluralism. The lasting remnants of the model of the melting pot—conceptually advocated accepting "the best" elements of each immigrant group but ultimately expected assimilation to a single American ideal. This was challenged by an alternative possibility offered by cultural pluralism, which posited overarching cultural values shared by all groups but also allowed for the retention of the particularities of distinct cultural groups. The two were conflated then and today, but the melting pot and pluralism represent different models of including minorities and help to think conceptually about implications of various ideologies and performances.

But there was also an internal battle among Jewish Americans regarding citizenship, religious practice, and Judaism within a democratic society. Jewish Americans simultaneously constructed two citizenships at the 1933 World's Fair: their own in the United States and that of a Jewish nation in Palestine. Citizenship exists in the performance of nationalism, in the texts, images, materials, and pageants that continually produce knowledge of citizenship. Although imagination of "the Orient" did help to build a physical place called Palestine located in the Middle East, Jewish Americans constructed a projection of "the Orient" from and onto the United States. One result of the performance of Jewish nationalism in the United States was the construction of both nations into a single Jewish American heritage. "The Orient" became almost simultaneously contemporary and contemporaneous. Contemporary for its role in the Jewish present, turning Palestine into "the Orient"—a contemporaneous perspective of life in Palestine—a cultural center and refuge for those fleeing Europe. But for the connection of these activities to a trajectory of the Jewish past and the imaginative vision of what it means to Jewish heritage, that is, what it was to be a Jew in the first half of the twentieth-century United States. Jewish life in Palestine in 1933 was quite different from Jewish American life and from Jewish visual culture of "the Orient," including differences in the forms of Zionism that existed in both places. But the idea of Jewish unity was important to the vision of heritage presented in both the Hall of Religion and in the Jewish Day pageant. Both narratives try to account for Jewish differences across time and space and to imagine a future Jewish unity by tracing an imagined thread through Jewish heritage. Comparing two presentations of visual culture at the same fair reveals the reality of differences in conceptions of Jewishness and the inability of any imagined heritage to overcome those differences.

Hall of Religion

The *Glimpses of the Jewish Exhibit* pamphlet by Rabbis Louis Mann and Gerson Levi printed for the exhibit in the Hall of Religion provided images of all the elements of the exhibit as finally executed. A central piece of the exhibit was an Ark featuring all the essential elements of material culture in synagogue life: Torah scrolls, a perpetual lamp, and two menorahs (fig. 5.2). Together with the abstract decorations and Hebrew and English inscriptions, these objects evoked a visual culture tied to Jewish religious life shaped by tradition and halakha. Yet the text of the pamphlet made a case for Jewish religious life beyond the space of the synagogue. Mann and Levi argued that Judaism had helped contribute to "Progress through Religion" in Chicago. Religion had cultivated "a deepening of

Figure 5.2. "The Ark."

social consciousness." Emphasizing the plural nature of American society, they noted that "in the past century the idea of religion as a social force has been given general support from organizations of worshippers of all creeds."[5] The social description of the "progress" achieved by religion and Judaism was disconnected from the rhythms of the Jewish calendar or the practices of the Jewish service. Social consciousness was the basis for the arguments of the significance of the contributions of Judaism to American life. Juxtaposing this argument with an image of a Torah Ark suggested a link between the values taught within the Torah and the social and civic activism described within the text, but the practices specifically described have little to do with the synagogue services that would employ the objects displayed. Mann and Levi explained neither weekday Torah readings and prayers, nor Shabbat, nor Jewish holidays. Progress and social consciousness thus provide a window into representation of a variety of other Jewish practices and the explicit claim that those practices are "religious."

In addition to the Ark, the exhibit featured a slideshow of 140 images depicting these practices. Topics of the slides, as categorized by Mann and Levi, included the people of Israel's Nobel Prize winners and their contributions to Peace, Social Service, Education, Religion, Literature, Medicine, Philanthropy, Agriculture, Statesmanship, Music, Science, Art, Drama, and Child Welfare. Each category mixed individuals and organizations in the United States, Palestine, and Europe alongside each other. This emphasized transnational Jewish peoplehood while also including Jewish activities in Palestine without making national or political claims on the land of Palestine. The display articulated Jewish peoplehood through the ideology of pluralism, emphasizing Jewish compatibility with and concern for other cultural groups. The Straus Health Center in Jerusalem and the Hadassah hospital in Tel Aviv, "maintained . . . free to all races and creeds," appeared alongside the YMHA and YWHA, the Jewish People's Institute in Chicago, and social service to soldiers and sailors by the Jewish Welfare Board under "Contribution to Social Service" (fig. 5.3). The Conservative Jewish Theological Seminary, Dropsie College, Reform's Hebrew Union College, the Orthodox Yeshiva College in New York, and Chief Rabbi of Palestine Abraham Isaac Kook appeared equal in their contributions to religion. And an extensive list of well-known international Jews appeared in the slides, such as Heinrich Heine, Israel Zangwill, Emma Lazarus, Ahad Ha'am, and Sigmund Freud. Other notable individuals included Julius Rosenwald, Moses Montefiore, Nathan Straus, Baron Edmond de Rothschild, Jacob Henry Schiff, Benjamin Disraeli, Chaim Weizmann, Samuel Gompers, Simon Wolf, Louis Marshall, Theodor Herzl, Gustav Mahler, Albert Einstein, Camille Pissarro, Ephraim Moses Lilien, Boris Schatz, and Rebecca Gratz.[6] Many of these names are recognizable from other chapters in this book. That recognition should also indicate how different their perspectives of Jewish heritage were.

Palestine was not presented as a unique nation or state, but contemporary life in Palestine was included in the Jewish exhibit of religion. All of the activities of Jews were framed within what Mann and Levi saw as the divisions of Jewish social-religious practice. By claiming these activities as "Israel's contribution" to each field, Mann and Levi implied the nature of peoplehood—membership as part of "Israel"—as religious or cultural but not national.[7] In this way, Ahad Ha'am did not represent cultural Zionism, but Jewish literature as a means to reinvigorate Jewish life and practice. Competing conceptions of Jewish heritage were flattened insofar as Ahad Ha'am, Heinrich Heine, and Israel Zangwill were simply represented alongside each other. The slideshow and Mann and Levi's frame of the general contributions of a variety of Jews achieved the appearance of unity among Jews—central to the discussions of the SCA prior to the exhibit—by placing names and images alongside each other. Viewers might easily have imagined a united, international religious community of Jews as a consequence of the absence of debates among individuals or groups

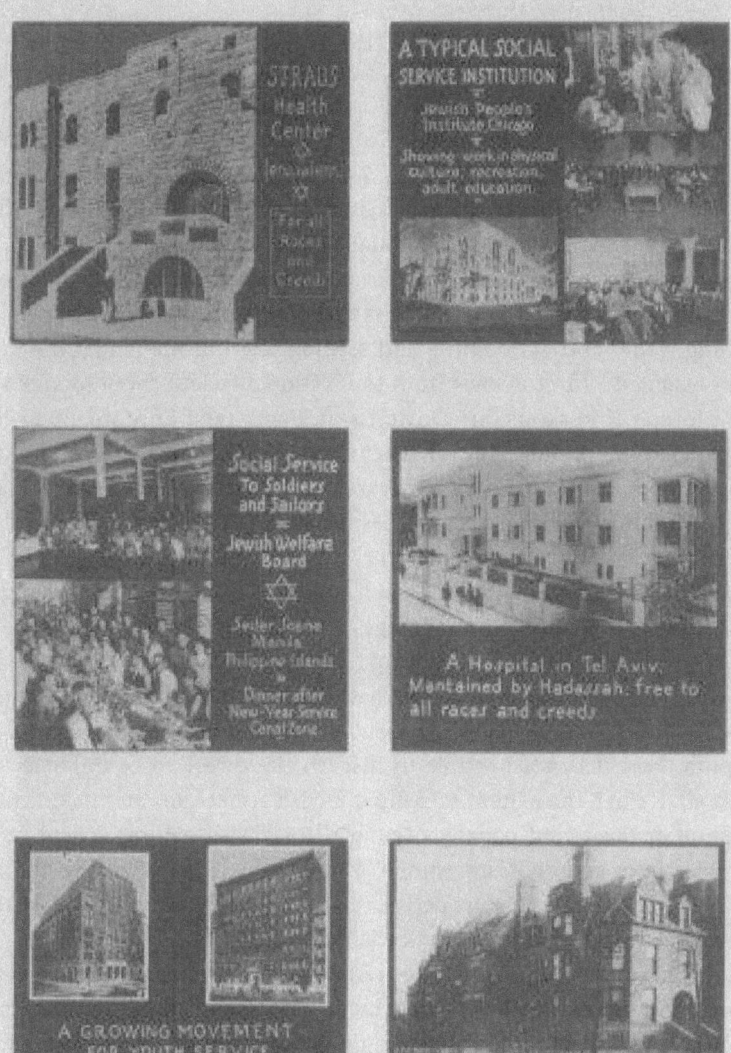

Figure 5.3. "Israel's Contribution to Social Service."

over the nature or future of Judaism, even as those individuals or groups might have opposed their designation as part of this religious framework, however broadly construed.

Many names and images drew specifically on Palestine, but they were always alongside diasporic activities. Beyond the aforementioned names of Jews whose work takes place in Palestine, photos of the land such as in "Israel's Contribution to Agriculture" appear in one of four slides, alongside other landscapes and portraits (fig. 5.4). The exhibit called David Lubin the "founder of the International Institute of Agriculture, the very first permanent movement for International Cooperation: the forerunner of the League of Nations." It described Baron Maurice de Hirsch as a "Friend of the Oppressed and Emigrant Jews [who] established Foundations for teaching trades and agriculture, and settling Jews on the land." The third slide presented "Three Scenes from the National Farm School founded by Rabbi Joseph Krauskopf [in] Doylestown, Penn," and only the final slide depicted several photographs of "Farm Scenes—Palestine."[8] Given no textual narrative, scenes from Pennsylvania and Palestine showed essentially the same thing: Jewish men's bodies at work. Whether on the land in America or Palestine, Jewish men were hard at work. This suggested the physical strength and cultural normalization of Jewish men that served as both motif and goal of Zionist images and ideology, but the side-by-side photos of Palestine and Pennsylvania implied equality of the two lands and of the Jews in each land. If Ahad Ha'am's cultural Zionism argued that a Jewish center in Palestine would radiate influence outward to the diaspora, here it is not possible to discern the direction of influence—if any at all. Rather, the exhibit presented Jewish Americans and Palestinians as simultaneously and equally capable. The Jewish exhibit articulated a future of Jews and Judaism similar to the NFTS art calendars: the era of vibrant Jewish life in Europe was ending, and America and Palestine offered the greatest promise for Jewish communities.

Jewish Americans sometimes relied on artistic images that depicted periods and places foreign to their own, as exemplified by the images of the NFTS art calendars that had originated with male artists and exhibits such as at the Fifth Zionist Congress; male bodies appeared more frequently in these images and men used these images in different ways from women. But the slides of the 1933 Jewish exhibit featured photographs of contemporary Jewish men. While artistic images may have been symbolic of various norms for Jewish men and women, these photographs

Figure 5.4. "Israel's Contribution to Agriculture."

represented Jewish men's physical strength in literal ways. These images claimed overtly that Jewish men had powerful bodies connected to the land (whether land in the United States or Palestine). Photographs offered symbolic proof of the fitness of Jewish men according to American gender norms: the rabbis and intellectuals who selected such images would most likely not have worked as farmers. This implicitly responded to Christian Orientalism and antisemitism that pictured Jewish men's bodies as effeminate. Like the Muscular Christianity movement that sought to create a new image of Christian men's bodies in the United States in the late nineteenth and early twentieth centuries, as discussed in chapter 2, the SCA sought to picture a Muscular Judaism. The SCA's Muscular Judaism was also a critique of Zionism's ideal of the New Jew or *Muskeljudentum*, as Max Nordau described it. The SCA's photographic exhibit in the Hall of Religion, unlike Nordau, envisioned muscular Jewish men who did not necessarily need Zionism to transform their bodies. Moreover, the lack of actual practice of farming or other physical labor by the rabbis of the SCA and most Jewish Americans indicates that the SCA's visual culture did not argue that Jewish Americans needed to transform their *bodies*, but the *image* of their bodies from the perspective of Americans. The SCA's exhibit presented an imagination of Jewish bodies for Jews and non-Jews at the 1933 World's Fair that suggested Jewish bodies were already "normal," as evidenced by its images, even if those images did not look like the viewers of those images.

The Romance of a People

Besides Chicago in 1933, several World's Fairs featured representations of Palestine as part of their displays. Chicago (1893) included actors and artifacts from Jerusalem and the region of Palestine within the Turkish village, St. Louis (1904) included a Protestant replica of Jerusalem, and New York (1939) included a Palestine Pavilion.[9] Engaging biblical heritage and subsequent years of suffering, on July 3, 1933, the Jewish Agency for Palestine held *The Romance of a People* in Soldier Field as the main feature of Jewish Day. The pageant attracted over 125,000 visitors, so many that it was restaged on July 6, 1933, under the sponsorship of the *Chicago Daily Tribune* and attracted 55,000 visitors to the encore performance. Pageants are productions of civic significance. "Hybrids of art and propaganda . . . not primarily motivated by commerce," they locate and dramatize significant moments of the past in order to direct the present. Thus they comment on the public realm and attempt to solidify community: at heart, they are political statements.[10] Pageantry has been a mainstay of American nationalism from the inception of the early republic. While broadcasting a vision of unity and consensus, pageants, parades, and celebrations have allowed Americans to project their partisan concerns—regarding race, region, religion, gender, or class—onto the American nation, at once affirming the Revolution and contesting its legacy.[11]

Jewish Americans were not the first to connect diasporic lands with the Holy Land and Jewish tradition. For example, Jewish immigrants to Poland and their descendants during the medieval period constructed legends of origin that Judaized Polish land, justifying their existence outside of Israel socially and theologically. Yet other legends addressed Jewish contributions to Poland, asserting Poles accepted Jews as residents as a matter of mutual benefit, not out of one-sided Polish graciousness.[12] In Poland, Jews had found a home and a good deal of freedom, if not the full citizenship and developing sense of pluralism articulated in early twentieth-century America. Many of the same tropes and motifs used in Jewish-Polish legends of origins were recast for *The Romance of a People*. The pageant thus functioned as a new legend of origin and of acceptance, engaging in Jewish traditions to make connections between a new physical space and the ongoing mystical Israel.

A broad number of Jewish American civic performances incorporated Jews and Jewish traditions into American myths around figures such as Christopher Columbus, George Washington, and Abraham Lincoln.[13] Yet even these stopped short of the history performed at *The Romance of a People*. Asserting Lincoln as the American Moses still worked within the larger frame of American history. In contrast, *The Romance of a People* worked American history into Jewish history and asserted that Jewish history, in its own right, was important for Americans, even as the pageant also accommodated American patriotism. The scale and audience of *The Romance of a People*, not to mention the bold claims for robust pluralism and the validity of a Jewish state, made the pageant a landmark moment. Performed almost entirely in English with the use of symbolic Hebrew songs, the pageant had the attention of a massive national and international Jewish and non-Jewish audience. The attendance on July 3, 1933, set the record for any single day of attendance that year, topping even the crowd the following day for Independence Day.[14] And the success at the fair spawned further productions: the pageant ran for a month later in

1933 in New York City, and it traveled throughout the United States to other cities including Detroit, Cleveland, Philadelphia, Baltimore, and Los Angeles. As it arrived in Los Angeles, in 1934, the *Los Angeles Times* even printed the hope that "the forthcoming tour will encompass practically every city with a population of 100,000 or more."[15]

The pageant featured a prologue and several episodes of Jewish history, whose significance were framed by the construction of two main stage elements, the Torah and the Temple. First, every episode was presented as a chapter of Torah, read from a massive Torah, "which in width was twice the height of two men," on an altar at center stage. As James O'Donnell Bennett reported the day after the performance, "One hundred and twenty-five thousand men, women, and children of Chicagoland's Jewry unrolled on Soldiers' field last night a gigantic scroll emblematic of the . . . Pentateuch and thereon they read the story, now tragic, now triumphant, of their race's march down forty centuries to the new Palestine of today."[16] Pageant chairman Harry Fisher proclaimed that these episodes represented not just a single moment of history, but all of history strung together, so that the pageant depicted "how a great idea had been kept alive during 40 centuries."[17] In the guidebook distributed for the pageant, Rabbi Solomon Goldman portrayed each moment of Jewish struggle to maintain a nation—the great idea Fisher referenced—as the vision of Moses upon his death. The construction of a narrative and stage structure that depicted all of Jewish history as the unfolding of the Torah and Moses' prophetic vision asserted that the covenant that lasted far beyond the destruction of the Temple. This implied a counterargument to the new covenant through Christ in Christianity, served as a historical claim to the land of Palestine, and emphasized Jewish unity. The guidebook remembers unity under the Maccabees against Antiochus, for example, rather than conflicts among various sects and differing degrees of Hellenization. But even as Jews—already an "old people"—united behind the Maccabees to restore the Temple and preserve ancient rites, they were able to undergo a vast change when the Temple fell several centuries later.

While the Torah altar stood at the center of the stadium, a replica of the Temple served as the stage for the history read from the Torah. In Chicago and in the later performances in New York, the Temple stage featured four tiers that provided space for the thousands of performers.[18] The Temple invoked ancient Palestine to claim both American citizenship, as a symbol of Jewish ethical contribution, and rights to the land of Palestine, as evidence of a nearly primordial presence of Jews there. As a claim on Palestine, the pageant also offered a physically strong representation of Jews. First, Jews worked hard as slaves in Egypt. Then, after the Exodus, Jews occupied and defended their land. Ultimately, "Titus captures Jerusalem with carnage unequaled in the long history of wars. Judah's sons fight like lions; they die, but do not surrender."[19] Though this depicted oppression and then the end of Jewish national life and military defeat, it asserted the physical strength of Jewish men. And because the narrative was expressed through the performance of the pageant, audience members view not only the physical strength of the warriors of antiquity but the contemporary Jews who embody them theatrically. Indeed, every element of the performance—"a mighty spectacle of color, dance, music, and light"[20]—suggested the physical mastery of contemporary Jews: not only warriors, but skilled dancers and actors individually and as a group. The slideshow at the Hall of Religion exhibited a few photographs of the physical abilities of Jews to counter stereotypes of weak and neurotic Jewish men, but on a much grander scale, the pageant portrayed the physical agility of Jewish Americans and Jews throughout history.

Physical elements of the land were important as well. Pageant planners and the press observed the ways the new Temple harmonized with the American landscape. In Chicago, Bennett observed that the elements of "synagogue-like temple" merged with its surroundings, including Greek influence such as the "Ionic loveliness of the Field museum, a temple of science," "stalwart Doric of the stadium's ranks upon ranks of columns," and "modernistic challenge of the overlooking parti-colored towers and silver domes of the Exposition." Bennett wondered, "Could any other city . . . provide a setting so touched with variety and with daring, with reverent replica and with insolent experimentation as is this setting of ours?"[21] (see figure 5.1). The fair elevated America in general and Chicago in particular, and a sense of competition to be the top city infused reports of both the Chicago and New York performances of *The Romance of a People*. Though the elements of the fair and the landscape of Chicago were obviously absent when the pageant was restaged in New York, the significance of the Temple remained equal. The *New York Times* reported the plans for building the Temple on the Polo Grounds:

> Early in the pageant, when the times of Solomon are being presented, the temple is the scene of the traditional services of the high priests. After the destruction of the temple by the Romans, the tumbled ruins remain in darkness until modern

times, when a crown of light illuminates the temple structure, to which has now been added a spire or cupola. The new building, patterned after the Hebrew University, is symbolic of the Jewish renaissance in Palestine.[22]

The Temple design was "assembled as a portable structure," perhaps reminiscent of the tabernacle the Israelites assembled in the wilderness before their final entry to the Promised Land[23] or God's heavenly chariot on wheels in Ezekiel 1: 15-21. Interpreters have seen this passage of Ezekiel to emphasize that God would go with Jews anywhere (including the United States?) and that God never abandoned God's covenant with Jews. But in this case, the wilderness is a Promised Land itself, featuring a replica of the Temple.

The pageant mainly relied on ancient symbols of and simulacra of relics from "the Orient," but it also included elements that gestured to the modern period, such as the architectural features of Hebrew University (which had been modeled on the ancient Temple). Chicago's stage included "blue six pointed star of the flag of the new Palestine," a "star theme . . . carried for 350 feet up and up and up the triple level stage proper to the super-neon six pointed star that gleamed above the pinnacle of the temple, which was the extreme background of the stage." This scale and its symbols portrayed Jewish past as grand and worth remembering and incorporating in world heritage. "Avenues of 32 steel flagstaffs from which swayed in the moonlight the blue and white banners of Palestine and the red, white, and blue of the United States."[24]

Blending ancient and modern symbols of Palestine with symbols of American nationalism presented an ideological statement that contracted the space between the United States and "the Orient," both as holy lands. The Bible became historical evidence for the national rights of Jews to the land of Israel. It symbolized covenant, but perhaps more importantly, it was proof of Jewish ties to the land, indicative of a primordial connection between Jews and territory specifically and Jews as a nation generally. Without invoking "political" rhetoric explicitly, save perhaps Chaim Weizmann's single speech prior to the Chicago performance, the pageant nevertheless implied the legitimacy of linking ancient Israel and modern nationalism, thus legitimizing the possibility to seek political sovereignty in Palestine.[25] Displays inspired by the American and Zionist flags argued for the authenticity of Jewish American heritage. Rather than presenting a philosophical argument for the legitimacy of multiple allegiances or cultural pluralism, the pageant simply performed it. European and Palestinian ideologies were translated into discourse and practices compelling for Americans, changing the very nature of Zionism. At the same time, the nature of America incorporated a space for "the Jewish Orient" as a performance of American heritage. The pageant simultaneously performed the right of Jews to Palestine and the right of Jewish Americans to support the right of Jews to Palestine without having their American loyalty questioned. By enacting these claims on the stage of the Temple, the pageant justified Jewish Americans' decision not to move to Palestine, even if they could. Through that construction, Jews were inserted into American heritage, linking Jewish heritage and American heritage.

The Romance of a People: Jewish History

In the space of the Temple, Jewish history unfolded. The prologue recalled creation, followed shortly by paganism and sacrifices to massive idols, including virgins heaved into a twenty-eight-foot fiery god Moloch. Idolatry was defeated by Abraham's affirmation of God's singularity and by God's intervention in the sacrifice of Isaac. Next, Moses led the Exodus, and then the Temple was built. Then the Romans destroyed the Temple and dispersed Jews throughout the world. Jews sought homes in Spain, Poland, and Germany. While each offered periods of peace and hope, each was violently shattered. In Germany, Jews experienced massive change during emancipation. Though it was not all at once and never quite complete, Jews received citizenship throughout Western Europe. Yet almost immediately, such promises were retracted: trouble brewed in Western Europe, and Russia not only failed ever to emancipate Jews but regressed to medieval mistreatment of Jews.[26] For example, one scene was described as "a Russian Cossack, in days of Czar, beats a Jew."[27] This muddied differences between Cossacks (Ukrainians) and ethnic Russians, suggesting a violent impulse and consolidated antisemitic front against Jews among all indistinguishable East Europeans (fig. 5.5). The scene also suggested that there is a clear and visible distinction between Jews who lived in Eastern Europe and non-Jews from Eastern Europe. This would not only confirm the distinctiveness of Jewish heritage and suffering of Jews at the hands of non-Jews—justifying the need for Jewish refuge in Palestine. This collapsed visions of "the Orient" and views of Russian and Ukrainian antisemitism. In addition, the performance asserted a

188　　　　　　　　The Hebrew Orient

(NEWS photo)
Harry Needleman, playing role of Russian Cossack in days of Czar, beats aged Jew, portrayed by Harry Cohen. This is in seventh episode.

Figure 5.5. "Russian Cossack, in Days of Czar, Beats a Jew."

distance—produced a difference—from ideologies and practices that many Americans considered problematic and associated with East Europe, from the imperialism of Czars to the Soviet Union.

One of the central scenes in the pageant featured a depiction of Hasidism in the form of a solo dance performance, "Dudele," by Nathan Vizonsky (1898–1968), a Jewish American choreographer as well as a socialist, Yiddishist, and Jewish nationalist. The performance highlighted emotive prayer, song, and a deeply personal, familiar relationship with God that developed amid Jewish struggle in Eastern Europe.[28] On the one hand, the pageant honored Orthodox Judaism as represented by the performance, but on the other hand, situating Hasidism in this historical narrative implied the anachronism of such Jewish practice. Further, as the image shows, Vizonsky's costume was highly stylized, including a sleeve and sock decorated with Hebrew letters, a partial tallis (prayer shawl), and half a long black coat (fig. 5.6).²⁹ This does not depict or attempt to depict

Figure 5.6. "Dudele."

a historically accurate image of Hasidic Jews. Rather his costume suited the emotional symbolic role that Hasidism played for many Jewish Americans in 1933. The use of a "costume" rather than an attempt at historical clothing typically associated with Hasidic East European Jews—such as in the ZOA's own periodicals, as demonstrated in chapter 2, or in the preceding image of a Jew beaten by a Cossack in the pageant—suggests a rejection of those modes of appearance and the practices and worldview to which they were linked. Thus within the performance we see the conversion of a historical moment, East European Jewish life, into an internalized, emotional symbol of collective Jewish memory, Vizonsky's performance. Each symbolic moment of the pageant transformed moments in Jewish history into a reservoir of Jewish heritage, decoupling moments from linear history and instead representing them as resources to Jewish Americans.

In response to the oppressive environments in Eastern and Western Europe, hundreds of thousands immigrated to the "most liberal place in the world," the United States. All of the actors, still in costume, participated in an Americanization scene, drawing a straight line from each moment of Jewish history to contemporary Jewish American consciousness. For example, Helena Ruth Kirstein (née Marks) retained an image of actors dressed like figures from antiquity holding American flags during this Americanization at the culmination of the pageant. This symbolically claimed Jewish antiquity as part of American heritage (fig. 5.7).[30] At long

Figure 5.7. Americanization scene.

last the United States offered new freedom and the Liberty Bell resonated with the same message as the message of Leviticus for the Temple, "Proclaim liberty throughout the land to all the inhabitants thereof."[31] This narrative distinctly reframed the origin of American civilization, shifting from Rome and Greece to Ancient Israel. Only this new form of liberty opened the possibility for the coming of the messiah and the rebuilding of Israel at the pageant's conclusion. Although thousands found freedom in the United States, the continued repression in Russia justified the need for a return to Palestine. Thus the liberalism of the United States remained intact, even as these East European refugees could not find a home in the United States. And Jewish Americans' patriotism was not threatened by Zionist hopes for Palestine because Palestine was not a destination for Jewish Americans who already had a homeland, but for East European Jews who did not, as they suffered pogroms and the First World War.[32]

The pageant's narrative was connected to the diaspora and halakhic Judaism, even as it concluded a Zionist future, despite the irrelevance of halakha to Labor Zionism. After dispersion it recalled Rome, Spain, Poland, and of course the United States. And in each, the major contribution of Jews to each curated moment in the past as well as the present of 1933 is something spiritual, such as philosophy, mysticism, or melody. These features placed the pageant in contrast to the national narratives that had already taken hold in Palestine by 1933. For the emerging national narratives in Palestine, almost nothing in history mattered since Jews had left the Holy Land. Diaspora meant "galut" or exile, something to shed in order to embody the new nation. Zionist myths in Palestine focused on the fall of Masada against the Romans in 73 CE, the Bar Kokhba revolt in 132–135 CE, and the Battle of Tel Hai in 1920. Each recalled the willing death of Jews fighting for the nation. While Masada and Bar Kokhba took place in antiquity, the Battle of Tel Hai took place during the period of Zionist settlement. Its memory recalled the death of several soldiers, including Joseph Trumpeldor, fighting to protect Tel Hai. Trumpeldor had first served in the tsarist Russian army and lost an arm in the Russo-Japanese War. His assimilated, soldier persona made him an easy symbol for Yishuv Zionists. When he died at Tel Hai, supposedly uttering the last words, "Never mind, it is good to die for our country," he quickly achieved legendary, martyred status in Jewish nationalism and became a centerpiece in the construction of Israeli nationalism from his death and through the formation of the state. His martyrdom was recalled as a means of rejecting the diaspora and willingness to immigrate to Israel and sacrifice for it at any cost.[33]

The Jewish American pageant concluded with the possibility for settlement in Palestine, portrayed with symbols such as the Hebrew-language folk song "Anu Banu Artzah" (translated as "We are building the land") and integrating architectural elements of Hebrew University into the rebuilt Temple.[34] These symbols indicated some cultural exchange with Jewish life on the ground in Palestine, such as the popularity of Zionist folk songs and the preference for Hebrew over Yiddish as the symbolic Jewish language in the pageant. Nevertheless the guidebook was printed in English, and English and Yiddish were the primary languages of Jewish daily life in the United States. Parallel Zionist narratives emerged in Palestine and the United States. Both valued building a new homeland, and both valued building new Jews. Yet the details of the new lands and new bodies were different. They shared a goal of remaking the image of Jews—especially Jewish men—over into physical strength, with a specific emphasis on soldiers. Jewish Americans drew primarily on ancient religious history, but Jews in Palestine constructed symbols based on ancient and contemporary national history. Steven Rosenthal argues that post-Zionist distancing between Israel and the United States beginning in the late twentieth century was the "result of the failure of Israelis and American Jews to create any great common cultural bonds."[35] This lack of connection is less a recent failure and more a direct result of distinct goals and understandings of diaspora/exile, Palestine, and "the Orient" from the beginning among Zionists in the United States and globally. Jewish Americans could never fully adopt the national narratives of pre-state Palestine or the State of Israel because those narratives did not affirm the diaspora in general or the significance of American citizenship specifically. While chalutzim helped Jewish Americans create a strong self-image, this served as a means to construct and partake in American pluralism, rather than preparing Jewish Americans for immigration to Palestine. Orientalized chalutzim served as an argument for the culmination of Jewish history and the import of that history for Jewish citizenship in the United States. This presented the new Jewish nation as once as a linear historical culmination of Jewish life *and* as vision of Jews and chalutzim as contemporaneous. As Jews "progressed" and modernized, between each scene, Arabs wandered lost in history with their camels. Lined up in a linear history, the pageant presented each stage of Jewish civilization as a time capsule that represented a core of Jewish values but also signaled Jewish "progress" through history in comparison to Arabs who never changed. Arabs and others living in Palestine for generations, unlike Zionist immigrants in most cases, had no voice in the representation of Palestine. Why would they, if they were contemporaneous and not located temporally in "the Orient" rather than contemporary inhabitants of Palestine?" Arabs, Bedouins, and others in Palestine had their histories and heritages silenced, obstructed from view, and effaced by arranging "the Orient" as Jewish heritage, i.e., Jewish and not Christian as well as Jewish and not Arab, Bedouin, Muslim, and so on. That Arabs had no legitimate history or progress per this telling was not lost on the audience. John Evans described what he saw: Arabs "were passive figures drawn into an exotic landscape. These nomads took over a portion of the metaphoric eternal wandering attributed to Jews. Jews were newly figured in *The Romance* as active, progressive, civilizing agents." Much like the ways Jews maintained a gendered binary in "the West" v. "the Orient" and sought to shift their categorization in that binary, Jewish Day sought to shift Jews across a binary of rootless ahistorical primitives to contemporary, progressive citizens. Furthermore, "Arabs replaced Jews in Jewish- and Christian-American Orientalism. Arabs were introduced as living outside of modern time and without direction or focused passion. Peacefully, the pageant suggested, they awaited modernist redemption. . . . If Jews were seen to be marching uphill together to advance civilization on behalf of both Christians and Jews, Bedouins were seen as trapped in an idyllic netherworld and made supplemental to the main story."[40] Evans collapsed Bedouin lifestyle with all Arabs, and discounted both the dynamic Bedouin lifestyle as well as possibility for Arabs—all of whom Evans assumed to be Muslim, though this is incorrect and overlooks the significant number of Christian Arabs and Palestinians—to join "modern progress" without the paternalism or "redemption" of Jews and Christians.

The Romance of a People: Religion and Race in Press Reception

The Romance of a People presents one example of how Palestine was portrayed in Jewish American public culture, but reports of the pageant in the press expand its window into American life in 1933. The descriptions and interpretations of the pageant reveal how Jewish and non-Jewish Americans attempted to integrate this new performance of American citizenship into their worldviews. The *Chicago Daily Tribune* announced the initial meeting of the cast of *The Romance of a People* in April 1933. Meyer Weisgal was to be executive director, Rabbi Solomon Goldman chairman of the pageant committee, and Isaac Van Grove the director. From the beginning, Weisgal and Van Grove planned for three thousand cast members and for the stage to be the largest ever. They also publicized initial support from several politicians. Judge Harry Fisher was chairman of the celebration, and four governors sponsored the pageant: Horner of Illinois, Seligman of New Mexico, Lehmann of New York, and Meyer of Oregon.[37]

The publicity for the pageant stretched to New York City. In June 1933, the *New York Times* printed an article explaining that the pageant was "the Jewish contribution to a century of progress" but that the significance of the pageant extended beyond Jews. Judge Harry Fisher and Meyer Weisgal pointed out that the event would be of vital interest to Christians of all sects. "We have not history, other than racial, that is exclusively our own as Jews," Judge Fisher said. "Our religious history belongs not only to Judaism, but also to Christianity and Mohammedanism. The 'Romance of a People' will be shared with our Christian friends as a common historical experience."[38] Race-as-heritage neutralized the threat to the maintenance of Jewish communal life by living with non-Jews in any territory and pretended to an equitable pluralism amongst Christians, Jews, and Muslims in the United States and "the Orient."

Publicity for the campaign embodied Kallen's concept of pluralism: through contributions unique to their group history, Jews benefited all Americans. Yet in juxtaposing Jews' racial differences from other Americans, Fisher differed from the representation of Jews and Judaism in the Hall of Religion. In the Hall of Religion, Jewish religion marked difference, while race was essentially unmarked. But Fisher claimed a shared core of religious history between Jews and Christians, while race marked difference. Discourse of race, religion, and pluralism all danced around similar ideas—Jews were like other Americans, but also had the right to be different—but negotiated the particular terms and configurations of identities differently. If religious contributions justified Jewish American citizenship as well as their rights to group heritage and practice, Van Grove did not consider this a new contribution. Rather, for Van Grove, the long history depicted in the pageant revealed that this had been Jews' contribution to the world throughout history: "This is not a pageant in the sense of a series of station scenes, nor is it a pictorial symbolization of the stages of religious thought." On the contrary, Van Grove has emphasized that it is "the enactment of the agonies through which a people passed in giving to the world the foundation of its religious concepts."[39]

This reference to Jewish suffering indicated a sense of moral insight as a result of the details of Jewish history. In this way, Van Grove claimed diaspora history as a viable element of Jewish memory, suggesting the importance of this memory in shaping contemporary Jewish heritage as morally conscientious and thus deserving of citizenship. Journalist John Evans echoed the idea, "One of the aims of the production will be to foster an understanding of the religious passion of a people in whose experience the belief in a compassionate God began." The emphasis on moral capital gained through suffering may explain why, beyond the simple depiction of scripture, Evans claimed in the *Chicago Daily Tribune*, "The pageant may be regarded as America's first attempt at a Passion Play."[40] Evans later added that the pageant was "more than mere spectacle, . . . It is religious, but is more than religion as such. It is also historical, but more than mere history: it is prophetic!" In this, he agreed with Van Grove that Jewish history founded contemporary heritage, and Evans suggested a comparison (or more?) with Christian heritage, "The 'Romance of a People' sways the emotions because it epitomizes 4,000 years of human life. But those 4,000 years of life were quickened by a big idea which through the years had been molding a Messianic Person who stumbles and staggers forward with sacrificial abandon to his destruction, only to rise again."[41] Christian viewers like Evans seem to have watched the pageant without concluding the same things about Jewish heritage as Jewish viewers. Evans still saw history and American heritage through a Christian frame. This type of thinking may have reinforced Christian Orientalism toward Jews and Jewish history. Jews and Christians' worldviews framed how they interpreted the pageant, while both Jewish American and Christian American interpretations rested on Orientalism. The only question was whose history could be reduced to contemporaneous "Oriental" heritage.

If Van Grove saw something unique about suffering for Jews' moral insight, Evans indicated that Christians and Jews could share in this "common historical experience." The Bible in history served simultaneously as an argument for Jewish peoplehood *and* to dissolve boundaries between Jews and Christians. But to cross the boundaries or to share in the morality drawn from Jewish history was an opportunity Christians had not capitalized on and thus was newly offered by the pageant. "George W. Dixon, chairman of the religious committee of the World's Fair, asserted that 'a new day not alone of religious tolerance but of religious cooperation has dawned,' and added 'that Jewish day will go down in history as one of religion's most significant moments.' "[42] Evans explained, "As a result of this expression of good will, Protestant and Catholic leaders have formed a Chicago committee of Christian friends who are cooperating actively in the preparation for the event."[43] Pressing the issue further, Evans quoted Chicago public schools superintendent William J. Bogan, who "declared the privilege granted to Christian friends to participate in the drama was 'an opportunity for Christians to regain their self-respect.' "[44] Without invoking the term itself, Evans, Dixon, and Bogan experimented with the idea of a shared "Judeo-Christian tradition" to express the relationship of various subcultures in America. Left-wing Christians who sought to fight other Christians' antisemitism, first in the 1930s and more broadly in the 1950s, popularized the term Judeo-Christian, but Van Grove also engaged the idea as a possibility for legitimizing Jewish American heritage.[45] A key difference in Van Grove's appeal to a shared religious history from his Christian counterparts was that for Van Grove religious and racial discourse existed alongside each other, while for Christians the Judeo-Christian tradition was an alternative to racial (antisemitic) discourse.

Similarly to the English-language press, the Yiddish newspaper *Forverts* (Forward) reported on the Chicago exhibition, noting both the pageant's concern with Jewish history and the large amount of money collected for Palestine, noting that Hadassah (the women's Zionist organization) had collected more than the Zionist Organization of America and the general support for Weizmann for president, the guest of honor in Chicago. Like the broader American press, *Forverts* noted that that the performance began with creation as rooted in *chumash* (the first five books of the Bible) and that it covered different eras in Jewish history, along with a report of the sports and athletic exercises in which Jewish youth partook during the day leading up to the pageant.[46] Coverage of the pageant in Chicago and New York emphasized the magnitude of "giant spectacle," in stage size, cast, audience, and significance.[47] The restaging of *The Romance of a People* in New York received much more coverage, as the paper was based in New York, and advertisement for the pageant called it the "richest, biggest, and most magnificent Jewish performance that will have been executed."[48] Advertisements in *Forverts* especially emphasized the visual element of the spectacle and its representation of Jewish history, highlighting the potential to see "the image rich [*bild rayche*] history of the Jewish people" and the "grandiose art-rich [*kinstliche-rayche*] performance."[49] The *Forverts* asserted the significance of the pageant in and beyond the Jewish community: "Not only a grandiose performance, nor only a grandiose Jewish Demonstration," the performance would "rejoice the land" of New York, the United States, and would "assemble for the first time in the history of New York, to manifest respect for their own history, to express the joy and the suffering of their own past and to help their brothers to settle in a new land—to burst all their hatreds."[50]

The pageant addressed a central question: What does it mean to be a people? Many conceptions circulated at the time. Were Jews a race, a religion, a nation, a culture? In order to determine the nature of Jewish peoplehood, the pageant's producers and audience also sought a usable past, dancing around which pieces of history would cohere well in Jewish Americans' sense of heritage. Considering the press before and after the pageant, the memories of planners and participants, the guidebooks, and the spectacle of the pageant's variety of visual and aural effects indicates that Jews considered each of these conceptions valuable yet incomplete. At times race, religion, and nation fused, and at times they broke down in the representation of Jews, Judaism, and Jewish history. The spectacle overwhelmed all the senses to create a feeling of unity, eliding the contradictions and frictions amongst Jews.

Finally, the production of *The Romance of a People* points to the ways that what we now call the Holocaust (to the extent that the event begins with the rise of Nazism in 1933) was entwined with American arguments favoring Jewish immigration to Palestine from the beginning of Jewish persecution in Germany. Zionist passion for the land of Palestine certainly predated Jewish persecution in Germany and was not predicated by it, but the broader American audience connected concern for Jews in Germany and Palestine with American civic performance. *The Romance of a People* complicates both the argument that Americans were inactive toward the plight of German Jews and the argument that there was no connection between the Holocaust and endorsement of Jewish Palestine. The pageant and especially its coverage in the press made very clear connections among America, Germany, Palestine, and Jews. The widespread coverage of the pageant in 1933 allowed Jewish and non-Jewish Americans to acknowledge increasing problems in Germany and hopes for Jewish Palestine publicly and regularly in the same context. Zionism predated Nazism in international Jewish communities. But in 1933, Zionism found a place on American stages (and audience numbers in the hundreds of thousands by the time the tour of American cities concluded) in direct connection to the plight of Jews under Nazism.

Stephen Whitfield argues that none of the several pageants performed throughout the 1930s and 1940s could have been expected to halt the actions of militaries and Sonderkommandos across Europe.[51] Had the United States' tolerance and freedom been as boundless as the pageant claims, the pageant might never have been held, or at least it would have appeared in a different form. If the United States had been a safe haven for *all* Jews, pleas for open Jewish immigration to Palestine would not have been necessary. But the near-total end of Jewish immigration through the Emergency Quota Act in 1920 and the Johnson-Reed Act in 1924 prevented the United States from serving as refuge for all of the oppressed of Europe. However, the pageant served the purpose not only to oppose the violence of the Nazi regime, but also to call for ongoing Jewish rights and citizenship in the United States and Palestine. The significance of the pageant lies as much in its appearance as an event within the pages of the American press as it does in the performances on July 3, 6, and thereafter or in its ability to raise funds for refugees or build a homeland in Palestine. Jewish Americans may not have convinced the American government to intervene during the 1930s and 1940s, but they did successfully find a space for their picture of themselves as Americans on the World's Fair stage. Its spectacle covered over the United States' major failure of refusing to accept immigrants or refugees in the interest of a narrative of Jewish heritage that could ground Jewish Americans' sense of self *and* serve as protection in the unstable 1930s as more non-Jewish Americans began to question Jews' belonging.

The Epic of a Nation

Following the success of the pageant in performing Jewish history and citizenship, the 1934 extension of the fair again held Jewish Day, though the pageant was reshaped. In 1934, I. B. Urya chaired, Blake Scott (who had assisted Van Grove in 1933) directed, and Samuel S. Oman produced *The Epic of a Nation*, which drew on the narrative and elements of *The Romance of a People*.[52] The 1934 pageant received a smaller audience than in 1933, but attendants still numbered in the tens of thousands.[53] Funded by the Orthodox Union and ORT rather than the ZOA, *The Epic of a Nation* included three main acts, "the first a youth demonstration of exercises and drills, the second a symphonic hour of Hebraic music, and the third part a pageant descriptive of the contribution of the Jewish race to the arts."[54]

The Epic of a Nation guidebook explained that ORT, an acronym for the Russian *Obshchestvo Rasprostranenia Truda*, was the Association for the Promotion of Trade and Agriculture. ORT's socialist principles of uplifting East European Jews, whether in Russia or in new lands and cultures to which they immigrated, reshaped the new production. Jewish Day became "Jewish People's Day."[55] Evans argued that although the 1933 pageant had been devoted "to Zionism and the creation of a national homeland of the Jews in Palestine," the 1934 production was both "lighter" and reoriented away from theology and politics toward "the unity of labor, thought and understanding exiting between Jews and their American countrymen," even as the new title boldly emphasized nation explicitly in place of more ambiguous peoplehood.[56]

The Epic of a Nation concluded with the scene "Tribute to Labor," which represented Jews from all countries and emphasized the redemption through work regardless of location.[57] Nation had become a more explicit feature of the title of the pageant, but Evans suggested that it was downplayed in the moral of the pageant. After the pageant, he concluded the Hasidic "mystic's consciousness of kinship with God" directed new labors in Palestine and internationally, serving as a foundation of unity. *The Epic of a Nation* concluded its depiction of united contributions of Jews with "The Star-Spangled Banner," echoing the 1933 pageant's performance of American patriotism and emphasis on the significance of Jewish contributions to American culture.[58] But national belonging was not a right: citizenship required certain groups, including Jews, continually to "earn" their place through productivity.

By centralizing the international unity of Jewish labor, artistic ability and physicality became even more central in *The Epic of a Nation* than in either the Jewish exhibit in the Hall of Religion or *The Romance of a People*. Music was also highlighted as a major Jewish contribution, asserting the vast success of Jews as musical artists. The orchestra included seventy-five pieces, and the pageant included five thousand children and adults performing liturgical, Spanish, Hasidic, and contemporary songs.[59] *The Epic of a Nation* advertised its feature of the musical ability of "The Street Singer" Arthur Tracy; violin prodigy Grisha Goluboff, who played on a Stradivarius loaned from Henry Ford; and Maude Key, descendent of "The Star-Spangled Banner" composer Francis Scott Key. These artistic displays countered antisemitic stereotypes that Jews had no soul and were not capable of art and fused that counternarrative with American patriotism.[60]

Finally and perhaps most importantly, *The Epic of a Nation* made demonstration of Jewish physical strength and masculinity an even more overt goal of the pageant than in 1933. While many Jewish children and athletes had participated in a field day prior to the pageant in 1933, the 1934 pageant integrated a boxing drill between world-famous Jewish heavyweight champion Max Baer and lightweight and welterweight champion Barney Ross.[61] Along with these celebrities, 150 boys reenacted the Dempsey-Tunney boxing match as a dance set to music, and 120 boys and girls performed tumbling and gymnastic feats.[62] While music marked a link to the ancient past, physicality marked contemporary "normality." Thousands of boys and girls spread across Soldier Field in a Star of David formation to perform a flag drill featuring both American and Jewish flags. The *Chicago Daily Tribune* explicitly linked these performances to Jewish physicality. "Jewish Community day will offer this youth pageant as a symbol of the Jew's belief in a strong body as well as a sane mind. The exhibition will be a symphony in skill and grace and will typify the important role youth plays in the Jewish people's life."[63] ORT's *The Epic of a Nation* espoused similar values of hegemonic Zionism as *The Romance of a People*, and by sponsoring a pageant that performed these values, Jewish Americans underscored their normalization and participation in American life, as other ORT organizations argued in various diaspora communities as well as in Palestine. The boxing performance in particular drew on American popular culture. Boxing was the sport in which numerous Jews sought to achieve fame, social mobility, and prove their physical prowess.[64] By emulating a well-known fight, the pageant suggested that even if not all Jewish children would grow up to be world-renowned boxers, they were thoroughly American as evidenced by their physical training and capabilities.

Conclusion

Separate from the Jewish exhibits, an "Oriental" village was at the center of the fair grounds. It included replicas of mosques and the visual elements often associated with them, such as domes and minarets. Alongside these visual elements associating Islam with "the Orient," the fair included displays of Arabian horsemanship, camel races, "Oriental theater," coffee, and more. Those who created the Oriental village considered it a "reproduction" of "native streets" from "the Orient" in the United States.[65]

Postcards from the World's Fair pictured these streets and the village sold souvenirs from "the Orient," offering fair visitors to purchase, take home, or share part of "the Orient" (fig. 5.8). One postcard showed a scantily clad woman seated on a divan, conjuring a fantasy of a harem. The woman looks up at a man in a "Western" suit, whose eyes we cannot

Figure 5.8. Two postcards from the Oriental Village.

see even though his view of the woman is nevertheless emphasized by a large pair of glasses as he seems to stare with desire at the woman. Domes and minarets appear in the background.[66] This exotic woman from "the Orient" symbolizes hypersexuality and femininity associated with the Arab "Orient," in stark contrast to the emphasis on Jewish bodily mastery and masculinity in *The Romance of a People*. The Oriental village made no distinction between different Arab lands, the difference between Arabs and non-Arabs, or between Muslims and non-Muslims in the Middle East. These were collapsed into a single undifferentiated "Orient" that stood outside the Hall of Religion and separate from Jewish Day. This vision of "the Orient" did not depict Arabs and Muslims as having a dynamic heritage, but as a contemporaneous way of life no different in the present than in the past. The Arabs who wandered on the stage of the Jewish Day pageant, lost in time, could be found in "the Orient"—either in the Oriental Village at the fair or in the American imagination of the Arab "Orient."

Both Jewish displays envisioned a different "Orient" from the essentially Protestant Oriental Village. However, the very presence of the separate Judaism exhibit created by the SCA at the Hall of Religion and the Jewish Day run by the ZOA that concluded with the pageant *The Romance of a People* indicates debate over and multiple understandings of what it meant to be Jewish and what "the Orient" meant to Jewishness in the United States, at times overlapping and at times in contradiction and even antagonism. A World's Fair was a unique stage for this type of debate because it displayed the debate not only for all Jewish Americans, but also non-Jewish Americans and Jews and non-Jews throughout the world. Of the representations of "the Orient" that I analyze in this book, the 1933 fair was the most visible with the largest audience. The Judaism exhibit and the Jewish Day pageant engaged Torah, Jewish history, and coexistence of diaspora and expanding Jewish life in Palestine. Both also claimed, in different ways, to eschew "politics," and both used visual media to assert and enact this attempt. The Judaism exhibit relied heavily upon material culture, such as a recreation of a Torah Ark and synagogue front to represent an imagined unity of the practice of Judaism. This apparent unity could only be achieved through the simulation of a synagogue that lacked seating, for example. Otherwise ideological and halakhic differences between the Reform, Conservative, and Orthodox constituents of the SCA and everyday Jewish life in the United States would be apparent. But the SCA eschewed these differences to present to its broad audience an image of a unified and vibrant Jewish American community. The SCA attempted to address the potential stiffness or appearance of a museum of Judaism-as-past by pairing the simulated synagogue with other visual culture, such as photographs of Jews around the world. Although the SCA firmly asserted they would address "religious" life, their interest in displaying Jews as good citizens blurred the lines between "religion," "ethnicity," and "nation." Like *The Romance of a People*, the Judaism exhibit displayed snapshots of Jewish history and contemporary life, though arranged in quite different categories. While the SCA represented Palestine, the SCA did not focus on it or exemplify Jewish life in Palestine as archetypal or American or international Jewish life. Even so, the SCA shared an interest in picturing Palestine with many other groups, mounting an Orientalism as a means of uniting Jews in the United States and the world.

The Judaism exhibit joined other traditions in the Hall of Religion throughout the entire summer of 1933, but the ZOA was forced by the fair to confine their display to a single Jewish Day. Surely the two shared many audience members, but the pageant *The Romance of a People* used different media to present their vision of Jewish heritage, including a theater with elaborate sets and the display of Jewish bodies. The pageant Orientalized all of the Jewish past as well as contemporaneous Jewish life. *The Romance of a People* performed even the most recent developments in Jewish life in Palestine-cum-"the Orient" as elements of Jewishness available to Americans. "The Orient" as heritage organized these places and moments as decoupling those moments from the past or geographic distance and instead presenting them as psychological elements that could be held together at once in the mind of the viewer. The very construction of the new Temple took place in Soldier Field in Chicago, suggesting not only the holiness of Palestine but the essential role of the United States and Jewish Americans in world heritage. The pageant translated European and Palestinian ideologies into discourse and practices compelling for Americans, changing the very nature of Zionism. At the same time, the nature of the United States incorporated a space for "the Jewish Orient" as a performance of American heritage. The practices of imagining "the Orient" and narrating Jewish history thus took a central place in the articulation of Jewish religious heritage. For many Jewish Americans, the study of Jewish law and traditional Jewish texts had ceased to be part of their practice, whether for ideological reasons or for practical ones, ranging from gender to social class. A vibrant visual culture that portrayed a proud Jewish heritage offered a foundation for Jewishness that required no theology and no training in rabbinics. The organizations, publications, and performances discussed in this book circulated multiple and contradictory images of "the Orient," making it possible to imagine several different visions within the Jewish American panorama. By juxtaposing multiple "Orients," these images constructed Jewish American heritage as a synthesis of the heritage of "the Oriental past" from the biblical period through the shtetl life of Eastern Europe and culminating with the transformation into the hypermuscular Jew of the new Palestine. Jewish American heritage did not give in to the excesses of the effeminate Arab and Jewish "Orients" of the past nor the Jewish hypermasculinity of the contemporaneous Jewish "Orient." American heritage contained and mastered all these images, filtering them through American democracy and progress.

Chapter 6

Making a Difference

Maternalism in Hadassah's "Propaganda"

We must remember that Zionism is a democratic movement, that its success depends upon the mass of Jewish women. Unfortunately there is no more serious charge made against Judaism than the charge that women are neglected. The Zionist organization, since it believes in the equality of men and women, must educate women not only to Judaism, but to a realization of their civic and of their national responsibilities.

—"Report of the Central Committee,"
Hadassah Convention, July 1915

Too much literature cannot be distributed both among Zionists and non-Zionists.

—"Report of the Central Committee,"
Hadassah Convention, 1917

Very few pupils coming from the Oriental communities of the Old City have the good fortune to be able to finish school.... Many of them are orphans or children deserted or neglected by their parents.... Only among the Sephardic children is there any visible sign of improvement.

—*Pupils from Poor Homes*,
Hadassah pamphlet, prewar

The cover of a 1934 Hadassah pamphlet invited its audience to "Join the Circle of Palestine's Children" (fig. 6.1). The pamphlet went on to ask the

Figure 6.1. "Join the Circle of Palestine's Children."

audience to "come visit the children of Palestine." The cover line suggests one can join without going to Palestine, perhaps even including readers within the "circle of Palestine's children." The opening paragraph reestablishes a boundary between "the children of Palestine" and the American audience. Through the pamphlet, "you peep into the twenty-five Hadassah child welfare centers where we take care of their health." The pamphlet suggests that without traveling to Palestine, Jewish Americans can nevertheless visit the children there through images, stories, and financial connections. This glimpse is not merely curious: it establishes a mutually beneficial relationship: "Hadassah's Child Welfare Fund is a double joy. It brings health and high spirits to the boys and girls of America who *give*, and to their pals in Palestine who *receive*" (fig. 6.2).[1] This verbal and visual text positions Jewish Americans as caretakers in relationship to young refugees in the land of Palestine. The pamphlet asks viewers to see Jewish American children as the "pals" of Jews in Palestine. But the relationship is reciprocal. Jewish Americans "*give*" and Jews in Palestine "*receive*." Additionally, the pamphlet frames or projects adults' action—cutting a check—on children, lending the imagined community an air of innocence.

This is paternalism, or maternalism. Naming this maternalism emphasizes the role gender plays in how Jewish Americans (and other activists) sought to "benevolently" control or change others for the "better," making a difference in the lives of those they saw as unsophisticated or uneducated. Men did not make space for women in their organizations, politics, or activism, and women and men sought to fulfill activism in distinct ways. I analyze how the "propaganda" of Hadassah used images of children to justify their involvement in politics as feminine caretakers. These women believed their activism was a "better" method than men's

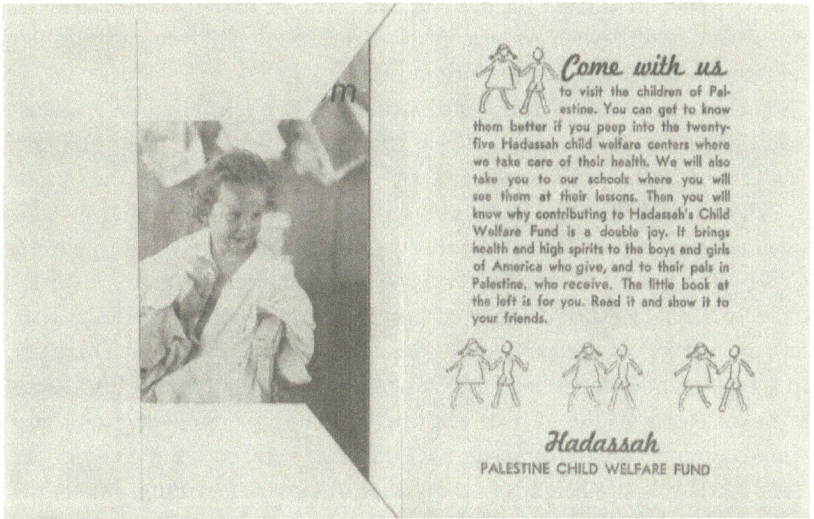

Figure 6.2. "Join the Circle of Palestine's Children."

activism, making a difference between men and women's activism and a difference between Jewish Americans and "Orientals."

Hadassah's "propaganda" served the role of expanding a place for women to participate in Jewish politics in the United States and Palestine by envisioning "the Orient" as the Jewish future via children.[2] The repeated trope of children in the pamphlets and literature that Hadassah distributed in an effort to increase its visibility and membership implicitly insists on the racial homogeneity and heteronormativity of the bodies of adult Jewish American men and women. Jewish men have historically been feminized in anti-Judaism and Orientalism. Hadassah's Orientalism subverts the presentation of femininity as problematic or as linked to Jewish men. Hadassah's visual culture positions Jewish Americans, especially women, at the top of a hierarchy of physical health and family relations. According to this vision of gender politics, Hadassah women are thereby in a position to inform Jews and non-Jews, in the United States and Palestine, as to how best to live. The visual culture in Hadassah's pamphlets used images of rescuing Jewish and non-Jewish children. Some were refugees from Nazi Europe, others were trapped in "the Orient" and needed to be trained in contemporary life and science. Physical threats did exist for children in Nazi Europe and inhabitants of the region of Palestine were affected negatively by World War I, colonialism, and conflicts in Middle Eastern politics under both the Ottoman Empire and the later British Mandate. However, the structure of their rescue and socialization in Palestine was not obvious and carried an imaginative sense of heritage and future for the lives of adult Jewish American women through children and mothers' representation in Hadassah's "propaganda."

Hadassah's visual culture sentimentalizes symbolic children and positions Hadassah as mother to these children, which ultimately visualizes Jewish Americans as the mature "West" and all inhabitants of "the Orient" as children to be directed under the watchful eye of Jewish Americans. Lee Edelman argues that, "in its coercive universalization, . . . the image of the Child [must] not be confused with the lived experiences of any historical children."[3] This view of children as symbol carries import for adult politics and the lives of children and adults. Visual and verbal rhetoric may purport to aid children while merely mobilizing images of children to political ends, or rhetoric may lead to or belie prioritizing some children over others, even while claiming to do the opposite. Excess is always embedded in the symbolic, and futurism is the height of that excess. Focus on the future insists that we change our past and present to work toward a perfect future. Futurism is most easily symbolically embodied by children. There may seem to be a tacit social consensus that we should protect children, yet it is essential to disentangle the excessive symbolism when politics turn to children. The heightened tendency to depict childhood in mid-twentieth-century Jewish visual culture focuses on the future and belies an embedded secularized messianism.[4] In the United States, such images dated to the colonial period of American mythology—paralleling the pre-state era of Palestine in the twentieth century. "The ability to tolerate pain was often held up as an ideal for the citizen in training." In this symbolic equation of childhood with young nations—whether American or Zionist—"children symbolize innocence, and national purity, regardless of actual American [or Zionist] political or military activities."[5] Images of "the Orient" tend to picture family life, especially juxtaposing mothers and their children, with the families barely holding on financially and physically, suffering the conditions of child labor, impoverishment, and neglect or, at best, appear in orphanages and perhaps summer camps.[6] In deliberate contrast, the FAZ/ZOA's images represented childhood in Palestine as a renewal and a redemption.

Hadassah was founded in 1913, and from the 1920s until World War II, it was both the largest Zionist organization in the United States—gaining more members than any men's organization, including the Zionist Organization of America—and the largest American women's volunteer organization with over one hundred thousand members by the 1940s. By the 1960s, it was one of the largest women's volunteer organizations in the world. The organization sought to allow women to work alongside other women, intentionally eschewing the perceived negative effects of cooperating with men. Hadassah drew women from diverse heritages—East European, German, and Sephardic—but most were born in the United States. These women sought to create a place for Jews, Judaism, and Zionism in the broader American context, yet they were rooted in the cultural, educational, social, and political structures of the United States before they founded their organization. However, Hadassah played an important role in constructing links across these familial backgrounds as well as class and other factors, as local chapters included "women irrespective of class, marital status, age, or immigrant background." Yet women still joined subgroups within their chapter, reflecting interests, such as study or sewing, and language, such as English or Yiddish.[7]

Hadassah members funneled much of their efforts into a major propaganda campaign, "propaganda" being their own term for pamphlets, literature, and education projects. They sought to establish Zionism as an indisputably democratic movement and familiarize the "non-Zionist public" with their vision of Palestine. Hadassah's leadership considered the distribution of "propaganda" integral in establishing that democratic image. However, Hadassah's conception of Palestine and democracy was very specific, and the equality of men and women in Judaism and the Jewish homeland was a central piece in Hadassah's ideal democracy. Many of the images in Hadassah "propaganda" do not focus on the *land* of Palestine, but on the women and children in it. This accomplishes several things at once: Israeli society is shown to be contemporary; women are made visible in Jewish life; motherhood is validated as essential and scientific; women are depicted as working, whether as nurses or as mothers.

Images of children are symbolic in a number of ways: their innocence stands in for that of the Jewish people; such innocence provokes a more emotional response morally, financially, and politically; the youth of these children mirrors that of the Israeli nation (still in its gestation as a hopeful future state); and images of children link American viewers as the "parents," especially "mothers," to these children.

"Too Much Literature Cannot Be Distributed": Hadassah's "Propaganda"

Hadassah's "propaganda" sought to establish women's care as work *equal* in importance to men's work, while it also offered an *alternative* to masculine conceptions of politics and Palestine. Though Hadassah and the FAZ/ZOA as well as other Zionist American movements diverged in their gendered approaches to Zionism in significant ways, their conceptions of pre-state Zionist movements also shared many themes and a critical endorsement of American values. Hadassah members "believed that women's biological potential to give life, together with their traditional responsibilities of caring for children, led them to be more pragmatic than men."[8] Jewish American women created their organization with this consciously gendered understanding. Founded in 1913 by thirty women, Hadassah immediately created official leadership positions for two-thirds of its original constituency and represented a powerhouse of Jewish American women. Commenting on Hadassah's quick rise to popularity, in 1920 Henrietta Szold, Hadassah's energetic first president, wrote to Alice Seligsberg (1873–1940), who later became Hadassah president herself, that it was "necessary to invent, actually invent, a specific Hadassah task to satisfy" Jewish American women.[9]

Hadassah members sought the professionalization of women's work: to see women's work as philanthropy not charity, domestic science not housework. Hadassah became the means of professionalization of many Jewish American women who became "public speakers, fiscal experts, administrators, technicians, and officials."[10] The professionalization of these types of work placed women as leaders in the Progressive movement, whose values drove the ZOA as well, as discussed in chapter 2. ZOA head Louis Brandeis's vision and practices of Progressivism influenced the ideas, actions, and policies by the women of Hadassah in their conceptions of Zionist and American values, even as their gendered performance of both Zionist and American values implicitly (and sometimes explicitly) challenged Brandeis. Zionism-as-Progressivism thus offered a vision of the possibility of a future uncorrupt society, a total cooperation between various social groups in one happy community, and a central role for American models of capitalism and government. Yet Hadassah also sought to carve out a space that existed alongside rather than in direct competition with men's projects, positioning itself as doing social and not political work, though Hadassah's philanthropy was in fact deeply political. Hadassah especially emphasized a family casework model of social work. An emphasis on social work capitalized on an accepted link between women's skills and family work, but sought to professionalize and thereby legitimize those skills, drawing on maternalist rhetoric while breaking down an idea of a link between domesticity and the "private sphere."[11]

The debate over naming Hadassah as an organization illustrates the complexities that emerged because of its goals for work in Palestine and the United States, and to attract as many women as possible. In 1914, Hadassah's constitution explicitly stated, "The purpose of this Association is to promote Jewish institutions and enterprises in Palestine, and to foster Zionist ideals in America."[12] In all projects, Hadassah maintained dual commitments to Jewish life in the United States and life in Palestine. Mary McCune argues that, unlike the National Council of Jewish Women, which "stressed the Americanness of their organization [and] its similarity to other [non-Jewish] women's organizations of the period . . . Hadassah . . . sought ways to create a Jewish identity that coincided with its feeling of connection to Jews throughout the world."[13] Though McCune is right that Hadassah's philanthropy focused on Jews around the world, especially "the Orient," Hadassah did assert an image of Jewish American heritage linked to Jews around the world. This grounded a conception of Jewish American heritage with roots in antiquity in ways that informed

American and "Western" heritage from an imagined origin to the present, as did the Orientalism seen in the other organizations' discussed throughout this book. And like those organizations, Hadassah's Orientalism managed any concerns about the appearance of worldwide Jewish communities as "backward" through Orientalism. Hadassah's Orientalism especially focused on women and children in "the Orient," which created a foil for Jewish American women and positioned Hadassah women as meaningful contributors to American and international society. By portraying itself through the lens of motherhood, Hadassah critiqued masculine visions of Jewish Americanness that excluded Jewish women from Jewish or American life and heritage. Hadassah's "propaganda" used Orientalism to picture Jewish American women as essential members of Jewish and non-Jewish life.

Visual culture played an important early role for the local meetings of Hadassah chapters: women would gather to view images of Palestine; to picture the plight of Jews, especially women; and to imagine plans for new projects meant to address these perceived needs.[14] At the first session of the First Annual Convention in June 1914, after discussing a program for nurses in Palestine, the organization create a "propaganda" program in the United States, resulting in eight societies in cities across the United States: Baltimore, Boston, Chicago, Cleveland, Newark, New York, Philadelphia, and St. Paul. From the beginning, Hadassah had the dual goal of working with other institutions in Palestine to create medical facilities and running a "propaganda" program in the United States.[15] The "propaganda" program was twofold, targeting the organization of chapters already established and more broadly the formation of new chapters and inculcation of new members.[16] Targeting new membership sought to Zionize America by bringing Jewish American women into Hadassah's vision. This vision could not have existed without images of Zion, but these images sought to transform the nature of Jewishness in the United States as much as on the ground in Palestine. To be Jewish in the United States, for Hadassah women, meant to be Zionized. This included a complex connection to Zionist ideologies that was negotiated via the more malleable medium of images of "the Orient" rather than explicit political platforms.

Hadassah's pamphlets, brochures, booklets, and other media frequently turned to relational tropes, especially family and motherhood, in verbal text as well as visual images. Many early Zionists in the land of Palestine considered propaganda a key strategy, and labeled "propaganda" as such. Later the State of Israel and its supporters in the United States developed *hasbara* or "explaining" projects, but during the first half of the twentieth century *ta'amulah* or "propaganda" was explicitly touted. Hadassah members participated in this widespread embrace of "propaganda," adjusting their printed materials to their American goals and audience. Hadassah's "propaganda," like its counterparts elsewhere, was designed to argue that Zionists were doing good work, not savagely taking over the land of Palestine.[17] "Propaganda" became a primary project for Hadassah from its earliest years. The "Report of the Central Committee" at the 1917 Hadassah convention insisted, "Too much literature cannot be distributed both among Zionists and non-Zionists." The Scholar Erica B. Simmons argues that "propaganda meant not only the promulgation of gripping images of Palestinian life but also the art of persuasion through personal contact between Hadassah members and other women." Hadassah women considered the visual culture of this "propaganda" "especially effective because of the emotional response of the audience to a presentation of Zionism" that images produced.[18]

Care for the children of Palestine constituted Hadassah's primary rhetorical posture in "propaganda" aimed at Jewish American women. Through that "propaganda," Hadassah defended Jewish life in Palestine while constructing Jewish practice in America that embraced democracy, Jewish heritage, and feminism. However, Hadassah's visual culture produced an image of Jews in the United States that revised the history of democracy, especially in conceptualizing an argument that democracy was born out of Judaism. Furthermore, while Hadassah women fought for women's rights to participate in Jewish communal life and created new spaces for women's practices, they did not do so through a revision of synagogue life. And although Jewish American women may have chafed at their exclusion from women's organizations by Christian American women, Hadassah's visual culture produced a vision of Jewish women's inclusion that shared much with middle-class white feminism. Despite visual and verbal rhetorical inclusion of Mizrahi Jews, Arabs, and others labeled "Oriental" in Hadassah excluded "Orientals" from their contemporary "propaganda," Hadassah's conception of community. The transformation of "Orientals" to join contemporary community was pushed to the future. Precisely through Hadassah's posture of "care" and the ways that "Orientals" were represented, Hadassah's "propaganda" represented a social hierarchy with Jewish American women at the top, and Mizrahi Jews and Arabs under Jewish American women's instruction.

Envisioning Motherhood in "the Orient" from the United States

Motherhood and "complementarity, the notion that to be whole, women must be partners with men," are at the center of Jewish canonical texts. Torah, Talmud, and other commentators assume that women's role is "enabling the continuity of the species" and only address women in relationship to men.[19] Hadassah's presentation of motherhood envisions an assumption of women's roles shared with these canonical texts produced by Jewish male elites. However, like many heterosexual Jewish feminists, Hadassah attempts to use that role of motherhood to create new roles for women, legitimizing women in "public spheres" such as education, medicine, and Jewish communal life. However, also like many heterosexual Jewish feminists, Hadassah's visual culture "assume[s] the centrality of male/female relationships, not to question their primacy." Women are legitimized, but only through rhetoric that positions women in relationship to men and takes for granted women's positions in heterosexual, reproductive relationship. Rebecca Alpert argues, "Value of women's biological roles is an important feminist concern. But it is too often the dominant concern in Jewish feminist circles and renders invisible those women who do not see biological roles as central to defining themselves as women."[20] Hadassah women may not have defined themselves as "feminist," but they did help construct new places for women in Jewish and American heritage that affirmed heteronormativity while challenging aspects of complementarity. The value of women-as-mothers to create a vision of the importance of women is important for understanding how maternalism created a hierarchy among Jewish women, and for how Hadassah created a vision of Jewish American women as better mothers than "Oriental" women. Although the trope of motherhood may have rhetorically implied heterosexual relationships to men, however, Hadassah's vision of motherhood renders women visible and in relationship to each other. If Jewish tradition frequently is silent about women-to-women interactions, these are at the center of Hadassah's visual culture.[21] But the representation of "Oriental" women suggests pitfalls in "visibility." By using images of women in "the Orient" to imagine Jewish American life in the United States, Hadassah's "propaganda" simultaneously made women in Palestine visible while disenfranchising them under a vision of Hadassah's intervening motherhood. In Hadassah "propaganda," women work together and teach each other. This challenged complementarity's emphasis on women existing to relate to men, it is precisely these woman-to-woman relationships that create a new hierarchy, in which white

Jewish American women are positioned above "Orientals" and others who are not as skilled at motherhood as the Jewish women of Hadassah. Jewish American difference produced in contrast to "the Orient"—Hadassah's particular form of Orientalism assuaged the anxiety of performing Jewish motherhood to be satisfactory or superior to other Americans proving the suitability of Jewish women and all Jews for citizenship.

The cover of the pamphlet *Health Welfare* features a photograph captioned, "A Child of the Colonies," sitting with a toy and smiling. As one opens the pamphlet, another photograph becomes visible, a hospital scene of four adult women and two babies, the "Interior of a Health Welfare Station" (fig. 6.3). Three are dressed as nurses, and one looks on, dressed in more "traditional" Middle Eastern clothing. There are cribs and scales, and plenty of sterile white tables and spaces. The pamphlet asks, "Did you know that Hadassah has lowered the maternity death rate among the mothers cared for in its institutions to 2.17 per 1,000, the lowest maternity death rate in the world?" The message is clearly that Jews have a special insight that positions them as unique leaders into scientific "modernity." This transfers theological chosenness onto scientific accomplishments that establishes Jewish difference yet in such a way that is compatible with contemporary citizenship. Not only are Jewishness and scientific modernity more than compatible—Jews excel in this, the pamphlet argues—but so are motherhood and science compatible. Hadassah also models its utopian society, attending to "the population already resident in Palestine" as well as "the new immigrant," especially "German refugees." The pamphlet offers more photographs, including one of two Hadassah nurses putting on a

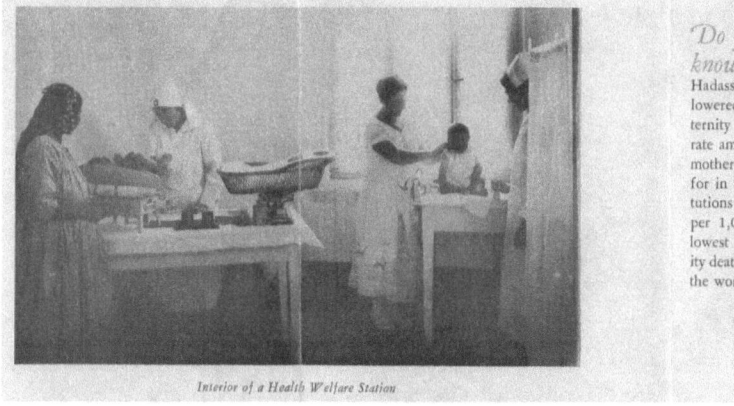

Figure 6.3. "Interior of a Health Welfare Station."

216   THE HEBREW ORIENT

demonstration for a roomful of women (some of whom pay more attention to the photographer than the demonstration) using a baby doll at the front of a classroom, and one of the Straus Health Center in Jerusalem, "in which a model Health Welfare Station is housed."[22]

The pamphlet *Doorway to Life* . . . (fig. 6.4) features a cover of two young girls walking out of the shadows and into the light. The photo

Figure 6.4. *Doorway to Life* . . . .

captures what seems like joy and vivacity, as the girl's swinging hair and posture suggest light playfulness. I imagine this girl calling me to join her, skipping ahead but looking back to make sure I'm following her lead. The jagged archway and stone building materials are visually continuous with other images of the old city of Jerusalem, though the girls are dressed in contemporary jumpers and have contemporary haircuts.[23] The inside of the pamphlet opens, "We wish you happiness." The pamphlet rhetorically assumes that any woman reading will be a mother and that her happiness will be stipulated by the health of her family. The pamphlet seeks to draw the reader in by saying, "You have just opened the doorway to life for your child." Motherhood itself is established as "the doorway to life." For whom is it the doorway to life? For both mother and child. But, the pamphlet goes on, "We know you would like to share this tenderness with other children who need it, with children whose well-being may affect *your* baby's development in the long run." The pamphlet suggests that any caring mother would help all mothers to share in health and privileges. (But just in case interest in others is not enough to persuade, the pamphlet argues that the welfare of others is ultimately in Jewish American women's self-interest.) Consider the similarity to Harriet Beecher Stowe's *Uncle Tom's Cabin*. Stowe appealed to a concept of family to argue against slavery: How could white American women treat slaves so inhumanely? Hadassah's trope of motherhood operates on the same principle. Motherhood and family are core American values. America's sociopolitical role is to ensure that all people may fulfill good family roles, as defined by American conceptions.

There are very different concepts of family. Amanda Porterfield argues, "Religious freedom, individual experience, family life, and social reform . . . have worked together over time to define virtually all of the particular religious traditions in America."[24] While individuals and groups have balanced these values in different ways, white Protestant conceptions of family have been hegemonic in defining American conceptions of family: "Concerns about the structure of the family and its relationship to both social stability and reform pervade American religious history." Porterfield argues that the emphasis on the nuclear family is a foundation of Puritan-Protestant conceptions of family and that "this originally Protestant emphasis on family life as the best context for religious life has shaped the development of American Catholicism, Hinduism, and Buddhism," along with many other traditions, "contributing to . . . increased emphasis within those traditions on the religious significance of ordinary life."[25] Hadassah's visual culture reproduces values of family, especially the nuclear family, secularizing this vision of family and deploying its use for political purposes. Secularism is frequently understood and critiqued as a universalized model of Protestantism. One way to understand American secularism is as Protestantism unmarked as Americanism, theoretically universal not only to Protestants but other religious and ethnic groups. However, the origins of American secularism in the structures and worldview of Protestantism limit the possibility of including others in a truly equally accessible secularism. Hadassah's visual culture suggests that this understanding of secularism covers over the participation in and production of secularism by non-Protestants. This pamphlet suggests that Jews are fully American because they are so naturalized in the care for nuclear family, a central value of Protestantism "universalized" in American secularism, that they can spread family values and instruct others who are unskilled. Protestant American women might not have seen Jewish American women as capable of that project. Like the NFTS, Hadassah argued for maternalism and the skills of Jewish mothers. But unlike the NFTS art calendars, which use biblical figures to depict Jewish motherhood, Hadassah frequently presented motherhood in visions of contemporary philanthropy. This furthered the secular quality of Hadassah's efforts, but images of Hadassah's unique achievements in "the Orient" continually asserted Jewish difference even as American secularism ostensibly presented motherhood as a shared value available to all religions and ethnicities.

Much of the visual culture of Hadassah addressed Jewish women in the United States, assuming that they would read and understand the needs of Jewish children in Europe and Palestine. Then Jewish American women would participate in Hadassah and transform those children. One fundraising pamphlet featured a place where a woman could record the financial gifts of individual contributors. As the pamphlet transformed Jewish American heritage, it also promised to transform the lives of Jewish children across the ocean. Each page described a different act: "to give you hope," "to rescue you," "to renew your faith," "to help you forget," "to restore your health," "to feed you," "to educate you," "to train you," "to prepare you," "to make you a fighter," "to help you live," and finally, "Through You I also give to Palestine, where as a Jew in your own homeland, you will face the future valiantly." Jewish American women imaginatively transformed themselves through the lives of Jewish children in Palestine, both through their financial contributions and the covenantal labor performed by those children. Hadassah's vision of Zionism transformed Jewish heritage into future-oriented practices.

The image on the cover of the pamphlet *Hadassah Mothers the Children of Erez-Israel* visually asserts a simultaneous connection through maternalism and distance from the residents of Palestine (fig. 6.5). The

Figure 6.5. *Hadassah Mothers the Children of Erez-Israel.*

photograph shows a family of a mother and her children. The father is conspicuously absent. The woman's dress notably marks her as not American. Her hair is covered, and her dress covers her full body, made from a patchwork of materials. One son sits on the floor, and the other sits in her lap. We have virtually no context for where she might be sitting, except for the title of the pamphlet. This same image appears elsewhere in Hadassah "propaganda with the background of the photo intact. Here the family's background has been clipped out.[26] Inside, the pamphlet explains that Hadassah has been the "Community Mother" to Palestine from 1913 to 1933. The implication is that the people of Palestine, here imaginatively portrayed from the view of Americans and thus transforming Palestine into "the Orient," had no good mothers prior to Hadassah's arrival. The pamphlet presents Hadassah as "a true mother, concerned . . . with the welfare of the children" of all people. This understanding of Hadassah's maternalism creates a dehumanizing Orientalism. The implication is that "Orientals"—no differentiation is made between Sephardi/Mizrahi Jews and non-Jews here—do not have even the basic faculties of family and motherhood much less the wherewithal to head a democratic government and complex society. A photograph of a "Pre-Natal and Infant Welfare Station, Jerusalem (Old City)" accompanies the narrative of Hadassah's motherhood. This image reinforces the distance between Hadassah as fully enlightened, modern "Western" women—marked by the attire of nurses in juxtaposition to the women to which they minister, who have no husbands and whose children seem scattered around in need of help. The absence of a father on the cover asserts not only the emphasis of Hadassah on motherhood and women but also the basic dysfunction of "Oriental" families. Men are absent; women do not know how to mother and must be told.

This image exemplifies Hadassah's visual culture as Orientalism rather than just "exoticism." Though Frederick Bohrer titled his book on the role of Mesopotamian architecture in "Western" imagination *Orientalism and Visual Culture*, he turns to the label of "exoticism" over Orientalism.[27] In an image such as this, Hadassah exoticizes this woman. But "exoticism" does not provide a full argument for what this picture is doing, whereas Orientalism locates the visions and ideas that Hadassah's "propaganda" can be seen as "correcting." Exoticism and Orientalism both create a social hierarchy, placing subjects such as this woman and her family as the object of "Western" view. Orientalism better schematizes not just how this photo distances the woman from "the West" and positions her as object rather than subject. The photo also shows Hadassah's "propaganda" as an example of the more significant role of exotic images from "the Orient" than any other place in Hadassah's production of visual culture. Hadassah's "propaganda" did not exoticize a variety of populations and places: Hadassah's "propaganda" repeatedly turned to "the Orient," that is, the organization's representation of Mizrahims, Arabs, or Muslims. Hadassah's philanthropic projects focused on Palestine, and for many Hadassah members, that philanthropy was part of an imagined state. Hadassah's image as medical and maternal savior both justified the place of Jews in the construction of a state and laid the groundwork for its infrastructure. The Orientalism in Hadassah's "propaganda" constructed the problem, to which Hadassah's "propaganda" positioned Jewish American women as the solution. Malaria and other diseases were a problem in Palestine, but inhabitants of Palestine did not welcome the hierarchical, maternalistic position of Jewish American women to come in without working together with Mizrahim, Arabs, and Muslims in Palestine to create a solution. Hadassah's Orientalist "propaganda" did not represent such conflict on the ground, instead visually representing Jewish American women as the solution to the "Oriental" population's position.

Moreover, seeing Hadassah's "propaganda" as Orientalism rather than mere exoticism connects the view of Hadassah's visual culture to the image of Hadassah women in the United States. Far more women viewed this "propaganda" than ever viewed Palestine in situ. The "propaganda" not only created a panorama through which Jewish American Hadassah women could imaginatively envision "the Orient," but the "propaganda" implicitly countered images of Jews as unproductive members of "Western" society. The specter of antisemitism haunts Orientalism: Christian Orientalism so often positioned Jews as the backward "Orientals." Seeing images in Hadassah's "propaganda" as examples of Orientalism reads them intertextually against non-Jewish antisemitism and Orientalism. Hadassah's Orientalism, like that of the other Jewish American organizations that I discuss, did not implode the lens of Orientalism but maintained its structure. This shifted Jewish Americans from a position as "Oriental" objects to "Western" viewers of "the Orient," placing Jewish Americans alongside Christian Americans. However, what Hadassah pictured in "the Orient" differed not only from Christians but also from other Jewish Americans, including the ZOA. Hadassah's "propaganda" positions Mizrahim ambivalently. Like the ZOA, Hadassah looked for nostalgic relics of the Jewish past, which they "found" in "Orientals," even as those "living relics" were problematic for the Jewish present because of the anachronistic or contemporaneous nature of "the Orient" according to a vision of "Western progress." But Hadassah's "propaganda" makes women visible as none of the other organizations I have discussed did. For Hadassah the Jewish Americans who were reenvisioned in contrast to "the Orient" were Jewish women. Jewish men often responded to antisemitic and Orientalist stereotypes of Jewish men as feminine by constructing Jews as hypermasculine as seen in chapters 2, 4, and 5. This hypermasculinity indicated that femininity was a problem to be eradicated and distrusted, a view that positioned Jewish American men as equals to Christian American men by degrading femininity not only when attached to men but also to women. Hadassah's "propaganda" countered this view, showing women as significant contributors to Jewish life and "Western" life and displacing mistrust from gender or women to ethnicity and geography. Hadassah's "propaganda" critiqued Jewish men's Orientalism, Christian Orientalism, and imagined Jews as valuable citizens in Palestine and in the United States all through the production of the organization's unique Orientalist perspective.

Seeing Jewish Americanness through Jewish Children

Images of children in Hadassah's "propaganda" stand in for Jewish Americans and for worldwide Jews as deserving of greater care and inclusion in society. Jodi Eichler-Levine argues that children are offered as a way to create universal commonalities among Americans, who in reality have "very real differences" in a fractured society. Though Eicher-Levine's work focuses on literature aimed at children, her analysis of the role of children in crafting national histories and arguing for the inclusion of minorities extends to representations of children well beyond children's literature. Multiple forms of visual culture present children as "our future," turning children and the future into a place "we" can go together. That idealized place becomes the site of consensus and unity. But the very need for such images suggests that "our" community is not unified: there is no "our." That is, the visual culture imagines a future wherein "our community" will be unified, although it is not now.[28] Hadassah's "propaganda" represents children as innocence incarnate. This innocence is implicitly a consensus amongst all decent people. Hadassah's visual culture then transfers this implicit innocence onto its own project aimed at children. Accordingly, Hadassah's visual culture uses the presumed consensus of children's innocence to suggest that their project is not political. But it is: Hadassah's visual culture addresses children symbolically in a vision of "the Orient," though their projects influenced the lives of children and adults in Palestine. Moreover, children (and adults) can and do suffer as a result of political decisions: not all political ideologies treat real children as innocent or all children as deserving of equal care. Focus on images of symbolic children-writ-future, children's suffering becomes a symbolic claim for Jewish American inclusion, in addition to being evidence of Jewish suffering and exclusion in Europe past and present. Past suffering legitimizes membership within the American polity and constructs a view of the future in which American values must be safeguarded. Children are a significant means of adult imagination that are emotionally powerful, and these overdetermined children are heavily mined as symbols of citizenship." In the Orientalism of Hadassah's "propaganda," the appearance of Jewish child refugees from Europe places them in a view that symbolically argues for including Jewish Americans in the American body politic. Images of Jewish children symbolize all Jews' innocence and need for recompense for Jewish suffering such as United States citizenship and autonomy in Palestine. For Jewish Americans who had lived in the United States for years, the vision of Jewishness through Jewish suffering in Europe and Jewish redemption through "the Orient" bolstered a sense of Jews as victims. Hadassah's visual culture depicts contemporary Jewish American women as empowered and worthy of American citizenship: visions of Jewish suffering relate to Jewish persecution outside the United States. Rhetorically and ethically, Hadassah positioned Jewish Americans as privileged, furthering a narrative of American exceptionalism as seen in other sources such as the NFTS art calendars and the Jewish exhibits at the 1933 World's Fair.

The cover of a postwar (ca. 1946–1947) pamphlet *Escape to Life* epitomized this vision of Jewishness through childhood suffering. A young boy with a shaved head holds a ball of cloth or a sack and an empty cup for food. He sits on a wooden crate in an empty village or detention camp, surrounded by nothing except ramshackle buildings. He is fenced in. His head tips downward and his eyes are closed, blinded by the sun. He seems only to have the clothes on his back, and no shoes. The child is completely defenseless, and the photograph begs us to consider his innocence and not condemn him to death. Inside, the pamphlet asks, "What is Youth Aliyah?"[29] Here the pamphlet constructs Jewish heritage through a narrative of Jewish past that acknowledges a shift in Jewish practice while still asserting continuity and progress from past to present and future. "The pamphlet explains that 'ALIYAH' is literally translated as 'to ascend,'" but "in Biblical times it referred to the annual pilgrimage or ascent to Jerusalem made by the Jews during the High Holidays." The pamphlet does not explain that this "ascent" was in holy status rather than geographical landscape. However, the pamphlet asserts this pilgrimage is no longer the meaning of aliyah. "Today 'aliyah' means immigration to Palestine." And, "Through Youth Aliyah, more than 15,000 Jewish children have already been snatched from a living death and helped to 'escape to life' in Palestine." The pamphlet's message hinges on a demonstration of the youth and innocence of children, asserting rights such as "to be young" and "to live in peace," presented as universal and nonpolitical rights. But by adding that these innocent children also have the right "to grow to maturity and a home of one's own," the full narrative is politicized. The pamphlet begins without placing children in space or time, the following pages discuss the political history of Nazi concentration camps, transport of Jewish children from Switzerland, France, Germany, Romania, Poland, Bulgaria, Turkey, Italy, Spain, and other "Central European Countries," as well as the role of the British Government and the American Jewish Joint Distribution Committees in approving and funding the transfer process. This picture of an "innocent" boy in need consolidates all these histories and places into Jewish heritage.

Additionally, the pamphlet's focus on children participates in a broader tendency that has persisted in Jewish American representations of the Holocaust and American ethics in general. Children are equated with innocence, but this does not interrogate what constitutes innocence. This vision of innocence may diminish the sense that Jewish adults and adult victims of other ethnic cleansings and tragedies are as innocent as children. Suffering under ethnic cleansing means that all victims have committed no crime related to their mistreatment, whether or not they can change the identities or labels that lead to that mistreatment. Hadassah argues for children's rights to full lives, but their focus on symbolic children's innocence and therefore rights detracts from conceptualizing genocide or ethnic cleansing as and crimes against the lives and bodies of members of the targeted group(s) of all ages. Focusing on symbolic children could imply that adults are less innocent in cases of crimes against humanity. Hadassah may have desired for the rights of adults, but its visual culture's focus on children and their programs such as "Youth Aliyah" may have unintentionally elided the postwar realities for all victims of the Holocaust. Many Jews languished in displaced persons camps after the war, a political problem for liberal democracies around the world. Children and adults alike needed homes, but liberal democracies failed to take them in. Hadassah's focus on Palestine argued, on the one hand, for a place for Jewish victims. But this politicized "Orient" masked a complaint Hadassah might have pressed upon the United States government: Why did children need to immigrate to Palestine in the first place? Not only or even primarily because it was their "homeland." Rather, even after the Allies defeated Nazi Germany, Jewish victims did not have the right to migrate to the United States or most of Western Europe. In Eastern Europe, many Jews faced outbreaks of pogroms or a general sense of discrimination from their neighbors as well as uncertainty about their place in the Communist futures coming into fruition all over the map. Hadassah's visual culture saw Jewish Americans in European children's victimhood, yet never explicitly addressed the ways in which Jewish Americans were not victims in the same way, *and* the United States displayed a hypocrisy of liberalism by failing to assist postwar refugees, as would continue through the early 1950s.

Lastly, in one pamphlet, we see a photograph of four girls eating at a table (fig. 6.6).[30] Though they appear young, perhaps twelve, they are dressed as nurses. Their clean table and healthy food offer evidence of the healthful lifestyle that Hadassah provides them. Their nurses' outfits feature white head coverings and white smocks, obviously clean and pressed. Their outfits mark them in several ways: they are dressed as tiny nurses, clearly linking them to Hadassah's vision of Jewish women. But they are also simultaneously marked as contemporaries, not "Orientals" or even immigrants from any West European nation. They are visually uniform, literally. Hadassah's visual association of nurses in Palestine with modern Jewish women thus created a way to mark Jewish women's bodies as Jewish, at least in their "propaganda." Dressing as a nurse would not necessarily mark one as Jewish in the United States, which is precisely the point. These girls could easily be Jewish or not, American or living in Palestine. The young nurses' attire, however, conjures visions of American patriotism, given the importance of women in the Red Cross and as nurses in the First and Second World Wars. Located in the context of Hadassah's "propaganda," attire that might be shared throughout many "Western" countries for those training in hospitals or medical care becomes a visual mark. Nurses uniforms mark Jewish girls and women as properly Jewish feminine caretakers, working with contemporary science, because of their juxtaposition to dark, tattered clothing presented as the abnormal state of "Oriental" life without Hadassah's intervention.

The cover of this same pamphlet features a "stamp" in the top right corner, with a "return address" from "Hadassah Youth Services" in "Jerusalem, Palestine" (fig. 6.7). The stamp is a facsimile of a real stamp used to send mail in Palestine. In "handwriting," it is addressed, "c/o Hadassah, U.S.A." and marked at the bottom, "(Please Forward)."[31] The image of the stamp, mass-produced handwriting, and closure present the "propaganda"

Figure 6.6. Four girls eating at a table.

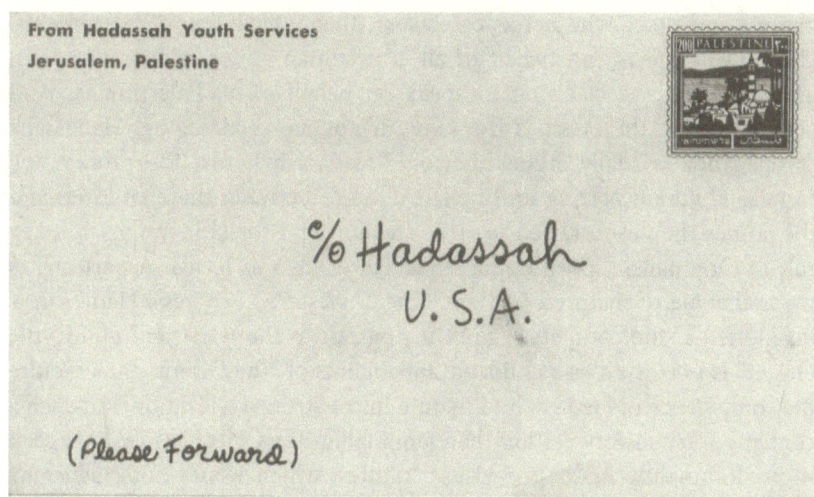

Figure 6.7. Cover with return address and stamp.

with an air of authenticity suggesting it comes directly from Palestine as an unmediated, on-the-ground account of life there, as might a personal letter. Any reader would recognize that this is not a personal letter, but the presentation nevertheless frames how Hadassah intends it to be read and the power these "authentic" images might have lent their "propaganda."

This visual presentation of the "letter" (pamphlet) as direct from Palestine also formally shapes the claims that the inner text makes about Hadassah's services. Because *we know that we speak on behalf of all of Palestine's younger generation, we add their thanks to ours, and express the hope that you will follow our efforts and continue to make even greater progress possible in the future via financial gifts* (italics mine). This further associates Hadassah's vision of Jewishness with its vision of "the Orient." Hadassah here claims to speak for all Palestinian children, transforming the dynamic life of those in Palestine into a silent, helpless "Orient." To speak for children is a deft strategy: it positions the women of Hadassah, whether in "the Orient" or in the United States, as caretakers or symbolic mothers. And in doing so, it elicits an emotional response. Who would not care for children's well-being? Speaking for children does not seem to abrogate the personal rights of Palestinians in the same way as other political rhetoric claiming to speak for adults, such as that of the ZOA claiming to speak for all Palestinians or that "Oriental" adults cannot understand logic. We might all agree that children require advocates, their parents and those who act as caretakers (theoretically) alongside parents. Claiming to speak "on behalf of all" Palestinian children does not seem as paternalistic as claiming to speak on behalf of all Palestinians. And yet, ultimately, the effect is the same, if not more damaging. Hadassah's "propaganda" visually argues that only Hadassah knows the proper way to raise children, placing an implicit distance between these children and the homes they were raised in. This creation of a social hierarchy is a key role of Orientalism, positioning Hadassah women as Jewish Americans as the archetype of matured and embodied "Western" Progress. Hadassah is positioned as the competent adult in contrast to the "Oriental" child: "the Orient" is portrayed as a child. All inhabitants of "the Orient" thus require the competence of Hadassah to mature into a strong civilization, but such a contemporary society. Rather than feminizing "the Orient" as we have seen in predominantly masculine visual cultures, which would not Hadassah's goal to elevate women's status, Hadassah "propaganda" infantilizes "the Orient" to insist on the need for motherhood and "Western" intervention.

Hadassah's images of medical philanthropy in "the Orient" mirror the position of Jewish Americans whose families arrived in the United States in large numbers from Germany from 1820 to 1880 toward Jewish Americans whose families immigrated in greater numbers from Eastern Europe following the 1880s. As Jenna Weissman Joselit has shown, German Jewish Americans launched a "systematic campaign to refashion the newly arrived East European immigrant, whose style, appearance, and personal hygiene differed markedly from [their] own." Through this "architecture of visible health," German Jewish Americans sought to alter practices of Judaism and other cultural norms among East European Jewish Americans. Joselit shows that health and home were the primary focuses of German Jewish American women in addressing this later wave of Jewish immigrants. Visual and material culture were prime means by which German Jewish Americans pictured the transformation of East European Jewish Americans. In this, German Jewish American women were especially concerned with the aesthetics of the home, and model apartments "offered a domestic vision that was as much ideological as it was physical." German Jewish American women saw East European immigrants as lower class. German Jewish American women wanted to replace East European Jewish American practices "with middle-class American notions of decoration, sanitation, and public hygiene."[32] Hadassah's "propaganda" thus projected middle-class Jewish American visions of home and ideology onto "the Orient." Hadassah did establish medical campaigns in Mandate Palestine, work that continued long after the State of Israel was established, that sought to alter the practices and norms of East European and Mizrahi Jews and to some extent Arabs and Muslims. But the representation of this work in the United States participated in a larger project to control norms and practices of Jews in the United States at the same time. Through language about Jewish homes and health, whether in the United States or in "the Orient," Hadassah performed Jewishness as white and middle class. Hadassah's "propaganda" attempted to "speak for immigrants" by describing Hadassah's idealized immigrant responses in "the Orient," which suggested how Hadassah's "propaganda" sought to construct the appropriate re-vision of East European Jewish Americans.

Conclusion

It is striking that the National Federation of Temple Sisterhoods' art calendars circulated by Reform Jewish American women contained images shared with the FAZ/ZOA and international Zionist culture. This is all the more fascinating since, in contrast, much of Hadassah's visual culture circulated images unique to Hadassah. This may be due to the tension between Hadassah and the FAZ/ZOA. Hadassah had to produce its own images in order for the women who joined Hadassah to distinguish themselves from Zionist American men in goals, practices, and visual culture. Reform Jewish women did not face a continual fight of being subsumed within masculine Zionist culture and thus could borrow from FAZ/ZOA visual culture, while that very borrowing subverted the meanings of the images the Reform women's art calendars shared with Zionist Americans or the culture of "fine art" for that matter. Hadassah's use of a unique visual culture helped differentiate Jewish American women in the organization from Zionist American men. Hadassah's "propaganda" represented a different strategy for viewing "the Orient" and thus for imagining Jewishness in the United States.

The women of Hadassah sought their own liberation within the United States and within Jewish communities, FAZ/ZOA circles in particular. Zionist men and Hadassah women's efforts intersected in seeking possibilities for the creation of a non-halakhic but vibrant Jewish heritage. For Zionists, men and women, the work to build a new Jewish nation was work in which women could at least theoretically participate in full, unlike the possibilities for women in the rabbinate, even in Reform Judaism, in the first half of the twentieth century.[33] If in practice women were frequently excluded or subjugated in Zionism, Zionism's theoretical and ideological inclusion of women distinguished it from Jewish halakha. Zionist ideals produced a system wherein Jewish women structurally could enter the conversation, as opposed to women's lack of options for debating or determining halakhic rulings at that time. Hadassah ultimately pushed the logic of Zionism's language of equality well beyond what most men had envisioned. Thereby Zionism did open up a space in which many women, including Jewish American women who had no intention to make *aliyah* (to "go up" in status by moving to Palestine), could find themselves.

Juxtaposing images of Jewish and non-Jewish children with multiple other "Oriental" characters, Hadassah's "propaganda" created a panorama that imagined Jewish American women as "Western" mothers in contrast to the infantilized "Orient." Adults often imagine children as powerless. In whatever ways this may be true, this construction of children's powerlessness positions adults as the powerful. "Children"—as imagined, that is—may be more "extensions of adult religious interiority" rather than the objects of investigation and understanding.[34] The power of adults' tendency to imagine children as "innocent" or "helpless" may make children harder to distinguish as subjects with their own religious existence separate from adults. Seeking to understand how a community draws boundaries around what it means to be a child, the needs of children, and what should be passed on to children from previous generations is a crucial part of the first-order production of heritage as well as the second-order academic study of religion. Visualizing children can make the need for heritage appear pressing; however, this can also mask the ways that heritage is created not necessarily for children but for the adults who envision those children materially and imaginatively.[35] Jewish American women desired a clear position of power within the Jewish community and as equals in American society. Hadassah's "propaganda" envisioned children and mothers as a means of creating a new Jewish future for themselves in the United States through "propaganda" for philanthropy in Palestine. The power Jewish American women sought to create for themselves depended on Orientalization of Mizrahim, Arabs, and other indigenous residents of Palestine. To escape the negative light in which non-Jews cast Jews and in which Jewish American men cast Jewish American women, the visual culture of Hadassah infantilized life in "the Orient." The success of Hadassah's efforts in the United States and Palestine influenced a lasting legacy of how Jewish and non-Jewish Americans have understood or imagined Palestine and Palestinians throughout the twentieth and twenty-first centuries."

Conclusion

In a job interview at the beginning of my career, I briefly described the contours of my research on Jewish American visual culture to an administrator. This person, who explained himself to be a Protestant Christian, asked me how my research could even be possible, given that Jews do not create images due to the Second Commandment. The directness of the question took me by surprise. Many things were tied up in this question: an administrative concern (skepticism?) over whether my scholarship is legitimate, a desire to better understand his Jewish American neighbors, and expanding his idea of the efforts of his colleagues in the humanities. This person could only see Jewish Americans through a Christian interpretation of how the Bible commands Jews, and the encounter is an example of how prevalent this conception of Jews and the Second Commandment remains. He is not alone in imagining a lack of Jewish American visual culture in contrast to Christianity. This idea stretches back several centuries and has shaped how Jews and non-Jews have seen the place of Jews in "modern heritage." For example, in the *Jewish Encyclopedia*, Immanuel Benzinger, a professor of Old Testament exegesis at the Berlin University, wrote that plastic arts were less developed among ancient Jews than pottery, seal-engraving, and metal-casting, and he claimed almost no sculpture existed among Jews because they did not know how to work with stone, though ivory- and wood-carvings were more common. He described only the carvings that served as decorations for the Temple, citing I Samuel and I Kings. Under the subheading "Religion as an Opponent of the Plastic Art," Benzinger explained, "Religion of the Jews . . . precluded the full development of the art of sculpture, and so confined it within . . . narrow limits. In the most ancient times, when images were not proscribed, the technical ability to make them artistically was lacking; and when in later periods this artistic skill might have been acquired from others, images were forbidden." Benzinger linked the myth of Jewish aniconism with both lack of skill and halakhic prohibition. Furthermore, he explicitly tied his conception of the Second Commandment to the Prophets as enforcers of his imagined interpretation of Jewish law. Finally, he claimed that "such a command as that of the Decalogue (Ex. xx. 4; Deut. v.8) would have been impossible to a nation possessed of such artistic gifts as the Greeks, and was carried to its ultimate consequences—as to-day in Islam—only because the people lacked artistic inclination with its creative power and formative imagination."[1] This assessment of the Second Commandment placed Judaism within a hierarchy. Benzinger ranked Greeks—it seems implicit that he means pre-Christian Greek society, though one could make connections to the very possibility for Christian imaging of God in a body—above Jewish contributions to arts and images. However, Benzinger asserted that contemporary Jewish participation in arts outranks those of contemporaneous Islam: while ancient Hebrews may have struggled to learn technical abilities or prevented the arts, Jews today have joined the other nations in the production of arts. For Benzinger, Muslims are trapped in primitive modes without any arts, suffering from the lack of creativity of generations past.

Like Benzinger, Reform Rabbi Kaufmann Kohler asserted in a different entry in the *Jewish Encyclopedia* that the Second Commandment prevented an indigenous Jewish art, and that the work of Jews was always influenced by their national and cultural context. This oddly separates Jews from the national and cultural contexts to which Kohler points, as if Jews were not contributing members of those contexts. Elsewhere, Kohler argued frequently and strongly for the success of Jewish Americans integrating in the United States. This did not lead him to look back across world history and see Jews as integrated into local life. Instead this narrative imagines Jews as insular and cut off in the past, persecuted and demeaned in such ways that Jews could not be creative at all. This narrative of Jewish heritage excludes Jewish visual culture in a certain way, suggesting it was not truly Jewish, even if made by Jews and used in Jewish life. In the *JE*, Kohler did indicate that rabbinical laws had been more relaxed in their interpretation of the Second Commandment. He claimed that the rabbis prohibited carved statues given their likeness to idols, but they allowed other arts such as portrait-painting. He also noted that Jews in the Middle Ages produced ecclesiastical and secular art.[2] Both Kohler and Eisenstein argued that the rabbis and medieval Jews considered figurative art in the synagogue a distraction from worship, yet both note decorations in the synagogue, especially on the doors of the synagogue, the Ark, and the Torah scrolls.³

As I have shown, the use of images in the *JE* itself belies the short-sightedness of Benzinger and Kohler's understanding of the Second Commandment and Jewish visual culture. The *JE* actively created new roles and spaces for images in Jewish life, and it drew on contemporary images and historical artwork as well. The preface proclaimed that the *JE* sought "to bring together as full a body of illustrative material as possible." All of these, the publishers believed, "would prove of great educational value in every Jewish household."⁴ Scholars such as Kalman Bland have shown that the concept that Jews produced no art before the nineteenth century due to the restriction under the Second Commandment is historically inaccurate. The concept of Jewish aniconism is a modern invention, a myth persistent among Jews and non-Jews for various reasons that did not always obtain but strongly influenced historical and cultural narratives once it took hold. Bland demonstrates that unlike the modern assertion that Jews produced little or no art, "premodern consensus" asserted Jews did not represent God in image or physical form, but other forms of representation and art were permitted.⁵ Despite the demonstrative evidence in primary and secondary sources of the rich history of Jewish visual culture, my encounter with the administrator gave me a strong sense of the significance of studying Jewish visual culture and disseminating that knowledge. Even highly educated Americans continue to misconceptualize Jewish American history and practice. This study seeks to reorient (no pun intended) understanding of Jewish American visual culture and to pay close attention to the ways the particular question of how to envision Jews and Palestine served as a possibility to work through other questions of what it meant to be Jewish in the United States in the first half of the twentieth century.

Envisioning a rich and varied panorama of the Jewish "Orient" provided an opportunity to reenvision the place of women in Jewish life in the United States. For example, the women of the National Federation of Temple of Sisterhoods offered a different vision of "the Orient" than the Zionist Organization of America, and thus an alternative vision of Jewish identity in the United States and a practice of Judaism that overtly included women. However, the NFTS shared significant elements of the ZOA's imagination of "the Orient." Both organizations contributed to the rapidly expanding market production of visual and material culture derived from imagining "the Orient." Many images included in the NFTS art calendars were first exhibited by the ZOA, though the NFTS selected images that nostalgically depicted the biblical period. By circulating these images, the NFTS raised money for its own organization and the Reform movement as a whole, integrating itself into the practice of Reform Judaism without challenging the existing structure of the Union for American Hebrew Congregations. Having established visual culture and women's contributions as significant aspects of Reform Judaism in America, later generations of Reform women used those practices to incorporate images of the State of Israel as resource for Orientalist visions, but simultaneously more overtly proclaiming American exceptionalism. In the second half of the twentieth century, the place for women's leadership alongside men's authority gave way to a more overt challenge to the structure of Reform and a push for further rights for women.

Through Hadassah, Jewish American women also created their own movement and conception of Zionism in the United States. Tenuously linked to the ZOA, Hadassah nevertheless did not require any particular political commitments as to Jewish nationalism in Palestine as the ZOA did, and thus drew from a far broader audience than the ZOA was able to create among Jewish American men. Founded shortly before World War I, Hadassah and the NFTS were part of a larger movement of Jewish- and non-Jewish American women who sought religious and cultural practice in auxiliary organizations alongside male-dominated institutions and movements. In 1915, Hadassah founder Henrietta Szold wrote to Mrs. Julius Rosenwald, "If you and [the National Federation of Temple Sisterhoods] do not follow us as Zionists so far, at least they will respond to the appeal for material help—at least they will recognize that for the sake of Jewish dignity and self-respect, even the purely philanthropic work in Palestine, for which so large a part of Jewry has long felt a keen responsibility, may never again be allowed to relapse into a pauperizing chaos."[6] Szold predicted many Jewish American women would never become as committed to laboring in Palestine as she was, though she still saw possibilities for women who remained in America to support those suffering for the good of the Jewish people. Hadassah's "propaganda" demonstrated a vision of the role of the imagined "Orient" not as a physical destination for Jewish Americans, but as an image of Jewish American women as mothers. This maternalism was the mechanism by which Hadassah "propaganda" transformed Palestine into "the Orient" and Jewish American women into "modern Westerners." Using children as symbols in Hadassah's visual culture depicted Jewish American women as equal to—even more skillful than—Jewish American men, as much as Hadassah's "propaganda" attended to the needs of Jewish children fleeing Nazi Europe or Jewish and non-Jewish children native to "the Orient." Real needs existed for many children and their families, but the Orientalist lens through which Hadassah's "propaganda" represented them at times blinded the organization to the self-images of Jewish refugees, Mizrahim, Arabs, Muslims, and other inhabitants of Palestine. Maternalism mediated all of Hadassah's visual representations of Palestine, producing an image of "the Orient" as part of Jewish Americanness and distancing Jewish American women from appearing "Oriental" to their Christian American neighbors. Hadassah's "propaganda" pictured Jewish American women as mothers to "the Orient," infantilizing and thereby excluding indigenous voices and visions for the future.

As a landmark in Jewish scholarship in America, the *Jewish Encyclopedia* also drew heavily on visual imagination to assert its significance for integrating "the Orient" into Jewish narratives of "Western" heritage. Published prior to a fuller development of Zionism and its conception of Jewish history, the *JE* is a particularly poignant time capsule of Jewish imagination of "the Orient" beyond the confines of Zionist ideology. Scholars who contributed to the *JE* belonged to varieties of Jewish organizations, self-identifying in a range of ways as secular and religious. The editors of the *JE* used images to create a connection to "the Orient" that could not be confined to a single slice of time. Idealized images of the Temple and ancient Israel became timeless when juxtaposed with articles of dynamic history, informing Jewish American identity in the present. Further, the lack of historical evidence for "scholarly" claims about ancient Jewish history indicates the ongoing importance of traditional conceptions of Jewish heritage for early twentieth-century history and other scholarship. Finally, the inclusion of Christian visual culture in the *JE*, similar to the NFTS art calendars, allowed the encyclopedia to redeem Christian claims on "the Orient" in the past and in the present as Jewish heritage. Because the Jewish editors of the encyclopedia selected the images and arranged them in a history of Jewish life, the *JE* had a formal authority over representation of biblical heritage and "the Orient," staking claims on the Hebrew Bible and "the Orient" as Jewish symbols. Acknowledging the shared place of these symbols in Christianity suggested a need for Christians to look to Jews as the source of biblical heritage and the correct understanding of "the Orient."

The place of a comparative view of Christian Orientalism has necessarily been limited in this study, but it is essential to seeing why and how

Jewish Americans engaged visual Orientalism. That Christians set their imaginative vision on "the Orient" was a double-edged sword. Christian Orientalism created a place for "the Orient" in the United States and a vision of American heritage. For many Protestants and Catholics alike, the biblical past and contemporaneous inhabitants of "the Orient" informed a trajectory of American heritage from ancient Israel as the home of Jesus to life on a new continent all guided by the hand of Providence. "The Orient" rivaled the place of ancient Greece and Rome as the origins of American democracy. These distinct claims on geographical and cultural origins have remained in tension in the imagined heritage of the United States for many Americans. To claim Greece and Rome as heritage was to carry European heritage to the United States, but to turn toward "the Orient" asserted the power of the Bible to guide American values and to temper the flaws of decadent Greco-Roman life. Concepts of "the West" were drawn against the foil of "the Orient" particularly since the Crusades, a battle for the right to control the Holy Land and Jerusalem, yet Greece and Rome appeared as sources of high culture from philosophy to drama. The tension between "the Orient" and Greece and Rome represented a tension between seeing Christianity as predominant in Europe and the United States and the secularism that emerged with the Enlightenment, which included many critics of the place of religion in a vision of nation-states. This tension has never been resolved, creating a broad panorama of the heritage of "the West" and the place of the United States in "Western heritage." This panorama opened up visions of "Western" heritage that saw Jews as part of American heritage through the biblical past, but in Christian Orientalism, Jews frequently appeared as a part of the contemporaneous "Orient." Christian Americans who viewed Jews through the lens of Orientalism, like Augustine in antiquity, saw all Jews as relics of ancient Israel and potential proof of the New Testament. If Jews suffered, this proved the truth of a new covenant. If Jews converted, this proved the power of Jesus to unite the world and to create God's kingdom on earth. Especially for postmillennial Christians, if Jews gathered in the land of Israel, this hastened the Second Coming of Christ. All of these visions of Jews positioned them as objects to be arranged by the power of Christian vision.

However, many Jewish Americans saw Orientalism as an opportunity to see themselves as part of American heritage and contemporary American life. Painting new ways of seeing "the Orient" made space for seeing dynamic Jewish religious practice and Jewish communal identity as condoned by the significance of the biblical past in the American present rather than freezing Jewish Americans in the past. These efforts to imagine "the Orient" as the future of Jewishness in the United States, within Jewish communities and within American cultural pluralism, reached a crescendo at the 1933 Century of Progress World's Fair in Chicago. Jewish Americans imagined Jewish unity in the face of Jewish difference through "the Orient." On the stage of the Temple on Jewish Day or in the Judaism exhibit in the Hall of Religion, from the origins of Israelite monotheism to Hasidic legends to Zionist pioneers, the soul of Jewishness derived from "the Orient" performed in "the West."

Many Jewish Americans shared a view of "the Orient" as a singular communal heritage. Few Jewish Americans ever traveled to the land of Palestine, though the technology to travel had developed rapidly since the antebellum period. Without ever laying eyes on the land of Palestine, many more Jewish Americans engaged visual culture that represented "the Orient." If Jews debated how to envision the Jewish future, it did not necessarily imply a permanent fragmentation in Jewish imaginations of community. Difference existed in the present, but if Jews had been united in the "Oriental" past, this implied they could be reunited under the right view of the future. However, no matter the power of imagining Jewish unity in Jewish American visual culture, I have shown the differences in how Jewish Americans imagined "the Orient" as heritage and thus the disagreements as to what Jewishness should look like in the future. Imagining unity did not create consensus, though many Jewish Americans continued to engage and debate other Jews with whom they disagreed about the future. This debate also created a sense of shared community and heritage even as it is evidence of differences between Jewish communities and their visions of Jewish life.

Jewish visual culture representing "the Orient" does not reflect the "reality" of everyday Jewish American life but the aspiration as to how Jewish Americans have wished to be seen. The twentieth and twenty-first centuries have not seen a resolution to conflict in Jewish American visions of their own heritage versus Christians views. In July 2012, a news story suggested how "the Orient" remains a touchstone for claiming religious authenticity in the United States. A fundamentalist Christian group announced plans for an antiabortion center in Wichita, Kansas. Plans included a scale replica of the Western Wall of the Temple, presenting the wall as a memorial to the "holocaust" of sixty million aborted fetuses. Thus, in addition to the full-size replica of the Western Wall, activists planned

Replica of Western Wall Planned in Kansas
Anti-Abortion Activists Plan Site as Part of Pro-Life Shrine

Whose Wall? A full-sized replica of the Western Wall, right, is planned as part of an anti-abortion center in Wichita, Kansas.

Figure C.1. "Replica of Western Wall Planned in Kansas."

sixty crosses, each representing one million aborted fetuses (fig. C.1). The *Jewish Daily Forward* editorialized that the comparison of suffering between abortions and genocide was "tenuous . . . offensive and inaccurate." And as to the use of the Western Wall, the newspaper asserted to Christian Americans, "Find your own symbols. Stay away from ours."[7] Though no fundraising had even begun for the projected multi-million-dollar project and nothing seems to have come of Spirit One Christian Ministry Church's plans, the announcement and the response are salient. There is more at stake in visual representations of "the Orient" than political claims on physical territory. At times, Jewish Americans have seen their concern with "the Orient" as a common bond between Jewish and Christian Americans. But Jewish Americans have also asserted their right to determine the meaning and legacy of ancient Israel, the Temple, and other relics to construct their own heritage and the place of that heritage in the United States. The Wall of the Temple has been a symbol of religious heritage, which in America has often been as much about what it means to be a citizen in the United States with rights to religious freedom as a claim to physical space in the Middle East.

The visual culture analyzed in the chapters of this book is significant for what it reveals about the internal construction of Jewish heritage and the roles images of Jews and "the Orient" have taken in American heritage. While the first half of the twentieth century saw a debate over how to imagine Palestine in Jewish American culture, the second half of the twentieth century the creation of the State of Israel, and Israeli soldiers have become more compelling icons for Jews and Christians. These images have been taken up by popular American culture at large, not only by a small segment of Jewish Americans, and they continue to say as much about being American as being Jewish or Israeli. When Paul Newman as Ari Ben Canaan swam up to the shore in the beginning of the film *Exodus*, it is as if he arrived from the United States, grappling with the issues of democratic citizenship and group identity within the context of cultural pluralism. When Israeli military troops took Jerusalem during the Six-Day War, images of chalutz-soldiers and the Western Wall were merged and became wildly popular. National periodicals such as the *New York Times*, *Life* magazine, and *Time* magazine selected photographs that deliberately framed Israeli soldiers and the Western Wall in an admiring view, and an abundance of ephemera to commemorate the moment was produced throughout the United States.[8] Many Jewish Americans saw the victory as stabilizing a political state that guaranteed Jewish safety after the Holocaust in Israel and for Jews around the world, but the emotional collective response suggests the extent to which such images also ground Jewish *American* visual heritage. Deborah Dash Moore attributes the representation of Israelis to selective use of biblical characters, such as descriptions of David as "ruddy-cheeked, bright-eyed, and handsome," in Hollywood depictions of heroes.[9] Both the Hebrew Bible and Hollywood influenced film and news media, but this traced back to the visual culture of the early twentieth century. The first half of the twentieth century shaped how Americans imagined "the Orient" and constructed the emotional connection between Jewish Americans and "the Orient" as heritage. As Jewish Americans produced and consumed a visual culture depicting "the Orient" in the second half of the twentieth century, they continued visual culture and viewing practices founded earlier.

Images of chalutzim have appeared in American films from Paul Newman's Ari Ben Canaan in *Exodus* (1960) to Adam Sandler's Zohan Dvir in *You Don't Mess with the Zohan* (2008), at the same time that Arabs and Muslims, by contrast, have frequently been demonized in American popular culture, and Palestinian narratives have by and large been absent.[10]

Yet the lack of a mainstream Palestinian American visual culture reveals more than a simple bias of many Americans toward Jews and Israelis over Palestinians. Nurith Gertz and George Khleifi argue that Palestinians have struggled to translate history into a viable medium for collective heritage in art, literature, and culture in the way that Jewish Americans, Zionists, and Israelis have. Although Gertz and Khleifi reject the sense that "history has forgotten our people" or its inverse, that "we are the people who have overlooked history," they echo other writers and scholars who argue "that the post-1948 Palestinian historical narrative has thus far not been told in its entirety or, at least, that it has yet to find its full artistic expression." Scholars' preoccupation with this artistic expression indicates the power of visualizing heritage, both in solidifying a people and in garnering that people's concern on international stages.[11] By contrast, the central place of "the Orient" in Jewish American visual culture indicates the success Jewish Americans have had in harnessing "the Orient" for the construction of heritage and in convincing the American public that Jewish heritage is an acceptable performance of American citizenship and valuable for American heritage in culture, politics, and religion.

In the summer of 2015, I gave a talk on Hadassah's early visual culture to a group of women from the tristate area around Brandeis University as a conclusion to my scholarship-in-residence related to gender and Judaism that summer at the Hadassah-Brandeis Institute. The Hadassah women who attended were deeply engaged with my research, though the idea that only a minority of Jewish Americans advocated Zionism in the first half of the twentieth century surprised them. Indeed, the State of Israel has become so prominent in such a range of Jewish American visual culture and conceptions of Jewish heritage that many forget the disagreement over the idea of a Jewish political entity in the region of Palestine that characterized Jewish life until after World War II, from the lingering of Holocaust victims in displaced persons camps to the creation of the State of Israel and the Arab-Israeli War in 1948–1949. *The Hebrew Orient* is a reminder that the United States and "the Orient" have only recently become linked in Jewish Americans' conceptions of their heritage. Visions of "the Orient," more than engagement with life on the ground in Palestine and later the State of Israel have informed Jewish Americans' views. For Jewish Americans from 1901 to 1938, the pressing question was whether and how to see "the Orient" and the United States intertwined. An international debate about the future of the region of Palestine and the disagreement among Jews and non-Jews about what their future should look like simultaneously took place, sometimes crossing with Jewish American questions and sometimes engaging alternative views of Jewish heritage and the place for Jews in Palestine.

Moreover, my audience of Hadassah members was shocked at the ways their organization had represented "the Orient" in the first half of the twentieth century. They did not resist seeing new ways to understand their organization's history, but obviously these intellectual and activist women did not understand Orientalism to be a part of their heritage. That scholarly analysis is not fully recognizable to religious participants is neither unique nor problematic. On the contrary, scholarship would be incomplete and offer little new if it did not elicit reactions of surprise. For one, scholars and popular practitioners are simply not interested in all the same questions. But a sense that heritage can be reevaluated in light of what academics uncover is a key piece of the import of scholarship. Jewish studies is somewhat unique in religious studies as a field and in the broader humanities and social sciences for the financial support of and communal engagement with scholarship. But in light of this overlap, *The Hebrew Orient* has the power to ask Jewish Americans, as well as non-Jewish Americans, how their own conceptions of Israel today might be seen anew in light of the history of Orientalism in Jewish American visual culture that I lay out. Of course, no linear link can be drawn from 1901–1938 to 2020. My research demonstrates the heterogeneity and dynamic evolution of Jewish American visual culture in the first half of the twentieth century. There is no singular line of influence between the Ottoman and Mandate Palestine to today, and the creation of the State of Israel as well as the occupation of territories after 1967 have deeply changed the international context in which Jewish Americans can imagine Jewish heritage. Prior to the creation of the state, the possibilities for the Jewish future were undetermined, while today Jewish Americans must construct their vision with some recognition of the reality of a hegemonic state. Additionally, Jews have been increasingly integrated into the American mainstream and have greater possibilities for social, educational, and professional inclusion and stability. But if the process of the construction of heritage selects and omits moments of the Jewish past, scholarly work uncovers that process and recovers those selections and omissions. What to make of the differences between the Jewish past and the Jewish present are not for scholars to say, but presenting these differences is possible in academic work in ways that normative practices of Jewishness do not include.

The Hebrew Orient also shows scholars the significance for viewing visual culture and Jewish studies together. Visual culture is not a mere decoration to verbal text. Visual texts have interacted with verbal texts and shaped how Jews have understood their heritage from antiquity to the present. Visual text must be analyzed alongside verbal text, from ancient canon to contemporary politics, to have a full picture of Jewish life. I have focused on visual culture because it complicates how to understand Jewish American engagement with Palestine and citizenship in the United States in the first half of the twentieth century. Seeing that engagement as the imaginative view of "the Orient" places greater attention on Jewish American life and goals rather than the influence of the United States on Palestine and, later, the State of Israel.

The gap between Palestine and "the Orient" constitutes the most serious implications of my study for understanding Jewish American life in the first half of the twentieth century and for extrapolating ideas about how to understand Jewish practice and visual culture more generally. A great number of circumstances produce that gap. Physical geographic distance creates changes in worldview. Emotional, historical, biblical, and scholarly attachments color the questions that Jewish and non-Jewish Americans have asked or hoped to answer by looking toward "the Orient." The problem of accessing any moment in the past frustrates the view from the present. The mediation of sites and sights through cultural lenses and new technologies sharpens focus on different aspects of past and present. Economics influence access or lack thereof to education. Dissatisfaction with the present and hope mixed with fear about the future frames how we see ourselves and others. Constructs such as gender, race, ethnicity, and religion order the world in shifting, competing categories, just as changing social and political systems structure the world in different ways. All of these together produce the gap between Palestine and "the Orient." These issues mediate and contextualize how we view all different spaces and times. The exotic is an attraction and a danger. But Jewish Americans have turned to the exotic "Orient" over and over to see themselves and their place in the world over and over again.

This book is not exhaustive in its analysis of visual culture produced by the groups I have selected for study. To try to address every single example would be an impossible task and miss the forest for the trees. I have assembled representative examples that serve to analyze the place of Orientalism in the visual construction of Jewish American heritage. Many more examples exist and merit greater attention, within these groups and among others. It is precisely to the diffuse but widespread visual engagement with "the Orient" that I wish to call attention. Neither the United States government policy toward Palestine nor the possibility for migration constituted the sole or perhaps primary goals of the production of Jewish American visual heritage. Jewish Americans sought to write themselves into American origins and the trajectory of the heritage of the United States by looking elsewhere, namely, to "the Orient." Each organization that I have evaluated represented "the Orient" according to its own view of Jewishness, views that were shaped and reshaped as new imaginations of "the Orient" took place in the United States. Thus visual culture representing "the Orient" was a constitutive aspect of the construction and maintenance of Jewish heritage in the United States, influencing the practice of Judaism as well as the sociopolitical realities of the United States and Palestine. When Jewish Americans sought goals in Palestine, they did so through the mediation of their imaginations of "the Orient."

Notes

Introduction

1. Images accompanying Ittamar Ben-Avi, "We Young Palestinians: To the Jewish Youth of America," *The Maccabaean* (hereafter, *TM*), June–July 1917, 259–261, 296–297.

2. Ben-Avi, "We Young Palestinians," 259.

3. For a longer study conceptualizing Jewish ethnicity and hyphenated terminology, see Jeffrey Lesser and Raanan Rein, "Challenging Particularity: Jews as a Lens on Latin American Ethnicity," *Latin American and Caribbean Ethnic Studies* 1, no. 2 (September 2006): 249–263.

4. Enda Duffy, *The Speed Handbook: Velocity, Pleasure, Modernism* (Durham: Duke University Press, 2009), 1.

5. Duffy, *The Speed Handbook*, 4.

6. Duffy, *The Speed Handbook*, 6–7.

7. Sara Horowitz, "The Geography of Memory: Haunting and Haunted Landscapes in Contemporary Canadian Jewish Writing," *Studies in American Jewish Literature* 35, no. 2 (2016): 217.

8. Duffy, *The Speed Handbook*, 34.

9. Alan Trachtenberg, *Reading American Photographs: Images as History, Mathew Brady to Walker Evans* (New York: Hill and Wang, 1989), 3.

10. Hubert Damisch, "Five Notes for a Phenomenology of the Photographic Image," in *Classic Essays on Photography*, ed. Alan Trachtenberg (Stony Creek, CT: Leete's Island Books, 1980), 287–290; Trachtenberg, *Reading American Photographs*, 5.

11. Trachtenberg, *Reading American Photographs*, 6.

12. Carol Zemel, *Looking Jewish: Visual Culture and Modern Diaspora* (Bloomington: Indiana University Press, 2015), 30.

13. Trachtenberg, *Reading American Photographs*, 6.

14. Benedict Anderson, *Imagined Communities: Reflections on the Origin and Spread of Nationalism* (New York: Verso, 2006), 6–7.

15. Barbara Kirshenblatt-Gimblett, "Intangible Heritage as Metacultural Production," *Museum International* 56, nos. 1–2 (2004): 56.

16. Andrea Siegel, "A Literary Perspective: Domestic Violence, the 'Woman Question,' and the 'Arab Question' in Early Zionism," in *Gender in Judaism and Islam: Common Lives, Uncommon Heritage*, ed. Firoozeh Kashani-Sabet and Beth Wenger (New York: New York University Press, 2015), 246; Claudia Sadowski-Smith, *The New Immigrant Whiteness: Race, Neoliberalism, and Post-Soviet Migration to the United States* (New York: New York University Press, 2018).

17. Beth Wenger, *History Lessons: The Creation of American Jewish Heritage* (Princeton: Princeton University Press, 1996), 1–2.

18. David Lowenthal, *The Past Is a Foreign Country—Revisited* (Cambridge: Cambridge University Press, 2015), 502.

19. David Lowenthal, *The Heritage Crusade and the Spoils of History* (Cambridge: Cambridge University Press, 1996), xvii; cited in Wenger, *History Lessons*, 5.

20. S. Brent Plate, "Introduction," in *Religion, Art, and Visual Culture: A Cross-Cultural Reader*, ed. S. Brent Plate (New York: Palgrave Macmillan, 2002), 5.

21. David Morgan, *The Sacred Gaze: Religious Visual Culture in Theory and Practice* (Berkeley: University of California Press, 2005), 27–31, 51, 55, 73, 258.

22. Rachel Gross, "Objects of Affection: The Material Religion of American Jewish Nostalgia," dissertation, Princeton University, 2014.

23. Ken Koltun-Fromm, *Imagining Jewish Authenticity: Vision and Text in American Jewish Thought* (Bloomington: Indiana University Press, 2015), 7.

24. Wenger, *History Lessons*, 1–2, 5.

25. Wenger, *History Lessons*, 10–12, 49.

26. Rita Gross, *Feminism and Religion: An Introduction* (Boston: Beacon Press, 1996), 16–20.

27. Judith Plaskow, *Standing Again at Sinai* (New York: HarperCollins, 1990), 51.

28. Joan W. Scott, "Gender: A Useful Category of Historical Analysis," *The American Historical Review* 91, no. 5 (December 1986): 1056.

29. R. Marie Griffith, *God's Daughters: Evangelical Women and the Power of Submission* (Berkeley: University of California Press, 1997); Saba Mahmood, *Politics of Piety: The Islamic Revival and the Feminist Subject* (Princeton: Princeton University Press, 2011).

30. Scott, "Gender," 1053.

31. Riv-Ellen Prell, *Fighting to Become Americans: Assimilation and the Trouble between Jewish Women and Jewish Men* (Boston: Beacon Press, 1999), 177–208.

32. Susannah Heschel, "Jewish and Muslim Feminist Theologies in Dialogue: Discourses of Difference," in *Gender in Judaism and Islam: Common Lives, Uncommon Heritage*, ed. Firoozeh Kashani-Sabet and Beth Wenger (New York: New York University Press, 2015), 15–16.

33. Scott, "Gender," 1059.

34. Sarah Imhoff, *Masculinity and the Making of American Judaism* (Bloomington: Indiana University Press, 2017), 8.

35. Richard Gregory, *Eye and Brain: The Psychology of Seeing*, 5th ed. (Princeton: Princeton University Press, 2015 [1966]), 1–13.

36. Dave Warner and Larry McShane, "Jewish Teen's Tefillin Sets Off Bomb Scare That Diverts US Airways Flight from LaGuardia Airport," *New York Daily News*, January 21, 2010, http://www.nydailynews.com/news/national/jewish-teen-tefillin-sets-bomb-scare-diverts-airways-flight-laguardia-airport-article-1.183107, accessed August 23, 2018.

37. Lisa Fishbayn Joffe, "Legislating the Family: Gender, Jewish Law, and Rabbinical Courts in Mandate Palestine," in *Gender in Judaism and Islam: Common Lives, Uncommon Heritage*, ed. Firoozeh Kashani-Sabet and Beth Wenger (New York: New York University Press, 2015), 204–205.

38. Joffe, "Legislating the Family," 209.

39. Kenneth Feldman, "Seeing Is Believing: U.S. Imperial Culture and the Jerusalem Exhibit of 1904," *Studies in American Jewish Literature* 35, no. 1 (2016): 98–101.

40. Jeffrey Gurock, *Orthodox Jews in America* (Bloomington: Indiana University Press, 2009), 148–149.

41. Edward Said, *Orientalism* (New York: Random House, 2003 [1978]), 12, 24.

42. Anderson, *Imagined Communities*, 6–7.

Chapter 1

1. Advertisement, *NP*, January 22, 1926, 93.

2. Jennifer Axsom Adler, "The Other Witness: Nineteenth-Century American Protestantism and the Material Gospel Theology," dissertation, Vanderbilt University, 2015, 3–4.

3. Rami Arav, "Archaeology in the Service of Ideology in Israel," in *"A Land Flowing with Milk and Honey": Visions of Israel from Biblical to Modern Times*, ed. Leonard Greenspoon and Ronald Simkins (Omaha: Creighton University Press, 2001), 85.

4. For more, see Yael Zerubavel, *Recovered Roots: Collective Memory and the Making of Israeli National Tradition* (Chicago: University of Chicago Press, 1995), 62–69.

5. Arav, "Archaeology in the Service of Ideology in Israel," 85–104.

6. "The Tower of David," *TM*, October 1906, 143; "The Tower of David, Jerusalem," in "Jerusalem, the Capital—from the Series, A Spy in the Land of Promise," *NP*, March 30, 1928, 370; "The Old City of Jerusalem," in "Our Painters: Israel Paldi: Sincere and Strong," *NP*, April 20, 1928, 426; "The Tower of David,"

in J. L. Avi-Sigla, "The Court House: Jurisprudence in Jerusalem," *NP*, May 31, 1929, 461; "Detailed Model of Holy City for Palestine Pavilion," in "J. H. Patteson Hails Pavilion Message," *NP*, March 24, 1939, 8.

7. Arav, "Archaeology in the Service of Ideology in Israel," 86.

8. Simone Ricca, "Heritage, Nationalism, and the Shifting Symbolism of the Wailing Wall," *Archives de sciences socials des religions* (July–September 2010): 170.

9. Michael Berkowitz, *Western Jewry and the Zionist Project, 1914–1933* (Cambridge: Cambridge University Press, 1997), 136.

10. Eyal Onne, *Photographic Heritage of the Holy Land, 1839–1914* (Manchester: Institute of Advanced Studies, Manchester England, 1980), 7–10.

11. John Efron, "Orientalism and the Jewish Horizontal Gaze," in *Orientalism and the Jews*, ed. Ivan Davidson Kalmar and Derek J. Penslar (Waltham: Brandeis University Press, 2005), 80.

12. Said, *Orientalism*, 273.

13. Jeffrey Librett, *Orientalism and the Figure of the Jew* (New York: Fordham University Press, 2015), 19.

14. Librett, *Orientalism*, 20, 23.

15. Yaron Peleg, *Orientalism and the Hebrew Imagination* (Ithaca: Cornell University Press, 2005), 5–10, 18.

16. Said, *Orientalism*, 216, 221.

17. James W. Carey, *Communication as Culture: Essays on Media and Society*, revised ed. (New York: Routledge, 2009), 119, 136–138.

18. Emily Alice Katz, *Bringing Zion Home: Israel in American Jewish Culture, 1948–1967* (Albany: State University of New York Press, 2015), 2–3, 11, 60–63, 79.

19. Lowenthal, *The Past Is a Foreign Country*, 25.

20. Arnold Lewis, "Phantom Ethnicity: 'Oriental Jews' in Israeli Society," in *Studies in Israeli Ethnicity: After the Ingathering*, ed. Alex Weingrod (New York: Gordon and Breach Science Publishers, 1985), 149.

21. Eric Goldstein, *The Price of Whiteness: Jews, Race, and American Identity* (Princeton: Princeton University Press, 2006), quote from 39; 17–19, 31–41, 50, 75–87.

22. Jonathan Z. Smith, "Differential Equations: On Construction the Other," in *Relating Religion: Essays on the Study of Religion* (Chicago: University of Chicago Press, 2004), 230–239, 245–246.

23. Jonathan Sarna, "A Projection of America as It Ought to Be: Zion in the Mind's Eye of American Jews," in *Envisioning Israel: The Changing Ideals and Images of North American Jews*, ed. Allon Gal (Detroit: Wayne State University Press, 1996), 41–42.

24. Horace Kallen, "Jewish Unity," in *The Zionist Idea: A Historical Analysis and Reader*, ed. Arthur Hertzberg (Philadelphia: Jewish Publication Society of America, 1997), 533.

25. Horace Kallen, "Zionism and Liberalism," in *The Zionist Idea*, 528–531.

26. Allon Gal, "Brandeis, Judaism, and Zionism," in *Brandeis and America*, ed. Nelson Dawson (Lexington: University Press of Kentucky, 1989), 65–94.

27. Louis Brandeis, "The Jewish Problem and How to Solve It," in *The Zionist Idea*, 519–522.

Chapter 2

1. "Give Today and Build For Ever!," *NP*, February 24, 1928, cover and 219.
2. David Levy, "Brandeis and the Progressive Movement," in *Brandeis and America*, 102–105.
3. Zerubavel, *Recovered Roots*, 16–36.
4. Evyatar Friesel, "The Meaning of Zionism and Its Influence among the American Jewish Religious Movements," in *Zionism and Religion*, ed. Shmuel Almog, Jehuda Reinharz, and Anita Shapira (Hanover, NH: Brandeis University Press by University Press of New England, 1998), 135–137.
5. Kalmar and Penslar, "Introduction," in *Orientalism and the Jews*, xviii.
6. Clifford Putney, *Muscular Christianity: Manhood and Sports in Protestant America, 1880–1920* (Cambridge: Harvard University Press, 2001), 11–44, 100, photographic insert following 126.
7. "Where the New and Old Jerusalem Meet: Here Is a Business Street in the Occidental Quarter, Photographed from the Jerusalem Wall, Near the Tower of David," *NP*, June 22, 1928, 653.
8. Ricca, "Heritage, Nationalism, and the Shifting Symbolism of the Wailing Wall," 170.
9. Berkowitz, *Western Jewry and the Zionist Project*, 136.
10. "A Survivor of Old Palestine," *NP*, December 30, 1927, 556.
11. Caitlen Carenen, "Zionism and American Jewish Relief Efforts during World War I," *American Jewish Archives Journal* 69, no. 2 (2017): 1–28.
12. Eliyahu Stern, *The Genius: Elijah of Vilna and the Making of Modern Judaism* (New Haven: Yale University Press, 2013), 6, 8.
13. Zerubavel, *Recovered Roots*, 39–47, 84–95.
14. Berkowitz, *Western Jewry and the Zionist Project*, 26–28.
15. *TM*, May 1917, 232.
16. *TM* Baltimore Convention Number, June 24–8, 1917, cover.
17. "Herzl as Moses: Window Design by Lilien in the B'nai B'rith House at Hamburg," *NP*, September 21, 1928, 188.
18. "Greetings to Dr. Weizmann," *NP*, March 2, 1923, cover; "The Zionist 'Big Three': Balfour, Weizmann, Sokolow Acknowledging an Ovation in Tel Aviv," *NP*, October 28, 1927, 284, 289; "Dr. Chaim Weizmann Arriving Here Mar. 6th for the United Palestine Appeal," *NP*, February 17, 1928, cover; "Man of the Hour," *NP*, March 28, 1945, 1; "After 2,000 Years!," *NP*, November 30, 1947, 5–6.

19. Meyer Weisgal, . . . *So Far: An Autobiography* (New York: Random House, 1971), 111.

20. "Martha Wolfenstein, Sketch Writer," *TM*, January 1906, 16.

21. "Son of the Ancient Race," by Josef Israels, *TM*, May 1916, cover.

22. For example, see Jeffrey Shandler, ed., *Awakening Lives: Autobiographies of Jewish Youth in Poland before the Holocaust* (New Haven: Yale University Press, 2002); Jeffrey Veidlinger, *In the Shadow of the Shtetl: Small-Town Jewish Life in Soviet Ukraine* (Bloomington: Indiana University Press, 2013).

23. Ben Cion Pinchuk, "Jewish Discourse and the Shtetl," *Jewish History* 15, no. 2 (June 2001), 170; Raphael Mahler, *Hasidism and the Jewish Enlightenment: Their Confrontation in Galicia and Poland in the First Half of the Nineteenth Century* (Philadelphia: Jewish Publication Society of America, 1985); Christoph Gassenschmidt, *Jewish Liberal Politics in Tsarist Russia, 1900–14: The Modernization of Russian Jewry* (New York: New York University Press, 1995); Steven Zipperstein, *The Jews of Odessa: A Cultural History, 1794–1881* (Stanford: Stanford University Press, 1985).

24. Becker, "HOW UNJEWISH!," *TM*, January 1916, cover.

25. Editorial, *TM*, January 1916, 1.

26. Berkowitz, *Western Jewry and the Zionist Project*, 20.

27. Five images illustrated an article by Nahum Sokolow, "Poland and the Jews," *TM*, October 1915, 94–96.

28. "Whither?," "Between the Hammer and the Anvil (An Appeal to the Hammer)," *TM*, November 1915, 122, 124.

29. "On the March," *TM*, January 1916, 6.

30. "Weary Wanderers" and "Goluth," *TM*, December 1915, 149, 151.

31. S. Maud, "For Whom?," *TM*, March 1916, cover.

32. Shmarya Levin, "The Living Dead," *TM*, March 1916, 54.

33. Becker, "Zion: Out of the Jungle!," *TM*, April 1916, cover.

34. Baer Epstein, "The Jewish National Fund," *TM*, April 1916, 89–90, 92.

35. For examples, see: *Yemenite Jew*, a painting by Hermann Struck, printed alongside James Salmark, "Hermann Struck: An Impression of Palestine's Foremost Jewish Painter," *NP*, November 25, 1927, 420; *A Yemenite Jew*, etching by Hermann Struck, provided as illustration for Jessie Sampter's story, "On the Stage and in Life: A Little Drama," *NP*, February 24, 1928, 228; Untitled image, *NP*, June 29, 1928, cover; "A Palestinian Jew," *NP*, September 7–14, 1928, cover.

36. Noah Isenberg, "To Pray Like a Dervish: Orientalist Discourse in Arnold Zweig's *The Face of East European Jewry*," in *Orientalism and the Jews*, 94–108.

37. For example, see A. Coralnik, "Jewish Hands: Relevant and Irrelevant Thoughts on the Struck Exhibition," including the etchings, *Havdalah* and *Kiddush*, *NP*, May 4, 1928, 485–486.

38. Reprinted courtesy of the *Scientific American*, Ernest Beaumont, "Farming in Palestine," images "Primitive Arab Farming," "Modern Jewish Farming Methods," *TM*, October 1915, 102–104.

39. "On Their Way," "Laborers," *NP*, March 9, 1923, iii–iv.

40. Joseph Brainin, "In the Land of the Koran: Ibn Sa'ud, 'The Story Petrel of the Arab Desert,'" *NP*, March 21, 1928, 338.

41. Peleg, *Orientalism*, 15–18, 40–74.

42. For just a few examples in addition to the aforementioned articles, which have included many images of farming, see Ittamar Ben-Avi, "The Founder of Mikveh Israel," *NP*, May 18, 1928, 540, 556; J. Rebelsky, "Industries in the Colonies," *NP*, November 2, 1928, 339–340; "The Girls' Training Farms," *NP*, December 21, 1928, 524.

43. Berkowitz, *Western Jewry and the Zionist Project*, 95.

44. Ivan Davidson Kalmar, "Jesus Did Not Wear a Turban: Orientalism, the Jews, and Christian Art," *Orientalism and the Jews*, 7, 10, 16.

45. Kalmar, "Jesus Did Not Wear a Turban," 3, 20.

46. For one example of an Arab, see "Ibn Saud," *NP*, March 21, 1928, 338. For one example of a Jew, see "An Immigration Camp," *NP*, March 9, 1923, v.

47. Smith, "Differential Equations," in *Relating Religion*, 230–239, 245–246.

48. Rafael Medoff, *Zionism and the Arabs: An American Jewish Dilemma, 1898–1948* (Westport: Praeger, 1997), 21–53; Lawrence Davidson, *America's Palestine: Popular and Official Perceptions from Balfour to Israeli Statehood* (Gainesville: University Press of Florida, 2001), 91–100.

49. Barbie Zelizer, *Remembering to Forget: Holocaust Memory through the Camera's Eye* (Chicago: University of Chicago Press, 1998), 33.

50. Adeed Dawisha, *Arab Nationalism in the Twentieth Century: From Triumph to Despair* (Princeton: Princeton University Press, 2003), 75–117.

51. *NP*, September 6, 1929, 140.

52. Berkowitz, *Western Jewry and the Zionist Project*, 94.

53. Richard I. Cohen, *Jewish Icons: Art and Society in Modern Europe* (Berkeley: University of California Press, 1998), 170.

54. Zerubavel, *Recovered Roots*, 92.

55. "The Chassidim in the Emek," *NP*, March 30, 1928, 373.

56. *NP*, May 14, 1926, xvi–xvii.

57. Anita Shapira, "The Fashioning of the 'New Jew' in the Yishuv Society," in *Major Changes within the Jewish People in the Wake of the Holocaust* (Jerusalem: Yad Vashem, 1996), 428–430.

58. Shapira, "Fashioning of the 'New Jew,'" 431–441.

59. "Scenes of Palestine Life," *NP*, November 16, 1934, 5.

60. "Chalutzim Erecting New Government Building at Ramallah," "Blazing the Trail—Chalutzim Migrating to a New Colony," *NP*, October 31, 1924, 275–277; "Chalutzim Engaged in Sinking a Well," *NP*, October 12, 1928, 236; "It Is the Chalutz-Immigrant That Builds the Country," *NP*, December 15, 1928, 489–490; "The New Pioneers in the Jewish Homeland," *NP*, September 11, 1936, 9.

61. Louis Golding, "Olive-Tree and Windy Hill: Pioneers Who Made the Supreme Sacrifice," *NP*, November 25, 1927, 417; "Split Tel Hai Fete to Avoid

Clashes: Separate Dates Set for Labor and Revisionist Pilgrimages to Trumpeldor's Grave," *NP*, March 8, 1935, 1; "Trumpeldor of Tel Hai," *NP*, March 8, 1935, 4; Max Rudensky, "15 Years after Tel Hai: A Personal Recollection of the 'Father of the Chalutz Movement,' " *NP*, March 8, 1935, 5.

62. Mark Raider, *The Emergence of American Zionism* (New York: New York University Press, 1998), 69–124.

63. Jodi Eichler-Levine, *Suffer the Little Children: Uses of the Past in Jewish and African American Children's Literature* (New York: New York University Press, 2013), 113.

64. George L. Mosse, *Nationalism and Sexuality: Middle-Class Morality and Sexual Norms in Modern Europe* (Madison: University of Wisconsin Press, 1985), 149–150; cited in Daniel Boyarin, *Unheroic Conduct: The Rise of Heterosexuality and the Invention of the Jewish Man* (Berkeley: University of California Press, 1997), 291.

65. "Ghaffirs Who Guard the Settlements: Intrepid Band of Jewish Men Help to Protect the Outlying Suburbs," *NP*, July 17, 1936, 13.

66. "With Zionist Youth," *NP*, November 1, 1940, 12.

67. For more on Reform and other Jewish summer camps, see Michael Lorge and Gary Phillip Zola, eds., *A Place of Our Own: The Rise of Reform Jewish Camping* (Tuscaloosa: University of Alabama Press, 2006).

68. "Beginning of an Epic of Rebuilding in Zion," *NP*, May 24, 1935, 3.

69. For one example, see "Bringing Health to Palestine," "Corps of Nurses, Hadassah Medical Organization," *NP*, March 9, 1923, x–xi.

70. "Woman in Palestine on Guard," *NP*, November 17, 1939, 1.

71. "An American Chalutz at Ain Ha'shofat," *NP*, November 4, 1938, 6.

72. Berkowitz, *Western Jewry and the Zionist Project*, 92–95.

73. "U.S. Chalutzim Dance Hora as They Sail for Palestine," *NP*, May 31, 1935, 3.

Chapter 3

1. All of the calendars are available at the Klau Library and American Jewish Archives at Hebrew Union College in Cincinnati.

2. Riv-Ellen Prell, "The Vision of Woman in Classical Reform Judaism," *Journal of the American Academy of Religion* 50, no. 4 (December 1982): 575–589.

3. Karla Goldman, *Beyond the Synagogue Gallery: Finding a Place for Women in American Judaism* (Cambridge: Harvard University Press, 2000), 2–37; Pamela Nadell and Rita Simon, "Ladies of the Sisterhood: Women in the American Reform Synagogue, 1900–1930," in *Active Voices: Women in Jewish Culture*, ed. Maurie Sacks (Urbana: University of Illinois Press, 1995), 63–64; Pamela Nadell, " 'The Synagog Shall Hear the Call of the Sister': Carrie Simon and the Founding of the NFTS," in *Sisterhood: A Centennial History of Women of Reform Judaism*, ed.

Carole B. Balin, Dana Herman, Jonathan D. Sarna, and Gary P. Zola (Cincinnati: Hebrew Union College Press, 2013), 19.

4. Friesel, "The Meaning of Zionism," 176.

5. Barbara Kirshenblatt-Gimblett, "From Ethnology to Heritage: The Role of the Museum," in *Museum Studies: An Anthology of Contexts*, ed. Bettina Messias Carbonell (Malden: Blackwell, 2012), 199.

6. "Report of the National Committee on Hebrew Union Scholarships," January 19, 1915, 70, *Proceedings of the National Federation of Temple Sisterhoods*, MS-73, Box A-1, Vol. 1, Jacob Rader Marcus Center of the American Jewish Archives.

7. Jenna Weissman Joselit, *The Wonders of America: Reinventing Jewish Culture, 1880–1950* (New York: Henry Holt and Company, 1994), 154, 161.

8. Joellyn Wallen Zollman, "Constructing Identity: Gift Shops and the NFTS Campaign for Home Observance," in *Sisterhood: A Centennial History of Women of Reform Judaism*, ed. Carole B. Balin, Dana Herman, Jonathan D. Sarna, and Gary P. Zola (Cincinnati: Hebrew Union College Press, 2013), 159–160, 165, 172.

9. Joselit, *Wonders of America*, 155–156; Zollman, "Constructing Identity," 166.

10. Gilya Gerda Schmidt, *The Art and Artists of the Fifth Zionist Congress, 1901: Heralds of a New Age* (Syracuse: Syracuse University Press, 2003), 48–49.

11. Schmidt, *Fifth Zionist Congress*, 47.

12. Sara Lipton, "Unfeigned Witness: Jews, Matter, and Vision in Twelfth-Century Christian Art," in *Judaism and Christian Art: Aesthetic Anxieties from the Catacombs to Colonialism*, ed. Herbert Kessler and David Nirenberg (Philadelphia: University of Pennsylvania Press, 2011), 45.

13. Arnold Eisen, *Rethinking Modern Judaism: Ritual, Commandment, Community* (Chicago: University of Chicago Press, 1998), 157–158, 166.

14. Eisen, *Rethinking Modern Judaism*, 176–177.

15. Milly Heyd, "Illustrations in Early Editions of the *Tsene-Urene*: Jewish Adaptations of Christian Sources," *Journal of Jewish Art* 10 (1984): 64–86.

16. Cohen, *Jewish Icons*, 160.

17. Cohen, *Jewish Icons*, 70–74, 91.

18. Colleen McDannell, *Material Christianity: Religion and Popular Culture in America* (New Haven: Yale University Press, 1995), 4–6, 68; Catherine Albanese, *A Republic of Mind and Spirit: A Cultural History of American Metaphysical Religion* (New Haven: Yale University Press, 2007), 4–17.

19. Lipton, "Unfeigned Witness," 46–49.

20. "Report of the National Committee on Religion," January 19, 1915, 61, *Proceedings of the National Federation of Temple Sisterhoods*, MS-73, Box A-1, Vol. 1, American Jewish Archives.

21. Ivan Marcus, *The Jewish Life Cycle: Rites of Passage from Biblical to Modern Times* (Seattle: University of Washington Press, 2004), 5–9, 51.

22. Susannah Heschel, "Jewish Studies as Counterhistory," in *Insider/Outsider: American Jews and Multiculturalism*, ed. David Biale, Michael Galchinsky, and Susannah Heschel (Berkeley: University of California Press, 1998), 105.

23. Heschel, "Jewish Studies as Counterhistory," 101–103.

24. "Report of the National Committee on Union Museum," Buffalo, 1921, 28, *Proceedings of the National Federation of Temple Sisterhoods Volume I 1913–1923* (1923), MS-73, Box A-1, Vol. 1, American Jewish Archives.

25. Bruce Feiler, *America's Prophet: Moses and the American Story* (New York: HarperCollins, 2009).

26. Schmidt, *Art and Artists of the Fifth Zionist Congress*, 33–38.

27. "An den Wassern zu Babylon saßen wir und weinen, wenn wir an Zion gedachten."

28. Jenny Franchot, *Roads to Rome: The Antebellum Protestant Encounter with Catholicism* (Berkeley: University of California Press, 1994), 34, 57–67, 81.

29. Burke Long, *Imagining the Holy Land: Maps, Models, and Fantasy Travels* (Bloomington: Indiana University Press, 2003), see especially 33, 69, 158–160.

30. "Art Calendar for 5697: Drawings by Hella Arensen," Cincinnati: National Federation of Temple Sisterhoods, 1936; and "Refugee's Art Work in New Calendar," *Topics and Trends* (March–April 1936): 3, Women of Reform Judaism Records, MS-73, Box 69, Folder 2, American Jewish Archives.

31. Howard Greenstein, *Turning Point: Zionism and Reform Judaism* (Chico, CA: Scholars Press, 1981), 24–30; 1937 Columbus Platform, CCAR, http://ccarnet.org/rabbis-speak/platforms/guiding-principles-reform-judaism/, accessed May 21, 2013.

32. On Zionism and masculinity, see Boyarin, *Unheroic Conduct*, 271–312; David Biale, *Eros and the Jews: From Biblical Israel to Contemporary America* (Berkeley: University of California Press, 1997), 176–203; Paula Hyman, *Gender and Assimilation in Modern Jewish History: The Roles and Presentations of Women* (Seattle: University of Washington Press, 1995), 134–169.

33. Wenger, *History Lessons*, 58–95; Lauren Love, "Performing Jewish Nationhood: *The Romance of a People* at the 1933 Chicago World's Fair," *TDR: The Drama Review* 55, no. 3 (Fall 2011): 57–67.

34. Ismar Elbogen, *Jewish Liturgy: A Comprehensive History* (Philadelphia: Jewish Publication Society of America, 1993), 26–28.

35. Kalman Bland, *The Artless Jew: Medieval and Modern Affirmations and Denials of the Visual* (Princeton: Princeton University Press, 200), 3–14, 59–60.

Chapter 4

1. "Temple, Plan of the Second" and "The Court of Priests," *Jewish Encyclopedia*, vol. 12 (New York: Funk & Wagnalls, 1905), 92.

2. Frederick N. Bohrer, *Orientalism and Visual Culture* (Cambridge: Cambridge University Press, 2003).

3. Joseph Jacobs, *The Jewish Encyclopedia: A Guide to Its Contents* (New York: Funk & Wagnalls, 1906), 118–134.

4. Jacobs, *The Jewish Encyclopedia*, 122.

5. Shuly Rubin Schwartz, *The Emergence of Jewish Scholarship in America: The Publication of the "Jewish Encyclopedia"* (Cincinnati: Hebrew Union College Press, 1991), 19–59.

6. Barry Trachtenberg, "From Edification to Commemoration: *Di Algemeyne Entsiklopedye*, the Holocaust and the Changing Mission of Yiddish Scholarship," *Journal of Modern Jewish Studies* 5, no. 3 (November 2006), 286; Jeffrey Veidlinger, "From Ashkenaz to Zionism: Putting Eastern European Jewish Life in (Alphabetical) Order," *AJS Review* 33, no. 2 (November 2009): 379–382.

7. Kirsten Belgum, "Translated Knowledge in the Early Nineteenth Century: Jews and Judaism in Brockhaus' *Conversation-Lexikon* and the *Encyclopedia Americana*," *Jahrbuch des Simon-Dubnow-Instituts* 9 (2010): 307–308.

8. Immanuel Wolf, "In the Concept of a Science of Judaism" (1822), in *Ideas of Jewish History*, ed. with introduction and notes by Michael A. Meyer (New York: 1974), 143; cited in Schwartz, *Jewish Scholarship*, 3.

9. "The Temple Area," "Court of Priests," and "Holy of Holies of the Temple at Jerusalem" (all reconstructed by Chipiez), *JE*, vol. 12 (1905), 90–92.

10. Charles Chipiez and Georges Perrot, *Histoire de l'art dans l'Antiquité, Égypte, Assyrie, Perse, Asie mineure, Grèce, Etrurie, Rome*, vol. 4: *Judée, Sardaigne, Syrie, Cappadoce* (Paris: 1887); *History of Art in Sardinia, Judaea, Syria, and Asia Minor*, vol. 1, ed. and trans. I. Gonino (London: 1890); *Le Temple de Jérusalem et la Maison du Bois-Liban restitués d'après Ézéchiel et le Livre des Rois* (Paris: 1889); cited in Sergey R. Kravtsov, "Reconstruction of the Temple by Charles Chipiez and Its Applications in Architecture," *Ars Judaica* (2008): 25–26.

11. Chipiez and Perrot, *History of Art*, 200, 222–241; cited in Kravtsov, "Reconstruction of the Temple," 26–27.

12. Crawford H. Toy, "Ezekiel," *Encyclopedia Britannica*, 11th ed., vol. 10 (Cambridge: 1911), 104; cited in Kravtsov, "Reconstruction of the Temple," 28. Additionally, Chipiez and Perrot influenced Joseph Barsky's design for the original Herzliya Gymnasium in Tel Aviv. Kravtsov, "Reconstruction of the Temple," 36–41.

13. Jacobs, *The Jewish Encyclopedia*, 81–101.

14. "The Temple at Jerusalem," "Utensils of the Temple," "Greek Inscription, Found on Site of the Temple Area, Forbidding Gentiles to Enter within the Inner Temple Walls," *JE*, vol. 12 (1905), 82, 83, 85.

15. Judah David Eisenstein, "Temple, Administration of," *JE*, vol. 12 (1905), 81.

16. Eisenstein, "Temple in Rabbinic Literature," *JE*, vol. 12 (1905), 96.

17. Rachel Neis, *The Sense of Sight in Rabbinic Culture: Jewish Ways of Seeing in Late Antiquity* (Cambridge: Cambridge University Press, 2013), 22.

18. Denise Piezynski, "Biographical Note" to the George A. Barton Papers, The University Archives and Records Center, University of Pennsylvania, November 1989, http://www.archives.upenn.edu/faids/upt/upt50/bartonga_guide.pdf, accessed August 17, 2012.

19. "Substructure of Temple of Herod, Now Called 'Solomon's Stables,' " from a photograph by the American Colony at Jerusalem; "View of the Temple of Solomon," reconstructed by Schick; "Sectional View of the Temple of Herod, Looking South," reconstructed by Sanday; "Column from the Temple of Herod," from a Palestine Exploration Fund photograph, *JE*, vol. 12 (1905), 86–89.

20. Frederick N. Bohrer, *Photography and Archaeology* (London: Reaktion Books, 2011), 15.

21. Bohrer, *Photography and Archaeology*, 22–23.

22. Alan Balfour, *Solomon's Temple: Myth, Conflict, and Faith* (Hoboken: Wiley, 2012), 208–209.

23. Arnold M. Eisen, "Off Center: The Concept of the Land of Israel in Modern Jewish Thought," in *The Land of Israel: Jewish Perspectives*, ed. Lawrence A. Hoffman (South Bend: University of Notre Dame Press, 1986), 263–296, especially 266.

24. "The Hereford Mappa Mundi, 1280, Showing Jerusalem in the Center of the World," G., "Jerusalem—Ancient," *JE*, vol. 7 (1904), 129.

25. Shai Ginsburg, *Rhetoric and Nation: The Formation of Hebrew National Culture, 1880–1990* (Syracuse: Syracuse University Press, 2014), 111–118.

26. Martin A. Meyer, "Jerusalem—Modern," *JE*, vol. 7 (1904), 149.

27. "Square Outside the Jaffa Gate, Jerusalem (from a Photograph by Dr. W. Popper)," *JE*, vol. 7, 150.

28. "Damascus Gate, Jerusalem (from a photograph by the American Colony, Jerusalem)," "The Golden Gate from within the City of Jerusalem (from a photograph by Bonfils)," "Zion Gate, Jerusalem (from a photograph by Bonfils)," "The Haram Area, Site of the Temple (from a photograph by Bonfils)," *JE*, vol. 7 (1904), 150–153.

29. *Remembrances of the Near East: The Photographs of Bonfils, 1867–1907*, exhibition prepared by Robert A. Sobieszek and Carney E. S. Gavin, International Museum of Photography at George Eastman House and the Harvard Semitic Museum, 1980, 6–8.

30. *Remembrances of the Near East*, 5.

31. Bohrer, *Photography and Archaeology*, 28.

32. "A Typical Street in Jerusalem (from a photograph by Bonfils)," *JE*, vol. 7 (1904), 154.

33. Meyer, "Jerusalem—Modern," *JE*, vol. 7 (1904), 150.

34. David Levy, "The Making of the *Encyclopaedia Judaica* and *The Jewish Encyclopedia*," in *Proceedings of the 37th Annual Convention of the Association of*

Jewish Libraries (Denver: June 2002), http://www.jewishlibraries.org/main/Portals/0/AJL_Assets/documents/Publications/proceedings/proceedings2002/levy.pdf, 4–5, accessed October 15, 2012.

35. "Map of Western Russia Showing the Jewish Pale of Settlement," *JE*, vol. 10 (1905), 531.

36. Herman Rosenthal, "Russia—Poland," *JE*, vol. 10 (1905), 562–563.

37. "General View of the Rishon Le-Zion Colony Palestine," "General View of Zikron Ya'akob Colony, Palestine," "Administration Building of the Zikron Ya'akob Colony," "General View of Rehoboth Colony, Palestine," "General View of Metullah Colony, Palestine," by I. Raffalovich and M. E. Sachs; map of "Jewish Agricultural Colonies in Palestine," by J. D. Eisenstein, *JE*, vol. 1 (1901), 246–252.

38. "Division of Fields in Modern Palestine," by Bonfils; "Plowing and Hoeing," from Wilkinson "Ancient Egyptians"; "Plowing in Palestine," after Benzinger, "Hebräische Archäologie." Images alongside "Agriculture—Historical Aspects," *JE*, vol. 1 (1901), 262–266.

39. In Argentina: "Mauricio—Russo-Jewish Colony in the Argentina Republic," "Mauricio—Administration Buildings," "Mauricio—Group of Colonists," "Clara Colony—Children on Horseback Starting for School," *JE*, vol. 1 (1901), 241–244; in the United States: "General View of Woodbine Colony, New Jersey," "The Schoolhouse, Woodbine Colony, New Jersey," "The Band of the Woodbine Colony," *JE*, vol. 1 (1901), 256–262.

40. "Bedouin Tent," from a photograph by Bonfils, *JE* vol. 12 (1905), 105; "Village Wells in Use in Palestine," *JE*, vol. 12 (1905), 499.

41. "Tashlik Ceremony in Galicia," *JE*, vol. 12 (1905), 66 (plate).

42. "Interior of the Great Synagogue at Teheran," from a photograph by E. N. Adler, *JE*, vol. 12 (1905), 73; "Interior of a Bet Ha-Midrash at Tripoli," from a painting by Israel Gentz, *JE*, vol. 12 (1905), 262.

43. "Costume of German Jews of the Thirteenth Century," from Herrad von Landsperg, "Luftgarten"; "German Jew of the Early Sixteenth Century," after Hans Burgkmair; "Jews of the Upper Rhine, End of Sixteenth Century," from the Basel "Stammbuch," 1612; "Costume of a Jew of Swabia, Early Seventeenth Century," after Daniel Meisner, "Politica Politice," 1700; "An English Jew of the Stock Exchange," from a caricature of the early eighteenth century; "Tunis Jewess in Street Costume," after a photograph; "Costume of a Jew of Algiers," from a photograph; "Jewess of Brusa, Turkey," after Racinet; "French Rabbi in Official Garb," from a photograph; "Costumes of Jews"; "Jews of Jerusalem," from a photograph by the American Colony, Jerusalem; "Jews of Constantinople, Eighteenth Century, Celebrating the Feast of Tabernacles," from an old print; "Rabbi of the Orient," from a photograph; "Jew of Kolomea, Austrian Galicia," after a photograph; "Jews of the Caucasus in Native Costume," after a photograph by Orden; "Polish Jewess and Jew of the Eighteenth Century," after La Prince, 1765; "Warsaw Jew and Jewess of the Early Nineteenth Century," from Hollaenderski, "Les Israelites de Pologne"; "Hassid

and Wife of the Early Nineteenth Century," from Hollaenderski, "Les Israelites de Pologne," *JE*, vol. 4 (1902), 293–303.

44. "Tunisian Jewess," "Tunisian Jewess," "Tunisian Jewesses, "Jewish Girls of Tunis," "Jews of Tunis in Native Costume," "Jewish Cemetery at Tunis," *JE*, vol. 12 (1905), 271–276.

45. "Types, Anthropological," *JE*, vol. 12 (1905), 293.

46. "Types, Anthropological," *JE*, vol. 12 (1905), 294 (plate).

47. *JE*, vol. 12 (1905), 293–294.

48. Jose Estrugo, "The Jewish Encyclopedia," *The American Israelite*, January 14, 1926, 5.

Chapter 5

1. Meyer Weisgal, *Meyer Weisgal . . . So Far: An Autobiography* (London: Weidenfeld and Nicolson, 1971), 109.

2. Rabbi Felix S. Mendelsohn, "Topics of the Week," *Sentinel*, Chicago, June 29, 1933, 5.

3. Barbara Kirshenblatt-Gimblett, "Performing the State: The Jewish Palestine Pavilion at the New York World's Fair, 1939/40," in *The Art of Being Jewish in Modern Times*, ed. Barbara Kirshenblatt-Gimblett and Jonathan Karp (Philadelphia: University of Pennsylvania Press, 2008), 98.

4. Kirshenblatt-Gimblett, "Performing the State," 99, 101.

5. Louis Mann and Gerson Levi, *Glimpses of the Jewish Exhibit in the Hall of Religion* (1933), 2. Material Distributed by Exhibitors, Box 22, Folder 16-309, Century of Progress Collection, University of Illinois at Chicago Special Collections.

6. Mann and Levi, *Glimpses of the Jewish Exhibit*.

7. Mann and Levi, *Glimpses of the Jewish Exhibit*.

8. Mann and Levi, *Glimpses of the Jewish Exhibit*.

9. Barbara Kirshenblatt-Gimblett, *Destination Culture: Tourism, Museums, and Heritage* (Berkeley: University of California Press, 1998), 118.

10. David Glassberg, *American Historical Pageantry: The Uses of Tradition in the Early Twentieth Century* (Chapel Hill: University of North Carolina Press, 1990), 1–3, 120–122; cited in and quoted from Stephen J. Whitfield, "The Politics of Pageantry, 1936–1946," *American Jewish History* 84, no. 3 (1996): 221.

11. David Waldstreicher, *In the Midst of Perpetual Fetes: The Making of American Nationalism, 1776–1820* (Chapel Hill: University of North Carolina Press, 1997), 3–19.

12. Haya Bar-Itzhak, *Jewish Poland: Legends of Origin—Ethnopoetics and Legendary Chronicles* (Detroit: Wayne State University Press, 2001), 28–34, 42–88. Beth Wenger has also noted the importance of Polish legends for Jewish settlement in Poland and alternative myths told by Jews in Amsterdam to articulate their place in Dutch society. Wenger, *History Lessons*, 21–22.

13. Wenger, *History Lessons*, 58–95.

14. Earl Mullin, "Holiday Throng at Fair Nears Monday Record: Morning Turnout Biggest So Far Admitted," *Chicago Daily Tribune*, July 5, 1933, 5.

15. "Pageant to Be Presented Here," *Los Angeles Times*, June 15, 1934, 14.

16. James O'Donnell Bennett, "125,000 Witness Jewish Spectacle: Mighty Drama Traces History Back 4,000 Yrs.," *Chicago Daily Tribune*, July 4, 1933, 1.

17. John Evans, "Fisher Explains the Idea Back [sic] of Jewish Pageant: Christian Friends Tell of Cooperation," *Chicago Daily Tribune*, June 21, 1933, 13.

18. "20,000 See Pageant of Jewish History," *New York Times*, September 25, 1933, 3.

19. Rev. John Evans, "Pageant Tells 4,000 Year Epic of a Great Race," *Chicago Daily Tribune*, July 2, 1933, 3.

20. Evans, "Fisher Explains the Idea Back of Jewish Pageant," 13.

21. Bennett, "125,000 Witness Jewish Spectacle," 4.

22. "Jewish Pageant to Use Vast Stage: Almost Entire Playing Field at Polo Grounds to Be Covered by Platforms," *New York Times*, September 3, 1933, N1.

23. "Jewish Pageant to Use Vast Stage," N1.

24. Bennett, "125,000 Witness Jewish Spectacle," 4.

25. My language for describing and concept of nationalism is here influenced by the *Stanford Encyclopedia of Philosophy*'s entry on nationalism, http://plato.stanford.edu/entries/nationalism/, first published November 29, 2001; substantive revision June 1, 2010, accessed December 5, 2011.

26. Solomon Goldman, "The Visionary on the Mountaintop," in *"The Romance of a People": A Pageant-Drama in Observance of Jewish Day at a Century of Progress*, ed. David Hirsch (Chicago: 1933; reprinted by the Chicago Jewish Historical Society, 2000), 5–16.

27. Helena Ruth Kirstein (née Marks), *The Romance of a People* scrapbook, 1933, American Jewish Historical Society Archives P-857, Box 1.

28. Evans, "Pageant Tells 4,000 Year Epic of a Great Race," 3; "Ball Park Pageantry," *New York Times*, September 10, 1933, X2.

29. "Dudele" performance, image reprinted in *Chicago Jewish History* newsletter, 2000.

30. Helena Ruth Kirstein (née Marks), *The Romance of a People* scrapbook, 1933, American Jewish Historical Society Archives, P-857, Box 1.

31. Evans, "Pageant Tells 4,000 Year Epic of a Great Race," 3.

32. Goldman, "The Visionary on the Mountaintop," 5–16.

33. Zerubavel, *Recovered Roots*, 39–76, 84–95.

34. "Jewish Pageant to Use Vast Stage," N1.

35. Steven Rosenthal, "Long-Distance Nationalism: American Jews, Zionism, and Israel," in *The Cambridge Companion to American Judaism*, ed. Dana Evan Kaplan (Cambridge: Cambridge University Press, 2005), 222.

36. John Evans, "3,600 Jews Hold Full Rehearsal of Fete Tonight," *Chicago Daily Tribune*, June 25, 1933, 10.

37. "Chorus of 1,200 Meets Director of Jewish Fete," *Chicago Daily Tribune*, April 28, 1933, 9.

38. "Pageant to Depict Rise of Religion: Cast of 3,500 on Jewish Day at Chicago Fair Will Enact 'The Romance of a People,'" *New York Times*, June 11, 1933, N1. The paragraph quoting Fisher was also printed two days earlier in Chicago. John Evans, "Jewish Pageant to Depict 40 Centuries of Religion," *Chicago Daily Tribune*, June 9, 1933, 10.

39. "Pageant to Depict Rise of Religion," N1.

40. Evans, "Jewish Pageant to Depict 40 Centuries of Religion," 10.

41. Evans, "Pageant Tells 4,000 Year Epic of a Great Race," 3.

42. Evans, "Fisher Explains the Idea Back of Jewish Pageant," 13.

43. Evans, "Jewish Pageant to Depict 40 Centuries of Religion," 10.

44. Evans, "Fisher Explains the Idea Back of Jewish Pageant," 13.

45. Mark Silk, "Notes on the Judeo-Christian Tradition in America," *American Quarterly* 36, no. 1 (Spring 1984): 64–85; cited in Stephen Prothero, *American Jesus: How the Son of God Became a National Icon* (New York: Farrar, Straus and Giroux, 2003), 258–259.

46. "Zionist Convention in Chicago Will Delegate to the World Congress Today," *Forverts*, July 4, 1933, 1 (Yiddish).

47. "Zionist Convention in Chicago Will Delegate to the World Congress Today," 1; [Advertisement] *Forverts*, September 1, 1933, 2 (Yiddish); [Full-page Advertisement] *Forverts*, September 2, 1933, 2 (Yiddish); "Biggest Stage in America Constructed in New York Jewish Performance," *Forverts*, September 9, 1933, 16 (Yiddish and English image captions); "Six Thousand Take Part in the Giant Spectacle This Evening," *Forverts*, September 14, 1933, 12 (Yiddish and English image captions).

48. [Advertisement] *Forverts*, September 1, 1933, 2 (Yiddish).

49. "Six Thousand Take Part in the Giant Spectacle This Evening," 12 (Yiddish and English image captions); "The Romance of a People," *Forverts*, September 13, 1933, 2 (Yiddish and English image captions).

50. [Full-page advertisement] *Forverts*, September 2, 1933, 2 (Yiddish).

51. Whitfield, "Politics of Pageantry," 224–225.

52. "Women Prepare for Jewish Day at World's Fair," *Chicago Daily Tribune*, June 3, 1934, SW2; John Evans, "'Epic of a Nation' Rehearsals Are Begun by Jews: 400 Youths Train; Cast Has 5,000," *Chicago Daily Tribune*, July 16, 1964, 8.

53. One article reported "nearly 100,000" audience members, while another suggested forty-five thousand attended. "'Disloyal Aliens' Are Held Menace," *New York Times*, July 30, 1934, 3; John Evans, "'Epic of a Nation' Tells Story of Jews to 45,000: Great Pageant Traces Life for 4,000 Years," *Chicago Daily Tribune*, July 30, 1934, 6.

54. "800 See Preview of Features in 'Epic of a Nation,'" *Chicago Daily Tribune*, July 20, 1934, 13.

55. *1934 Jewish People's Day: The Epic of a Nation* Guidebook, Chicago, 1934, Chicago, Illinois, Jacob Rader Marcus Center of the American Jewish Archives, Nearprint—Geography, Box 1, File 1.

56. Evans, "Mighty Pageant Will Tell Story of Jews Tonight," 13.

57. Evans, "'Epic of a Nation' Rehearsals Are Begun by Jews," 8.

58. Evans, "'Epic of a Nation' Tells Story of Jews to 45,000," 6.

59. Edward Moore, "Music Program Depicts History of Jewish Race: Native Tunes Will Be Background for Hebrew Pageant at Soldiers' Field," *Chicago Daily Tribune*, July 29, 1934, D7.

60. Vivian B. Mann, *Jewish Texts on the Visual Arts* (Cambridge: Cambridge University Press, 2000), 4; Schmidt, *Art and Artists of the Fifth Zionist Congress*, 15; Bland, *Artless Jew*.

61. John Evans, "Noted American Jews on Way to Great Pageant: Special Trains Bringing Hundreds to City," *Chicago Daily Tribune*, July 28, 1934, 5.

62. Evans, "'Epic of a Nation' Tells Story of Jews to 45,000," 6; "Jewish Youths Rehearsing for Fair Spectacle," *Chicago Daily Tribune*, July 8, 1934, NW5.

63. "Jewish Youths Rehearsing for Fair Spectacle," NW5.

64. David Biale, "The Body and Sexuality in American Jewish Culture," in *The Cambridge Companion to American Judaism*, ed. Dana Evan Kaplan (Cambridge: Cambridge University Press, 2005), 255; Stephen Whitfield, "Unathletic Department," in *Jews, Sports, and the Rites of Citizenship*, ed. Jack Kugelmass (Urbana: University of Illinois Press, 2007), 56.

65. Letter to Hotel Allenby from M. P. Kerr, Asst. Director of Concessions—Century of Progress, February 6, 1933; Letter from March 6, 1933; Palestine—Information, Box 65, Folder 2-1170, Century of Progress Collection, University of Illinois at Chicago Special Collections.

66. "Oriental Village. Chicago World's Fair" and "Big Attractions at the Oriental Village," A Century of Progress, Chicago, 1933, postcards from the author's private collection.

Chapter 6

1. "Join the Circle of Palestine's Children," 1934, Box 1, Folder 5—Child Welfare Fund, 1920s–1940s, RG17—Printed Material—Pamphlets, Brochures, Booklets, American Jewish Historical Society at the Center for Jewish History.

2. Lee Edelman, *No Future: Queer Theory and the Death Drive* (Durham: Duke University Press, 2004), 8–9.

3. Edelman, *No Future*, 11.

4. Zemel, *Looking Jewish*, 76.

5. Anna Mae Duane, *Suffering Childhood in Early America: Violence, Race, and the Making of the Child Victim* (Athens: University of Georgia Press, 2010), n.p.; Eichler-Levine, *Suffer the Little Children*, 122.

6. Zemel, *Looking Jewish*, 37–38.

7. Deborah Dash Moore, "Hadassah in the United States," in *Jewish Women's Archive Encyclopedia*, https://jwa.org/encyclopedia/article/hadassah-in-united-states, accessed July 3, 2015.

8. Mary McCune, *"The Whole Wide World, without Limits": International Relief, Gender Politics, and American Jewish Women, 1893–1930* (Detroit: Wayne State University Press, 2005), 96.

9. Henrietta Szold to Alice Seligsberg, New York, January 7, 1920, in Marvin Lowenthal, ed., *Henrietta Szold: Life and Letters* (New York: Viking Press, 1942), 119; Erica B. Simmons, *Hadassah and the Zionist Project* (Lanham: Rowman & Littlefield, 2006), 21.

10. Joyce Antler, "Zion in Our Hearts: Henrietta Szold and the American Jewish Women's Movement," in *American Jewish Women's History: A Reader*, ed. Pamela Nadell (New York: New York University Press, 2003), 144.

11. Simmons, *Hadassah*, 29, 31, 35–36, 47, 49, 63.

12. "Report of the Proceedings of the First Annual Convention of the DAUGHTERS OF ZION OF AMERICA," 8, Box 1, Folder 1—1914. Hadassah Conventions (RG3), American Jewish Historical Society at the Center for Jewish History.

13. McCune, *"Whole Wide World,"* 114.

14. Moore, "Hadassah in the United States"; Simmons, *Hadassah*, 22.

15. "Report of the Proceedings of the First Annual Convention of the DAUGHTERS OF ZION OF AMERICA," 1, 4, Box 1, Folder 1—1914. Hadassah Conventions (RG3), American Jewish Historical Society at the Center for Jewish History.

16. "Report of the Proceedings," Box 1, Folder 3—1916. Hadassah Conventions (RG3), American Jewish Historical Society at the Center for Jewish History.

17. Liora Halperin, *Babel in Zion: Jews, Nationalism, and Language Diversity in Palestine, 1920–1948* (New Haven: Yale University Press, 2014), 163, 170.

18. Simmons, *Hadassah*, 22; "The Healing of the Daughter of My People," *TM*, May 1913, 135.

19. Rebecca Alpert, "Challenging Male/Female Complementarity: Jewish Lesbians and the Jewish Tradition," in *People of the Body: Jews and Judaism from an Embodied Perspective*, ed. Howard Eilberg-Schwartz (Albany: State University of New York Press, 1992), 362.

20. Alpert, "Challenging Male/Female Complementarity," 363.

21. Alpert, "Challenging Male/Female Complementarity," 365.
22. *Health Welfare*, 1934. Box 1, Folder 5—Child Welfare Fund, 1920s–1940s.
23. *Doorway to Life* . . . , Box 1, Folder 5—Child Welfare Fund, 1920s–1940s.
24. Amanda Porterfield, *American Religious History* (Malden: Blackwell, 2002), 2.
25. Porterfield, *American Religious History*, 5.
26. *Hadassah Mothers the Children of Erez-Israel*, printed at Goldeberg's Press; blocks by M. Pikovsky, Jerusalem; supervision and photos by J. Schweig, Jerusalem, 1933, RG17 Pamphlets, Child Welfare Fund, 1930s, 1940s, Hadassah, WZOA, American Jewish Historical Society at the Center for Jewish History.
27. Bohrer, *Orientalism and Visual Culture*, 10–36.
28. Eichler-Levine, *Suffer the Little Children*, xix–xx.
29. *Escape to Life*, Box 1, Folder 5—Hadassah Youth Aliyah, American Jewish Historical Society at the Center for Jewish History.
30. "c/o Hadassah, U.S.A.," Box 1, Folder 5—Child Welfare Fund, 1920s–1940s, American Jewish Historical Society at the Center for Jewish History.
31. "c/o Hadassah, U.S.A.," Box 1, Folder 5—Child Welfare Fund, 1920s–1940s, American Jewish Historical Society at the Center for Jewish History.
32. Joselit, *Wonders of America*, 137, 139.
33. Anita Shapira, "Religious Motifs of the Labor Movement," in *Zionism and Religion*, ed. S. Almog, Jehuda Reinharz, and Anita Shapira (Hanover, NH: Brandeis University Press by the University Press of New England, 1998), 254; Halperin, *Babel in Zion*, 33.
34. Robert Orsi, *Between Heaven and Earth: The Religious Worlds People Make and the Scholars Who Study Them* (Princeton: Princeton University Press, 2006), 15.
35. Orsi, *Between Heaven and Earth*, 17, 77.

Conclusion

1. Immanuel Benzinger, "Art among the Ancient Hebrews," *JE*, vol. 2 (1902), 141.
2. Kaufmann Kohler, "Art, Attitude of Judaism Toward," *JE*, vol. 2 (1902), 142.
3. In addition to Talmudic passages, Eisenstein also cites later *responsim*, postrabbinic halakhic rulings that interpreted Jewish law and guided Jewish practice. Judah David Eisenstein, "Art in the Synagogue," *JE*, vol. 2 (1902), 143.
4. "Preface," *JE*, vol. 1 (1901), xix.
5. Bland, *Artless Jew*, 3–14.
6. Letter to Mrs. Julius Rosenwald, from New York, January 17, 1915, in Lowenthal, ed., *Henrietta Szold: Life and Letters*, 86–87.

7. Editorial, "The Wrong Symbol," *Jewish Daily Forward*, published online July 17, 2012, http://forward.com/articles/159252/the-wrong-symbol/, accessed July 23, 2012; print issue of July 20, 2012.

8. For example, *Life*, June 16, 1967, and June 23, 1967, http://books.google.com/books?id=lVYEAAAAMBAJ&source=gbs_all_issues_r&cad=1 and http://books.google.com/books?id=wlUEAAAAMBAJ&source=gbs_all_issues_r&cad=1, accessed March 15, 2011; "Hero of the Israelis: Itzhak Rabin," *New York Times*, June 8, 1967, 16; *Time*, June 16, 1967.

9. I Samuel 16: 12, *Tanakh* (Philadelphia: Jewish Publication Society of America, 1985); cited in Deborah Dash Moore, "From David to Goliath: American Representations of Jews around the Six-Day War," in *The Six-Day War and World Jewry*, ed. Eli Lederhendler (Bethesda: University of Maryland Press, 2000), 70–75.

10. Jack Shaheen, *Reel Bad Arabs: How Hollywood Vilifies a People* (Northampton: Olive Branch Press, 2001).

11. Yezid Sayigh, "Reflections on Al Nakba," *Journal of Palestine Studies* 28, no. 1 (Autumn 1998): 19–23; Emile Habibi, *The Six-Day Sextet* (*Sodasyyato-l-Ayyami-s-Sitta*) (Haifa: Dar Alitihad, 1968a) (Arabic); cited in Nurith Gertz and George Khleifi, *Palestinian Cinema: Landscape, Trauma, and Memory* (Bloomington: Indiana University Press, 2008), 1–2.

Bibliography

Archives

American Jewish Historical Society (Center for Jewish History)
Asher Library at Spertus Institute
Chicago Public Library
Dorot Jewish Division, New York Public Library
Jacob Rader Marcus Center of the American Jewish Archives
Klau Library at Hebrew Union College–Jewish Institute of Religion
University of Illinois at Chicago Special Collections
YIVO Institute for Jewish Research (Center for Jewish History)

Periodicals

Chicago Daily Tribune
Der Tog (Yiddish)
Forverts (Yiddish)
Jewish Daily Forward
Los Angeles Times
The Maccabaean
The New Palestine
New York Times
Sentinel

Published Primary Sources

1934 Jewish People's Day: The Epic of a Nation Guidebook. Chicago, 1934. Jacob Rader Marcus Center of the American Jewish Archives. Nearprint—Geography. Box 1. File 1.

Afro-American Encyclopaedia. Compiled by James T. Haley. Nashville: Haley & Florida, 1895.

Artemas Ward. *The Grocer's Encyclopedia*. New York: 1911.

Catholic Encyclopedia. New York: Robert Appleton Company, 1907–1912.

Chicago Jewish History 24, no. 3 (Summer 2000). Asher Library at Spertus Institute. Printed by the Chicago Jewish Historical Society.

Encyclopaedia Judaica.

Encyclopaedia of Missions. Edited by Edwin Munsell Bliss. New York: Funk & Wagnalls, 1891.

Goldman, Solomon. "The Visionary on the Mountaintop." In *"A Romance of a People": A Pageant-Drama in Observance of Jewish Day at A Century of Progress*, edited by David Hirsch. Chicago: 1933; reprinted by the Chicago Jewish Historical Society, 2000.

Hadassah Subconvention, Hadassah: The Women's Zionist Organization. Bulletin No. 12. July 1915. 7. Box 1. Folder 2. RG3 Hadassah Conventions. American Jewish Historical Society (Center for Jewish History).

———. 1917. 15. Box 1. Folder 4. RG3 Hadassah Conventions. American Jewish Historical Society (Center for Jewish History).

Herzl, Theodor. "A Solution of the Jewish Question." *Jewish Chronicle*, January 17, 1896, 12–13; reprinted in *The Jew in the Modern World*, 2nd ed., edited by Paul Mendes-Flohr and Jehuda Reinharz, 533–538. New York: Oxford University Press, 1995.

Jacobs, Joseph. *The Jewish Encyclopedia: A Guide to Its Contents*. New York: Funk & Wagnalls, 1906.

Jewish Encyclopedia. Edited by Isidore Singer. New York: Funk & Wagnalls, 1901–1906.

Judaism at the World's Parliament of Religions, vol. 1. Cincinnati: 1894.

Mann, Louis, and Gerson Levi. *Glimpses of the Jewish Exhibit in the Hall of Religion*. Chicago: 1933. Century of Progress Collection. University of Illinois at Chicago Special Collections.

New Schaff-Herzog Encyclopedia of Religious Knowledge, 1st ed. Edited by Philip Schaff. New York: Funk & Wagnalls, 1882–1884.

Official Pictures of a Century of Progress Exposition, Chicago, 1933. Chicago: Century of Progress International Exposition, 1933, 1934.

Opinions of the World's Press on Volume 1 of the Funk & Wagnalls Jewish Encyclopedia. New York: Funk & Wagnalls, 1901.

Proceedings of the National Federation of Temple Sisterhoods. Vol. 1, 1913–1923. Jacob Rader Marcus Center of the American Jewish Archives.

Pupils from Poor Homes. n.d. RG17—Printed Material—Pamphlets, Brochures, Booklets. 3–4. Box 1, Folder 5. Child Welfare Fund, 1920s–1940s. American Jewish Historical Society (Center for Jewish History).

Realencycklopädie für protestantische Theologie und Kirche. Edited by Johann Jakob Herzog. Hamburg: Rudolf Beffer, 1853–1868.
Schottenstein Edition of the Bavli Talmud. New York: Mesorah Publications, 2004.
The Sentinel History of Chicago Jewry. Chicago: Sentinel Publishing Company, 1961. Jacob Rader Marcus Center of the American Jewish Archives.
Szold, Henrietta. *Henrietta Szold: Life and Letters.* Edited by Marvin Lowenthal. London: Greenwood Press, 1976.
Weisgal, Meyer. . . . *Facts about the Jewish Palestine Pavilion at the N. Y. World's Fair—1939.* New York: Palestine Exhibits, 1939.
———. *Meyer Weisgal . . . So Far: An Autobiography.* London: Weidenfeld and Nicolson, 1971.

Secondary Sources

Abu-Lughod, Lila. "Do Muslim Women Really Need Saving? Anthropological Reflections on Cultural Relativism and Its Others." *American Anthropologist* 104, no. 3 (September 2002): 785–788.
Albanese, Catherine. *A Republic of Mind and Spirit: A Cultural History of American Metaphysical Religion.* New Haven: Yale University Press, 2007.
Alexander, Michael. *Jazz Age Jews.* Princeton: Princeton University Press, 2001.
Alpert, Rebecca. "Challenging Male/Female Complementarity: Jewish Lesbians and the Jewish Tradition." In *People of the Body: Jews and Judaism from an Embodied Perspective*, edited by Howard Eilberg-Schwartz, 361–377. Albany: State University of New York Press, 1992.
Alpert, Rebecca Trachtenberg. "Jewish Participation at the World's Parliament of Religions, 1893." In *Jewish Civilization: Essays and Studies*, vol. 1, edited by Ronald Brauner, 111–121. Philadelphia: Reconstructionist Rabbinical College, 1979.
Anderson, Benedict. *Imagined Communities: Reflections on the Origin and Spread of Nationalism.* New York: Verso, 2006.
Antler, Joyce. "Zion in Our Hearts: Henrietta Szold and the American Jewish Women's Movement." In *American Jewish Women's History: A Reader*, edited by Pamela Nadell, 129–149. New York: New York University Press, 2003.
Arav, Rami. "Archaeology in the Service of Ideology in Israel." In *"A Land Flowing with Milk and Honey": Visions of Israel from Biblical to Modern Times*, edited by Leonard Greenspoon and Ronald Simkins, 85–104. Omaha: Creighton University Press, 2001.
Axsom Adler, Jennifer. "The Other Witness: Nineteenth-Century American Protestantism and the Material Gospel Theology." Dissertation. Vanderbilt University, 2015.

Balfour, Alan. *Solomon's Temple: Myth, Conflict, and Faith.* Hoboken: Wiley, 2012.
Bar-Itzhak, Haya. *Jewish Poland: Legends of Origin—Ethnopoetics and Legendary Chronicles.* Detroit: Wayne State University Press, 2001.
Bayart, Jean-François. *The Illusion of Cultural Identity.* Chicago: University of Chicago Press, 2005.
Belgum, Kirsten. "Translated Knowledge in the Early Nineteenth Century: Jews and Judaism in Brockhaus' *Conversations-Lexikon* and the *Encyclopedia Americana*." *Jahrbuch des Simon-Dubnow-Instituts* 9 (2010): 303–322.
Ben Dov, Meir, Mordechai Naor, and Ze'ev Aner. *The Wailing Wall.* Tel Aviv: Ministry of Defense Publishing House, 1983.
Ben-Ur, Aviva. *Sephardic Jews in America: A Diasporic History.* New York: New York University Press, 2009.
Berkowitz, Michael. *Western Jewry and the Zionist Project, 1914–1933.* Cambridge: Cambridge University Press, 1997.
Berman, Lila Corwin. *Speaking of Jews: Rabbis, Intellectuals, and the Creation of an American Public Identity.* Berkeley: University of California Press, 2009.
Bernstein, Deborah, ed. *Pioneers and Homemakers: Jewish Women in Pre-State Israel.* Albany: State University of New York Press, 1992.
Biale, David. *Eros and the Jews: From Biblical Israel to Contemporary America.* Berkeley: University of California Press, 1997.
Bland, Kalman. *The Artless Jew: Medieval and Modern Affirmations and Denials of the Visual.* Princeton: Princeton University Press, 2000.
Blumenthal, David. "Where Does 'Jewish Studies' Belong?" *Journal of the American Academy of Religion* 44, no. 3 (September 1976): 535–546.
Bodian, Miriam. *Hebrews of the Portuguese Nation: Conversos and Community in Early Modern Amsterdam.* Bloomington: Indiana University Press, 1991.
Bohrer, Frederick N. *Orientalism and Visual Culture.* Cambridge: Cambridge University Press, 2003.
Boyarin, Daniel. *Unheroic Conduct: The Rise of Heterosexuality and the Invention of the Jewish Man.* Berkeley: University of California Press, 1997.
Brubaker, Rogers. *Ethnicity without Groups.* Cambridge: Harvard University Press, 2004.
Buber, Martin. "The Spirit of the Orient and Judaism." In *On Judaism*, edited by Nahum Glazer, 56–78. New York: Schocken Books, 1967.
Butler, Jon. *Awash in a Sea of Faith: Christianizing the American People.* Cambridge: Harvard University Press, 1990.
———. "Historiographical Heresy: Catholicism as a Model for American Religious History." In *Belief in History: Innovative Approaches to European and American Religion*, edited by Thomas A. Kselman, 286–309. Notre Dame: University of Notre Dame Press, 1991.
Butler, Judith. *Gender Trouble.* New York: Routledge Classics, 1990.

Carey, James W. *Communication as Culture: Essays on Media and Society*, rev. ed. New York: Routledge, 2009.

Carlebach, Elisheva. *Palaces of Time: Jewish Calendar and Culture in Early Modern Europe*. Cambridge: The Belknap Press of Harvard University Press, 2011.

Chipiez, Charles, and Georges Perrot. *Histoire de l'art dans l'Antiquité, Égypte, Assyrie, Perse, Asie mineure, Grèce, Etrurie, Rome, vol. 4: Judée, Sardaigne, Syrie, Cappadoce*. Paris: 1887.

———. *History of Art in Sardinia, Judaea, Syria, and Asia Minor*, vol. 1. Edited and translated by I. Gonino. London: 1890.

———. *Le Temple de Jérusalem et la Maison du Bois-Liban restitués d'après Ezéchiel et le Livre des Rois*. Paris: 1889.

Cohen, Naomi. *The Americanization of Zionism, 1897–1948*. Hanover, NH: Brandeis University Press, 2003.

———. *The Year After the Riots: American Responses to the Palestine Crisis of 1929–30*. Detroit: Wayne State University Press, 1988.

Cohen, Richard I. *Jewish Icons: Art and Society in Modern Europe*. Berkeley: University of California Press, 1998.

Damisch, Hubert. "Five Notes for a Phenomenology of the Photographic Image." In *Classic Essays in Photography*, edited by Alan Trachtenberg, 287–290. Stony Creek, CT: Leete's Island Books, 1980.

Davidson, Lawrence. *America's Palestine: Popular and Official Perceptions from Balfour to Israeli Statehood*. Gainesville: University Press of Florida, 2001.

———. "The Past as Prelude: Zionism and the Betrayal of American Democratic Principles, 1917–48." *Journal of Palestine Studies* 31, no. 3 (Spring 2002): 21–35.

Davis, John. "Catholic Envy: The Visual Culture of Protestant Desire." In *The Visual Culture of American Religions*, edited by David Morgan and Sally M. Promey, 107–128. Berkeley: University of California Press, 2001.

Dawisha, Adeed. *Arab Nationalism in the Twentieth Century: From Triumph to Despair*. Princeton: Princeton University Press, 2003.

Dawson, Nelson, ed. *Brandeis and America*. Lexington: University Press of Kentucky, 1989.

de Certeau, Michel. *The Practice of Everyday Life*. Berkeley: University of California Press, 1984.

Diner, Hasia. *The Jews of the United States, 1654–2000*. Berkeley: University of California Press, 2006.

Dinnerstein, Leonard. *Uneasy at Home: Antisemitism and the American Jewish Experience*. New York: Columbia University Press, 1987.

Duane, Anna Mae. *Suffering Childhood in Early America: Violence, Race, and the Making of the Child Victim*. Athens: University of Georgia Press, 2010.

Du Bois, W. E. B. *The Souls of Black Folk*. New York: Dover, 1994 (1903).

Edelman, Lee. *No Future: Queer Theory and the Death Drive*. Durham: Duke University Press, 2004.

Eichler-Levine, Jodi. *Suffer the Little Children: Uses of the Past in Jewish and African American Children's Literature*. New York: New York University Press, 2013.

Eisen, Arnold. "Off Center: The Concept of the Land of Israel in Modern Jewish Thought." In *The Land of Israel: Jewish Perspectives*, edited by Lawrence A. Hoffman, 263–296. South Bend: University of Notre Dame Press, 1986.

———. *Rethinking Modern Judaism: Ritual, Commandment, Community*. Chicago: University of Chicago Press, 1998.

Elbogen, Ismar. *Jewish Liturgy: A Comprehensive History*. Philadelphia: Jewish Publication Society, 1993 (1913).

Fanon, Frantz. *Black Skin, White Masks*. New York: Grove Press, 1967.

Feeding America: The Historic American Cookbook Project. Michigan State University Libraries. http://digital.lib.msu.edu/projects/cookbooks/html/books/book_63.cfm. Accessed January 7, 2013.

Feiler, Bruce. *America's Prophet: Moses and the American Story*. New York: Harper Collins, 2009.

Finkel, Jori. "Jean-Léon Gérôme's 'The Snake Charmer': A Twisted History." *Los Angeles Times*, June 13, 2010. http://articles.latimes.com/2010/jun/13/entertainment/la-ca-geromeatgettysidebar-20100613. Accessed January 25, 2017.

Fishberg, Maurice. "Materials for the Physical Anthropology of the Eastern European Jews." *Memoirs of the American Anthropological and Ethnological Societies* 1 (1905–1907): 1–146.

———. "North African Jews." *Boas Anniversary Volume* (1906): 55–63.

———. "Physical Anthropology of the Jews. II—Pigmentation." *American Anthropologist* 5 (1903): 89–106.

———. *Science* 17 (1903): 470.

Franchot, Jenny. *Roads to Rome: The Antebellum Protestant Encounter with Catholicism*. Berkeley: University of California Press, 1994.

Friesel, Evyatar. "Ahad Ha-amism in American Zionist Thought." In *At the Crossroads: Essays on Ahad Ha-am*, edited by Jacques Kornberg, 133–141. Albany: State University of New York Press, 1983.

———. "The Meaning of Zionism and Its Influence among the American Jewish Religious Movements." In *Zionism and Religion*, edited by Shmuel Almog, Jehuda Reinharz, and Anita Shapira, 175–186. Hanover, NH: Brandeis University Press by University Press of New England, 1998.

Gassenschmidt, Christoph. *Jewish Liberal Politics in Tsarist Russia, 1900–14: The Modernization of Russian Jewry*. New York: New York University Press, 1995.

Gertz, Nurith, and George Khleifi. *Palestinian Cinema: Landscape, Trauma, and Memory*. Bloomington: Indiana University Press, 2008.

Ginsburg, Shai. *Rhetoric and Nation: The Formation of Hebrew National Culture, 1880–1990*. Syracuse: Syracuse University Press, 2014.

Glassberg, David. *American Historical Pageantry: The Uses of Tradition in the Early Twentieth Century*. Chapel Hill: University of North Carolina Press, 1990.
Goldman, Karla. "The Ambivalence of Reform Judaism: Kaufmann Kohler and the Ideal Jewish Woman." *American Jewish History* 79, no. 4 (Summer 1990): 477–499.
———. *Beyond the Synagogue Gallery: Finding a Place for Women in American Judaism*. Cambridge: Harvard University Press, 2000.
Goldstein, Eric. *The Price of Whiteness: Jews, Race, and American Identity*. Princeton: Princeton University Press, 2006.
Golden, Jonathan. "From Cooperation to Confrontation: The Rise and Fall of the Synagogue Council of America." Dissertation. Brandeis University, May 2008.
Greenstein, Howard. *Turning Point: Zionism and Reform Judaism*. Chico, CA: Scholars Press, 1981.
Griffith, R. Marie. *God's Daughters: Evangelical Women and the Power of Submission*. Berkeley: University of California Press, 1997.
Gruber, Ruth Ellen. *Virtually Jewish: Reinventing Jewish Culture in Europe*. Berkeley: University of California Press, 2002.
Guralnik, Nehama. *Maurycy Gottlieb, 1856–1879: Meisterwerke*. Edited by Georg Heuberger. Frankfurt a.M.: Tel Aviv Museum of Art and Jüdisches Museum Frankfurt, 1991.
Halperin, Liora. *Babel in Zion: Jews, Nationalism, and Language Diversity in Palestine, 1920–1948*. New Haven: Yale University Press, 2014.
Hartenau, Walter [pseud.]. "Höre Israel!" *Zukunft* 18 (March 16, 1897): 460; translated in Paul Mendes-Flohr and Jehuda Reinharz, eds. *Jew in the Modern World*, 2nd ed. New York: Oxford University Press, 1980.
Havrelock, Rachel. *River Jordan: The Mythology of a Dividing Line*. Chicago: University of Chicago Press, 2011.
Heinze, Andrew. *Adapting to Abundance: Jewish Immigrants, Mass Consumption, and the Search for American Identity*. New York: Columbia University Press, 1990.
———. *Jews and the American Soul: Human Nature in the 20th Century*. Princeton: Princeton University Press, 2004.
Hertzberg, Arthur, ed. *The Zionist Idea: A Historical Analysis and Reader*. Philadelphia: Jewish Publication Society of America, 1997.
Heschel, Susannah. *Abraham Geiger and the Jewish Jesus*. Chicago: University of Chicago Press, 1998.
Hirsch, Marianne. "Projected Memory: Holocaust Photographs in Personal and Public Fantasy." In *Acts of Memory: Cultural Recall in the Present*, edited by Mieke Bal, Jonathan Crewe, and Leo Spitzer. Hanover, NH: Dartmouth College Press, 1999.
Hollywood, Amy. "Performativity, Citationality, Ritualization." *History of Religions* 42, no. 2 (November 2002): 93–115.

Horowitz, Elliott. *Reckless Rites: Purim and the Legacy of Jewish Violence*. Princeton: Princeton University Press, 2006.

Hyman, Paula. *Gender and Assimilation in Modern Jewish History: The Roles and Presentations of Women*. Seattle: University of Washington Press, 1995.

Jick, Leon. *The Americanization of the Synagogue, 1820–1870*. Hanover, NH: Brandeis University Press, 1992.

Jones, Jonathan. "Jean-Léon Gérôme: Orientalist Fantasy among the Impressionists." *The Guardian*, July 3, 2012. https://www.theguardian.com/artanddesign/jonathanjonesblog/2012/jul/03/jean-leon-gerome-orientalism-impressionists. Accessed January 25, 2017.

Joselit, Jenna Weissman. "The Special Sphere of the Middle-Class American Jewish Woman: The Synagogue Sisterhood, 1890–1940." In *The American Synagogue: A Sanctuary Transformed*, edited by Jack Wertheimer, 206–230. Cambridge: Cambridge University Press, 1987.

———. *The Wonders of America: Reinventing Jewish Culture, 1880–1950*. New York: Hill and Wang, 1994.

Kalman, Julie. "Going Home to the Holy Land: The Jews of Jerusalem in Nineteenth-Century French Catholic Pilgrimage." *Journal of Modern History* 84, no. 2 (June 2012): 335–368.

Kalmar, Ivan Davidson, and Derek J. Penslar, eds. *Orientalism and the Jews*. Waltham: Brandeis University Press, 2005.

Kaplan, Dana Evan, ed. *The Cambridge Companion to American Judaism*. Cambridge: Cambridge University Press, 2005.

Katriel, Tamar, and Eliza Shenhar. "Tower and Stockade: Dialogic Narration in Israeli Settlement Ethos." *Quarterly Journal of Speech* 76 (1990): 359–380.

Katz, Emily Alice. *Bringing Zion Home: Israel in American Jewish Culture, 1948–1967*. Albany: State University of New York Press, 2015.

Katz, Maia Balakirsky. *The Visual Culture of Chabad*. Cambridge: Cambridge University Press, 2010.

Kaufman, David. *Shul with a Pool: The "Synagogue-Center" in American Jewish History*. Hanover, NH: Brandeis University Press by University Press of New England, 1999.

Kaufman, Menahem. *An Ambiguous Partnership: Non-Zionists and Zionists in America, 1939–1948*. Jerusalem: The Magnes Press, 1991.

Kirshenblatt-Gimblett, Barbara. *Destination Culture: Tourism, Museums, and Heritage*. Berkeley: University of California Press, 1998.

———. "From Ethnology to Heritage: The Role of the Museum." In *Museum Studies: An Anthology of Contexts*, edited by Bettina Messias Carbonell, 199–205. Malden: Blackwell, 2012.

———. "Intangible Heritage as Metacultural Production." *Museum International* 56, nos. 1–2 (2004): 52–65.

Kirshenblatt-Gimblett, Barbara, and Jonathan Karp, eds. *The Art of Being Jewish in Modern Times*. Philadelphia: University of Pennsylvania Press, 2008.

Klapper, Melissa. "'Those by Whose Sides We Have Labored': American Jewish Women and the Peace Movement between the Wars." *Journal of American History* 97, no. 3 (2010): 636–658.
Kolsky, Thomas. *Jews Against Zionism: The American Council for Judaism, 1942–1948.* Philadelphia: Temple University Press, 1990.
Koltun-Fromm, Ken. *Material Culture and Jewish Thought in America.* Bloomington: Indiana University Press, 2010.
Kravtsov, Sergey R. "Reconstruction of the Temple by Charles Chipiez and Its Applications in Architecture." *Ars Judaica* (2008): 25–42.
Lambert, Frank. *Inventing the Great Awakening.* Princeton: Princeton University Press, 2001.
Lederhendler, Eli, ed. *The Six-Day War and World Jewry.* Bethesda: University of Maryland Press, 2000.
Leiter, Andrew. "Summary." *Afro-American Encyclopaedia, Documenting the American South.* Chapel Hill: University Library, the University of North Carolina, 2004. http://docsouth.unc.edu/church/haley/summary.html. Accessed January 7, 2013.
Lesser, Jeffrey, and Raanan Rein. "Challenging Particularity: Jews as a Lens on Latin American Ethnicity." *Latin American and Caribbean Ethnic Studies* 1, no. 2 (September 2006): 249–263.
Levy, David. "The Making of the *Encyclopaedia Judaica* and *The Jewish Encyclopedia*." In *Proceedings of the 37th Annual Convention of the Association of Jewish Libraries* (Denver: June 2002), 3–5. http://www.jewishlibraries.org/main/Portals/0/AJL_Assets/documents/Publications/proceedings/proceedings2002/levy.pdf. Accessed October 15, 2012.
Lewis, Arnold. "Phantom Ethnicity: 'Oriental Jews' in Israeli Society." In *Studies in Israeli Ethnicity: After the Ingathering*, edited by Alex Weingrod, 133–158. New York: Gordon and Breach Science Publishers, 1985.
Long, Burke. *Imagining the Holy Land: Maps, Models, and Fantasy Travels.* Bloomington: Indiana University Press, 2003.
Lorge, Michael, and Gary Phillip Zola, eds. *A Place of Our Own: The Rise of Reform Jewish Camping.* Tuscaloosa: University of Alabama Press, 2006.
Love, Lauren. "Performing Jewish Nationhood: *The Romance of a People* at the 1933 Chicago World's Fair." *TDR: The Drama Review* 55, no. 3 (Fall 2011): 57–67.
Lowenthal, David. *The Heritage Crusade and the Spoils of History.* Cambridge: Cambridge University Press, 1996.
———. *The Past Is a Foreign Country—Revisited.* Cambridge: Cambridge University Press, 2015.
Lowenthal, Marvin, ed. *Henrietta Szold: Life and Letters.* New York: Viking Press, 1942.
Maffly-Kipp, Laurie. "Assembling Bodies and Souls: Missionary Practices on the Pacific Frontier." In *Practicing Protestants: Histories of Christian Life in*

America, 1630–1965, edited by Laurie Maffly-Kipp, Leigh Schmidt, and Mark Valeri, 51–76. Baltimore: Johns Hopkins University Press, 2006.

Magid, Shaul. *American Post-Judaism: Identity and Renewal in a Postethnic Society*. Bloomington: Indiana University Press, 2013.

Mahler, Raphael. *Hasidism and the Jewish Enlightenment: Their Confrontation in Galicia and Poland in the First Half of the Nineteenth Century*. Philadelphia: Jewish Publication Society of America, 1985.

Mann, Michael. *The Darkside of Democracy: Explaining Ethnic Cleansing*. Cambridge: Cambridge University Press, 2004.

Mann, Vivian B. *Jewish Texts on the Visual Arts*. Cambridge: Cambridge University Press, 2000.

Marcus, Ivan. *The Jewish Life Cycle: Rites of Passage from Biblical to Modern Times*. Seattle: University of Washington Press, 2004.

McCune, Mary. "Social Workers in the *Muskeljudentum*: 'Hadassah Ladies,' Manly Men' and the Significance of Gender in the American Zionist Movement, 1912–1928." *American Jewish History* 86, no. 2 (1998): 164.

———. *"The Whole Wide World, without Limits": International Relief, Gender Politics, and American Jewish Women, 1893–1930*. Detroit: Wayne State University Press, 2005.

McDannell, Colleen. *Material Christianity: Religion and Popular Culture in America*. New Haven: Yale University Press, 1995.

Medoff, Rafael. *Militant Zionism in America: The Rise and Impact of the Jabotinsky Movement in the United States, 1926–1948*. Tuscaloosa: University of Alabama Press, 2002.

———. *Zionism and the Arabs: An American Jewish Dilemma, 1898–1948*. Westport: Praeger, 1997.

Mendes-Flohr, Paul. *Divided Passions: Jewish Intellectuals and the Experience of Modernity*. Detroit: Wayne State University Press, 1991.

Metcalf, Barbara, ed. *Making Muslim Space in North America and Europe*. Berkeley: University of California Press, 1996.

Meyer, Michael. *Response to Modernity: A History of the Reform Movement in Judaism*. Detroit: Wayne State University Press, 1995.

Miller, Perry. *The Life of the Mind in America*. New York: Oxford University Press, 1965.

Miller, Rory. *Divided Against Zion: Anti-Zionist Opposition in Britain to a Jewish State in Palestine, 1945–1948*. London: Frank Cass, 2000.

Moore, Deborah Dash. *At Home in America: Second Generation New York Jews*. New York: Columbia University Press, 1981.

———. "Hadassah in the United States." *Jewish Women's Archive Encyclopedia*. https://jwa.org/encyclopedia/article/hadassah-in-united-states. Accessed July 3, 2015.

Morgan, David. *The Sacred Gaze: Religious Visual Culture in Theory and Practice*. Berkeley: University of California Press, 2005.

Mosse, George L. *Nationalism and Sexuality: Middle-Class Morality and Sexual Norms in Modern Europe*. Madison: University of Wisconsin Press, 1985.

Myers, David. "Of Marranos and Memory: Yosef Hayim Yerushalmi and the Writing of Jewish History." In *Jewish History and Jewish Memory*, ed. Elisheva Carlebach, John Efron, David Myers, 1–21. Hanover, NH: Brandeis University Press, 1998.

Nadell, Pamela. "'The Synagog Shall Hear the Call of the Sister': Carrie Simon and the Founding of the NFTS." In *Sisterhood: A Centennial History of Women of Reform Judaism*, edited by Carole B. Balin, Dana Herman, Jonathan D. Sarna, and Gary P. Zola, 19–48. Cincinnati: Hebrew Union College Press, 2013.

Nadell, Pamela, and Rita Simon. "Ladies of the Sisterhood: Women in the American Reform Synagogue, 1900–1930." In *Active Voices: Women in Jewish Culture*, edited by Maurie Sacks, 19–48. Urbana: University of Illinois Press, 1995.

"Nationalism." In *Stanford Encyclopedia of Philosophy*. http://plato.stanford.edu/entries/nationalism/. First published November 29, 2001; substantive revision June 1, 2010. Accessed December 5, 2011.

Neulander, Judith. "Tchotchkes: A Study of Popular Culture in Tangible Form." In *Studies in Jewish Civilization, Volume 17: American Judaism in Popular Culture*, edited by Leonard Greenspoon and Ronald Simkins, 175–199. Omaha: Creighton University Press, 2006.

Neusner, Jacob. *The Way of Torah*, 2nd ed. Encino: Dickenson, 1974.

Novick, Peter. *The Holocaust in American Life*. Boston: Houghton Mifflin Company, 1999.

Onne, Eyal. *Photographic Heritage of the Holy Land, 1839–1914*. Manchester: Institute of Advanced Studies, Manchester England, 1980.

Orsi, Robert. *Between Heaven and Earth: The Religious Worlds People Make and the Scholars Who Study Them*. Princeton: Princeton University Press, 2006.

———. *The Madonna of 115th Street: Faith and Community in Italian Harlem, 1880–1950*. New Haven: Yale University Press, 1985.

Peleg, Yaron. *Orientalism and the Hebrew Imagination*. Ithaca: Cornell University Press, 2005.

Pellegrini, Ann. *Performance Anxieties: Staging Psychoanalysis, Staging Race*. New York: Routledge, 1997.

Peters, Francis Edward. *Jerusalem*. Princeton: Princeton University Press, 1985.

Pew Forum. "A Portrait of Jewish Americans." October 1, 2013. http://www.pew-forum.org/2013/10/01/Jewish American-beliefs-attitudes-culture-survey/.

Pianko, Noam. *Zionism and the Roads Not Taken: Rawidowicz, Kaplan, Kohn*. Bloomington: Indiana University Press, 2010.

Piezynski, Denise. "Biographical Note" to the George A. Barton Papers. The University Archives and Records Center, University of Pennsylvania. November 1989. http://www.archives.upenn.edu/faids/upt/upt50/bartonga_guide.pdf. Accessed August 17, 2012.

Pinchuk, Ben Cion. "Jewish Discourse and the Shtetl." *Jewish History* 15, no. 2 (June 2001): 169–179.
Plaskow, Judith. *Standing Again at Sinai*. New York: HarperCollins, 1991.
Plate, S. Brent. "Introduction." In *Religion, Art, and Visual Culture: A Cross-Cultural Reader*, edited by S. Brent Plate. New York: Palgrave Macmillan, 2002.
Prell, Riv-Ellen. *Fighting to Become Americans: Assimilation and the Trouble between Jewish Women and Jewish Men*. Boston: Beacon Press, 1999.
———. *Prayer and Community: The Havurah in American Judaism*. Detroit: Wayne State University Press, 1989.
———. "The Vision of Woman in Classical Reform Judaism." *Journal of the American Academy of Religion* 50, no. 4 (December 1982): 575–589.
Prothero, Stephen. *American Jesus: How the Son of God Became a National Icon*. New York: Farrar, Straus and Giroux, 2003.
Raider, Mark. *The Emergence of American Zionism*. New York: New York University Press, 1998.
Raider, Mark, Jonathan Sarna, and Ronald Zweig, eds. *Abba Hillel Silver and American Zionism*. London: Frank Cass, 1997.
Reinharz, Shulamit, and Mark Raider, eds. *American Jewish Women and the Zionist Enterprise*. Waltham: Brandeis University Press, 2004.
Remembrances of the Near East: The Photographs of Bonfils, 1867–1907. Exhibition prepared by Robert A. Sobieszek and Carney E. S. Gavin. International Museum of Photography at George Eastman House and the Harvard Semitic Museum, 1980.
Ricca, Simone. "Heritage, Nationalism, and the Shifting Symbolism of the Wailing Wall." *Archives de sciences socials des religions* (July–September 2010): 169–188.
Rosenthal, Steven. "Long-Distance Nationalism: American Jews, Zionism, and Israel." In *The Cambridge Companion to American Judaism*, edited by Dana Evan Kaplan, 209–224. Cambridge: Cambridge University Press, 2005.
Rubaschoff, S. "Erstlinge der Entjudung: Drei Reden von Eduard Gans im "Kulturerein.'" *Der jüdische Wille* 2 (1919): 109–115.
Said, Edward. *Orientalism*. New York: Random House, 2003 (1978).
Sarna, Jonathan. *American Judaism: A History*. New Haven: Yale University Press, 2004.
———. "Converts to Zionism in the American Reform Movement." In *Zionism and Religion*, edited by Shmuel Almog, Jehuda Reinharz, and Anita Shapira, 188–203. Hanover, NH: Brandeis University Press by University Press of New England, 1998.
———. "A Projection of America as It Ought to Be: Zion in the Mind's Eye of American Jews." In *Envisioning Israel: The Changing Ideals and Images of North American Jews*, edited by Allon Gal, 41–59. Detroit: Wayne State University Press, 1996.

Sayigh, Yezid. "Reflections on Al Nakba." *Journal of Palestine Studies* 28, no. 1 (Autumn 1998): 5–35.
Schmidt, Gilya Gerda. *The Art and Artists of the Fifth Zionist Congress, 1901: Heralds of a New Age.* Syracuse: Syracuse University Press, 2003.
Schmidt, Leigh. *Consumer Rites: The Buying and Selling of American Holidays.* Princeton: Princeton University Press, 1995.
Schorsch, Ismar. *From Text to Context: The Turn to History in Modern Judaism.* Hanover, NH: University Press of New England, 1994.
Schwartz, Shuly Rubin. "From the Ladder to the Umbrella: The Metaphors of American Jewish Religious Life." *American Jewish History* 90:1 (March 2002): 27–34.
———. *The Emergence of Jewish Scholarship in America: The Publication of the "Jewish Encyclopedia."* Cincinnati: Hebrew Union College Press, 1991.
———. "They Married What They Wanted to Be." *Women's League Outlook* 76, no. 2 (Winter 2005).
Scott, Joan W. "Gender: A Useful Category of Historical Analysis." *American Historical Review* 91, no. 5 (December 1986): 1053–1075.
Shaheen, Jack. *Reel Bad Arabs: How Hollywood Vilifies a People.* Northampton: Olive Branch Press, 2001.
Shandler, Jeffrey, and Beth Wenger, eds. *Encounters with the "Holy Land": Place, Past and Future in American Jewish Culture.* Hanover, NH: National Museum of American Jewish History and the Trustees of the University of Pennsylvania through the University Press of New England, 1997.
Shapira, Anita. *Land and Power: The Zionist Resort to Force, 1881–1948.* New York: Oxford University Press, 1992.
Shapiro, Yonathan. *Leadership of the American Zionist Organization, 1897–1930.* Urbana: University of Illinois Press, 1971.
Shenhav, Yehouda. *The Arab Jews: A Postcolonial Reading of Nationalism, Religion, and Ethnicity.* Stanford: Stanford University Press, 2006.
Shmeruk, Chone. *The Esterke Story in Yiddish and Polish Literature.* Jerusalem: Zalman Shazar Center, 1985.
Silk, Mark. "Notes on the Judeo-Christian Tradition in America." *American Quarterly* 36, no. 1 (Spring 1984): 64–85.
Simmons, Erica B. *Hadassah and the Zionist Project.* Lanham: Rowman & Littlefield, 2006.
Smith, Anna Deavere. *Fires in the Mirror: Crown Heights, Brooklyn, and Other Identities.* New York: Anchor-Doubleday, 1993.
Smith, Anthony. "The Question of Jewish Identity." In *A New Jewry? Studies in Contemporary Jewry*, vol. 8, edited by Peter Medding, 219–235. Oxford: Oxford University Press, 1992.
Smith, Jonathan Z. *Imagining Religion: From Babylon to Jonestown.* Chicago: University of Chicago Press, 1982.

———. *Relating Religion: Essays on the Study of Religion*. Chicago: University of Chicago Press, 2004.

Stanislawski, Michael. *Zionism and the Fin de Siècle: Cosmopolitanism and Nationalism from Nordau to Jabotinsky*. Berkeley: University of California Press, 2001.

Stern, Eliyahu. *The Genius: Elijah of Vilna and the Making of Modern Judaism*. New Haven: Yale University Press, 2013.

Stow, Kenneth. *Alienated Minority: The Jews of Medieval Latin Europe*. Cambridge: Harvard University Press, 1992.

Trachtenberg, Alan. *Reading American Photographs: Images as History, Mathew Brady to Walker Evans*. New York: Hill and Wang, 1989.

Trachtenberg, Barry. "From Edification to Commemoration: *Di Algemeyne Entsiklopedye*, the Holocaust and the Changing Mission of Yiddish Scholarship." *Journal of Modern Jewish Studies* 5, no. 3 (2006): 285–300.

Troen, S. Ilan. *Imagining Zion: Dreams, Designs, and Realities in a Century of Jewish Settlement*. New Haven: Yale University Press, 2003.

Tweed, Thomas, ed. *Retelling U.S. Religious History*. Berkeley: University of California Press, 1997.

Urofsky, Melvin. *A Voice That Spoke for Justice: The Life and Times of Stephen S. Wise*. Albany: State University of New York Press, 1982.

Veidlinger, Jeffrey. "'Emancipation: See Anti-Semitism': The Evreiskaia entsiklopediia and Jewish Public Culture." *Simon Dubnow Institute Yearbook* 9 (2010): 405–426.

———. "From Ashkenaz to Zionism: Putting Eastern European Jewish Life in (Alphabetical) Order." *AJS Review* 33, no. 2 (November 2009): 379–389.

———. *Jewish Public Culture in the Late Russian Empire*. Bloomington: Indiana University Press, 2009.

Waldstreicher, David. *In the Midst of Perpetual Fetes: The Making of American Nationalism, 1776–1820*. Chapel Hill: University of North Carolina Press, 1997.

Weber, Max. "Ethnic Groups" (1922). In *Theories of Ethnicity: A Classical Reader*, edited by Werner Sollers, 52–66. New York: New York University Press, 1996.

Weinryb, Bernard. *The Jews of Poland: A Social and Economic History of the Jewish Community in Poland from 1100 to 1800*. Philadelphia: Jewish Publication Society of America, 1972.

Wenger, Beth. *History Lessons: The Creation of American Jewish Heritage*. Princeton: Princeton University Press, 2010.

———. "Jewish Women of the Club: The Changing Role of Atlanta's Jewish Women, 1870–1930." *American Jewish History* 76 (March 1987): 311–333.

White, Richard. *The Middle Ground: Indians, Empires, and Republics in the Great Lakes Region, 1650–1815*. New York: Cambridge University Press, 1991.

Whitfield, Stephen J. "The Politics of Pageantry, 1936–1946." *American Jewish History* 84, no. 3 (1996): 221–251.

———. "Unathletic Department." In *Jews, Sports, and the Rites of Citizenship*, edited by Jack Kugelmass, 51–71. Urbana: University of Illinois Press, 2007.

Wolf, Immanuel. "In the Concept of a Science of Judaism" (1822). In *Ideas of Jewish History*, edited with introduction and notes by Michael A. Meyer, 141–155. New York: Behrman House, 1974.

Yerushalmi, Yosef Hayyim. *Zakhor: Jewish History and Jewish Memory*. New York: Schocken Books, 1989.

Young, Iris Marion. "The Ideal of Community and the Politics of Difference." In *Feminism/Postmodernism*, edited by Linda J. Nicholson, 300–323. New York: Routledge, 1990.

Zemel, Carol. *Looking Jewish: Visual Culture and Modern Diaspora*. Bloomington: Indiana University Press, 2015.

Zerubavel, Yael. *Recovered Roots: Collective Memory and the Making of Israeli National Tradition*. Chicago: University of Chicago Press, 1995.

Zipperstein, Steven. *The Jews of Odessa: A Cultural History, 1794–1881*. Stanford: Stanford University Press, 1985.

Zola, Gary P. "Sisterhood and the American Synagogue: An Introduction." In *Sisterhood: A Centennial History of Women of Reform Judaism*, edited by Carole B. Balin, Dana Herman, Jonathan D. Sarna, and Gary P. Zola, 1–16. Cincinnati: Hebrew Union College Press, 2013.

Zollman, Joellyn Wallen. "Constructing Identity: Gift Shops and the NFTS Campaign for Home Observance." In *Sisterhood: A Centennial History of Women of Reform Judaism*, edited by Carole B. Balin, Dana Herman, Jonathan D. Sarna, and Gary P. Zola, 159–182. Cincinnati: Hebrew Union College Press, 2013.

Index

abortion, 237–238, *238*
Adler, Jennifer Axsom, 31
aestheticism, 97
"Agricultural Colonies in Palestine," 158
agricultural fair, *3*
agricultural modernity, 70, *71*, 72–73
agriculture, *71*
   antisemitism related to, 159–160
   of Arabs, 70, *70*
   in diaspora, 160
   in Hall of Religion, 180, *181*
   historical, *158*, 158–160, *160*, *161*
   ORT and, 198–199
   photographs of, 161
   stereotype related to, 159–161
   of U.S., 161
   visual culture of, 160
Ahad Ha-am, 79, 178, 180
'aliyah' (ascend), 223–224, 230
Alpert, Rebecca, 214
America. *See* United States
The American Israelite, 166, 168
American Jewish Committee, 61, *62*
American Protestantism, 218
Americanization scene, *190*
Americanness, 122–123
Anderson, Benedict, 8
aniconism, 232, 233

antisemitism, 34–35
   agriculture related to, 159–160
   in Europe, 22, 191
   of Jerome, 91
   Orientalism related to, 221–222
   in Russia, 187, *188*
   in U. S., 22
anxieties, 83, 242
appropriation, in art calendars, 107–108
Arabs, 43, 45, 202
   agriculture of, 70, *70*
   Arago on, 155
   chalutzim and, 82
   Christians and, 193
   in Jewish history, 192–193
   Jews compared to, 161–162
   manipulation of, 75–76
   Mizrahim and, 73–74
   Muslims as, 76, 193
   in Orientalism, 35–36, 121, *121*
   violence of, 74–75
   voice of, 193
   ZOA and, 87
Arago, François, 155
Arav, Rami, 32
archaeological photography, 146, 155
   decisions in, 168–169
archaeologists, 133–134

archetypes, photographs as, 154
architectural heritage. *See also*
    Western Wall
  Tomb of Rachel as, 33
  Tower of David as, 32–33
  as visual culture, 32–34
architectural relics, 25
Arensen, Hella, 123, *123*–124
"The Ark," 176–177, *177*
art
  Bezalel art school, 1, *3*, 92, 109, 114, 139
  on East European Jews, 68, 70
  halakha and, 231–233
  Jewish visual culture and, 232–233
  sculpture as, 231–232
  stereotype and, 199
art calendars, 25–26, 233–234
  acculturation related to, 108
  aestheticism and, 97
  American exceptionalism in, 96, 131
  Americanness from, 122–123
  anachronism of, 102
  appropriation in, 107–108
  biblical stories in, 100–101, *101*
  The Boy David, *118*, 118–119
  Christian Americans and, 107
  Christian influence in, 102–109, 131
  Christian Orientalism and, 91–92
  counterhistory related to, 92–93, 108–109, 131
  The Crowning of Esther in, 100–103, *101*
  democracy in, 128–129
  Fervently We Invoke Thy Blessing, *127*, 127–128
  fiction in, 102–103
  format of, 114–115
  fundraising with, 96
  Gypsy Arabs in Sephardic Quarter—Jerusalem, 121, *121*
  halakha and, 94–95, 129–130, 131
  heritage and, 97–98
  home observance and, 97
  Jeremiah on the Ruins of Jerusalem, 111, *113*
  Jewish heritage and, 92–93
  Jews Taken Captive into Babylon, 111, *112*, 114
  Jochebed in, 109, *110*, 111
  Michelangelo and, 89–90, *90*, 91
  Midnight Prayer, 114, *116*
  motherhood and, 109, *110*, 111, 218
  Mystic Safed, 119–120, *120*, 121–122
  nationalisms and, 126–129, *127*
  Nazism related to, 123
  nostalgia in, 102, 103
  Old Jewish Quarter, 123, *123*
  pictorial messages in, 96
  recontextualization of, 95, 102, 103–104
  selective remembrance in, 103
  symbols in, 98
  women and, 93, 131, 229
  The Workers' Village, 129, *130*
  Zionist artists and, 92
arthouse photography, 155
artisans, 3, 92
Ashkenazi, Jacob ben Isaac, 103–104
Ashkenazim, 38, 50–51, 103–104
  East European Jews as, 39–40
  in *JE*, 162, 164, 168
Association for the Promotion of Trade and Agriculture (*Obshchestvo Rasprostranenia Truda*) (ORT), 198–199
Assyria, 133–134
attachments, 242
authenticity, 14
  in history reconstruction, 134
  of Western Wall, 32

Baer, Max, 200
Balfour, Lord Arthur, 52, *53*
Balfour Declaration, 75
Baltimore Convention Number cover of The Maccabaean, *54*
Barsky, Joseph, 1, 138–140, 255n12
Barton, George A., 144
Battle of Tel Hai (1920), 191
"Bedouin Tent," 162, *163*
Bedouins, 36, 43–44, 72. *See also* Arabs
Ben Canaan, Ari (fictional name), 239
Ben Yehuda, Ben-Zion. *See* Ben-Avi, Ittamar
Ben Yehuda, Eliezer, 1, 4
Ben-Avi, Ittamar, 1, *2–3*, 4
Bendemann, Eduard, 104–105, 111, *112*, *113*, 114
Bennett, James O'Donnell, 184, 185
Ben-Shetah, Shimeon, *3*
Benzinger, Immanuel, 231–233
Berkowitz, Michael, 52
Bezalel art school, 1, *3*, 92, 109, 114, 139
biblical stories, 100–101, *101*
Bland, Kalman, 233
Bogan, William J., 196
Bohrer, Frederick, 144, 220
bomb scare, 19
Bonfils (firm), 152–155
Bonfils, Félix, 152
Bonfils, Lydie, 152
Boris Schatz, *117*
Born, Berthe, 89
boxing, 200
The Boy David, *118*, 118–119
boys, 48, 166, *167*
  boxing by, 200
  clothing of, 223
Brandeis, Louis, 10–11, 41–42, 211
"Bringing Health to Palestine," 84
Britain, 20–21, 75
British Mandate, 20–21

By the Waters of Babylon, 115

Carey, James, 37
Catholics, 90–91
Cavafy, C. P., 29
Century of Progress International Exposition. *See* World's Fair
chalutzim (Zionist pioneers), 1
  in American films, 239
  Arabs and, 82
  hypersymbolization of, 81
  Jewish Americans as, 83, 86
  manual labor of, 83, *85*, 86
  as objects of Orientalism, 76–81
  spectacle of, 82
  visual culture and, 76–77, 80–81
Chassidism. *See* Hasidism
Chicago. *See* World's Fair
children, 27, 84, *85*. *See also* Jewish children
  Hadassah Mothers the Children of Erez-Israel, 218, *219*, 220
  innocence of, 224
  men's and women's activism for, 207–208
  powerlessness of, 230
  rights of, 224
  symbol of, 208–209, 210
  visit with, 205–207
Chipiez, Charles, 133–135, *134*, 138, 255n12
Christian American fundamentalists, 237–238, *238*
Christian American women, 93–94
Christian Americans, 21–22, 47–48
  art calendars and, 107
  material gospel of, 31
  NFTS and, 90–91, 93–94
  Protestants, 122, 218, 231
  visual culture of, 90–91, 108, 109
Christian Orientalism, 221–222
  art calendars and, 91–92

Christian Orientalism *(continued)*
　Jewish Orientalism compared to, 10, 235–237
　photographs related to, 168
Christian presses, 103–104
Christianity, 47–48, 182
　JE related to, 135, 136–137, 141–142, 147, 149–152, 162, 168–169
　Jerusalem mapping related to, 149–152, 155
Christians
　Arabs and, 193
　Catholics, 90–91
　Romance and, 194, 195–196
　Torah and, 91
Ciseri, Antonio, 100
civilizations, 1, 25–26, 49, 51, 75, 90, 94, 109, 133, 136, 157, 173, 191–193, 228
clothing, 57, *58*, 100, 119
　of boy, 223
　in dance, *189*, 189–190
　of girls, 225, *226*
　kaffiyehs, 29, 68, 73
　motherhood and, 220
　types of, 162, *163*, 164
Cohen, Naomi, 12
Cohen, Richard, 104
colonialism, 34–35, 158
competition, 147, 200, 242
"Composite Portraits," 166, *167*
Conrad, Joseph, 36
contemporary and contemporaneous, definitions of, 10
"Corps of Nurses, Hadassah Medical Organization," 85
costumes. *See* clothing
counterhistory, 92–93, 108–109, 131
"Court of Priests," *133–134*, 134
Cover with return address and stamp, 225, *227*
The Crowning of Esther, 100–103, *101*

Crusades, 9, 102
cultural pluralism, 10–11, 41
　at World's Fair (1933), 26–27, 175, 186–187
culture, 37–38, 40. *See also* visual culture
　of Jewish Americans, 4
　material, 51, 97–98, 176, *177*, 202

daguerreotypes, 33–34, 155
Damisch, Hubert, 7
dance performance, 188–190, *189*
David (king), *118*, 118–119, 239
　Stars of, 61, *62*, *127*, 128–129, 186
David's Tower in Jerusalem, 125
Dawisha, Adeed, 75–76
democracy, 12, 52
　in art calendars, 128–129
　from Judaism, 213
　Romance as, 27
　of Zionism, 205
The Destruction of Jerusalem, 104–106, *105*
diaspora, 60, 180, 182
　agriculture in, 160
　in Jewish history, 191–192
diasporic photo-eulogy, 60
"Division of Fields in Modern Palestine," 158–159, *160*
Dixon, George W., 195–196
"documentary" photographs, 7
Doorway to Life . . ., *216*, 216–217
Doré, Gustave, 73
"Dudele," 188–190, *189*, 189
Duffy, Enda, 5
Duma, 64, 66

East European Jewish American women, 228
East European Jews, 228–229
　art on, 68, 70
　as Ashkenazim, 39–40

diasporic photo-eulogy of, 60
differences among, 158
FAZ/ZOA and, 47, 57
Hasidim in, 157
without images, 158
Maskilim in, 157
from Russia, 157–158, 161
in Russia, 187–188, *188*
socialism of, 61–62
Eastern Europe, 122
Edelman, Lee, 208
Efron, John, 34
Eichler-Levine, Jodi, 81–82, 222
Eisen, Arnold, 103, 149–150
Eisenstein, Judah David, 138, 158, 232–233, 263n3
Emergency Quota Act (1921), 23, 198
Encyclopedia Britannica, 138
encyclopedias, 137–138. See also *Jewish Encyclopedia*
The Epic of a Nation
  Jewish physicality in, 200
  Romance compared to, 175, 198–199, 203
  "The Star-Spangled Banner" in, 199
  "Tribute to Labor" in, 199
Epstein, Baer, 68
Escape to Life, 223–224
Esther (queen), 100–103, *101*
Estrugo, Jose, 166, 168
Europe. See also East European Jews
  antisemitism in, 22, 191
  Britain, 20–21, 75
European royalty, 100–101, *101*
Evans, John, 193, 195–196, 199
exile (*galut/goluth*), 43, 46, 50, 64, 67, 73, 93, 99, 111, 122, 140, 191, 192. See also diaspora
Exodus, 72
Exodus (film), 239
"explaining" projects (*hasbara*), 212–213

Ezechiel, *106*, 106–107
Ezekiel (prophet), 106–107, 138
Ezekiel 1: 15-21, 186

family, 217–218
  genetics related to, 166, *167*
"A Farm of the New Era," 70, *71*
farming. See agriculture
Federation of American Zionists (FAZ), 45. See also Zionist Organization of America
feminism
  as academic lens, 16–17
  of Jewish men, 208
  motherhood and, 213, 214
  protofeminism, 17
Fervently We Invoke Thy Blessing, *127*, 127–128
fiction, 102–103
Fisher, Harry, 184, 194
"For Whom?," 64, 66, *66*
Forverts (Forward), 196–197
Foucault, Michel, 14–15
"Four girls eating at a table," 225, *226*
French Chamber of Deputies, 155
fundraising
  with art calendars, 96
  for Hadassah, 207
  modernity related to, 52
future from past
  Ashkenazim in, 38–39, 39–40
  comparison in, 39
  culture in, 40
  Mizrahim in, 38
  theorization of, 37

galut/goluth. See exile
Gavin, Carney E. S., 154–155
gender, 207–208
gender and Jewish American visual culture
  bomb scare in, 19

gender and Jewish American visual
    culture *(continued)*
  feminism in, 16–17
  feminist scholarship in, 16
  gender plurality in, 20
  grammar in, 17
  heterosexuality in, 20
  Islam and, 18
  JAP in, 17–18
  masculinity in, 18–19
  Orientalism in, 18, 20
  protofeminism in, 17
  Temple Sisterhoods and, 16–17
  visual change in, 19–20
  visual sources in, 16, 17
"General View of Rehoboth Colony, Palestine," 158, *159*
genetics, 166, *167*
geographic distance, 242
geography of identity, 31
German Jewish Americans, 228
German Jews, 104, 114, 123, 162, 187, 197
German language, 3
Gertz, Nurith, 240
girls, 164, *216*, 216–217, 225, *226*
"Give Today and Build For Ever!," 43, *44*, 45
Glimpses of the Jewish Exhibit (Mann and Levi), 176–178, *177*, *179*
God, 72, 119–120, 128, 186
Golding, Louis, 82
Goldman, Solomon, 171, 184, 194
Goldstein, Eric, 39
"Goluth," 64, *65*
Gottlieb, Maurycy (Moshe David), 98–100
grammars, 14–15, 17
Grätz, Heinrich, 159–160
Greece, 236
"Greetings to Dr. Weizmann," 56

Griffith, R. Marie, 17
Gross, Rachel, 14
Gross, Rita, 16
"Group of Yemenite Jews," 162
Grove, Isaac Van, 173, 194–195, 196
guards. See *shomrim*
Guirafossian, Abraham, 152–153
gymnastics, 200
Gypsy Arabs in Sephardic Quarter—Jerusalem, 121, *121*

Hadassah Medical Organization (Hadassah), 17, 85, 196. See also children; motherhood
  as alternative, 210
  description of, 209
  fundraising for, 207
  health and, *84*
  heritages within, 209
  inclusion in, 213
  maternalism from, 207–208
  medical campaigns of, 228–229
  National Council of Jewish Women compared to, 211
  Orientalism of, 208, 211–212
  professionalization of, 211
  "propaganda" of, 27, 207–208, 212–213, 234–235
  U.S. related to, 209
  visual culture of, 212–213
  Zionism and, 209–210, 212–213
  Zionism-as-Progressivism in, 211
  ZOA compared to, 27, 234
Hadassah Mothers the Children of Erez-Israel, 218, *219*, 220
Hadassah-Brandeis Institute, 240–241
Haggadahs, 143–144
halakha, 13, 40, 79, 191
  art and, 231–233
  art calendars and, 94–95, 129–130, 131

INDEX 287

Hall of Religion, 173. See also *The Romance of a People*
  agriculture in, 180, *181*
  Ark in, 176–177, *177*
  international Jews in, 178
  "Israel's contribution" in, 178, *179*
  Jewish men in, 180, 182
  the Orient at, 174
  Palestine with diaspora in, 180, 182
  pluralism in, 178
  slideshow in, 177–178
  social consciousness in, 176–178, *179*
  Torah and, 177
  transnationalism in, 177–178
Haluzah, 125
happiness, 216–217
harem fantasy, *201*, 201–202
hasbara ("explaining" projects), 212–213
Hasidism, 60, 81, 199
  in East European Jews, 157
  in Jewish history, 188–190, *189*
  as pioneers, 77, *78*, 79
Haskalah (Jewish Enlightenment), 157
head coverings, 29, 68, 73
health, 84, 85. See also Hadassah Medical Organization
Health Welfare, *215*, 215–216
Heart of Darkness (Conrad), 36
Hebrew Bible. See Torah
Hebrew language, 1, 3, 4
Hebrew University, 186
Hellenization, 184
Herbert, Leon M., 64
"The Hereford Mappa Mundi, 1280, Showing Jerusalem in the Center of the World" ("Hereford Mappa Mundi"), 150–152, *151*
heritage. See also architectural heritage; Jewish American heritage
  art calendars and, 97–98

  definition of, 6, 9–10, 12
  of the Orient, 5, 126–127, 203–204
  in Orientalism reimagined, 9–10, 11
  Polish synagogue and, 98–100, *99*
  Romance as, 26–27
  scholarship on, 241
  space related to, 6
  Western Wall as, 29, *30*
Herod's Temple, 32, 46, 140, 142, 144, *145*. See also Second Temple; Western Wall
Herzl, Theodor, 24–25, 52, 54–55, *55*
"Herzl as Moses," 55, *55*
Herzliah, 1
Herzliya Gymnasium, 138–139, 255n12
Heschel, Susannah, 108–109
heterosexuality, 20, 214
Heyd, Milly, 103–104
Hiram of Tyre, 138
Hirsch, Maurice de, 180, *181*
historical agriculture, *158*, 158–160, *160*, *161*
historicism, 35–38
historization, 26
history, 33–34. See also counterhistory; Jewish history
  ZOA and, 46–47, 87
History of the Jews (Grätz), 159–160
history reconstruction, 134. See also *Jewish Encyclopedia*
Holland, 258n12
Holocaust, 123, 197–198, 234–235
  abortion compared to, 237–238, *238*
  Jewish children and, 224
Holy Land photographs
  history of, 33–34
  subjectivities and, 34
  technologies for, 34, 130

"Holy of Holies," 100, 138, *139*
home observance, 97
homeland, 9–11, 82, 86, 126–127
"HOW UNJEWISH!," 61, *62*
hypermasculinity, 204, 222
hypersexuality, *201*, 201–202

identity, 76, 79, 97
  geography of, 31
"Images of Chassidism," 78
Imhoff, Sarah, 19
immigration, 10–11
  to U.S., 22, 129, 191, 198
  World's Fair related to, 172
"In Rabbinical Literature," 160, *161*
In the Synagogue (Jews Praying in the Synagogue on Yom Kippur), 98–100, *99*
"Interior of a Bet Ha-Midrash [a synagogue] at Tripoli," 162
"Interior of a Health Welfare Station," 215
Isaiah, 128
Isenberg, Noah, 68
Islam, 18, 76, 200, 232
Israeli Defense Ministry, 33
Israeli soldiers, 239
"Israel's Contribution to Agriculture," 180, *181*
"Israel's Contribution to Social Service," 179, *179*

Jabotinsky, Vladimir, 52, 79
Jacobs, Joseph, 133, 135, 140
JAP. *See* Jewish American Princess
JE. *See Jewish Encyclopedia*
Jeremiah on the Ruins of Jerusalem, 111, *113*
Jerome, 91
Jerusalem, 48–49. *See also specific images*

Jerusalem mapping
  changelessness in, 155–156
  Christianity related to, 149–152, 155
  demystification of, 149–150
  earthly compared to above in, 149
  Eisen on, 149–150
  Guirafossian and, 152–153
  "Hereford Mappa Mundi" in, 150–152, *151*
  Martin in, 152, *153*
  Meyer on, 152, 156
  Muslim Empire and, 150–152
  Orientalism in, 151–152
  photographs and, 152–155
  power in, 156–157
  significance of, 149
  stereotyping in, 156
  "Zion Gate" in, 152, 154, *154*
  Zionism and, 149–150
"Jerusalem—Modern," 152, *153*, 156–157
Jesus Christ, 109, 111, 236
Jewish American heritage, 6, 12–15, 83, 86, 175
  Orientalism in, 242–243
Jewish American imagination, 86
  the Orient in, 40–42
  Zionism in, 41–42
Jewish American Princess (JAP), 18–19
Jewish American women. *See also* Hadassah Medical Organization; National Federation of Temple Sisterhoods
  motherhood and, 93, 111, 221, 230
Jewish Americanness. *See* Jewish children
Jewish Americans, 10, 40
  as *chalutzim*, 83, 86
  culture and politics related to, 37–38

culture of, 4
differences among, 237
dual citizenship of, 175–176
inclusion of, 241
loyalty of, 41–42
medical campaigns and, 229
in *NP*, 83
political issues of, 6
privilege of, 223
speed technologies of, 5–6
technologies of, 5
word order of, 4
in World War II, *127*, 127–128
Jewish boys, 166, *167*
strength of, 200
"Jewish Cemetery at Tunis," 164
Jewish children, 1, 4
    Cover with return address and stamp related to, 225, *227*
    Escape to Life about, 223–224
    Holocaust and, 224
    "Join the Circle of Palestine's Children," 205–207, *206*
    politics of, 222–223
    "propaganda" on, 222, 225, *227*, 227–228, 230
    symbol of, 222–223, 234–235
    voice of, 227–228
    Youth Aliyah for, 223–224
Jewish citizenship, 175
Jewish Day, 195–196, 198. See also *The Romance of a People*
Jewish Encyclopedia (*JE*), 26. See also Jerusalem mapping; Temple reconstruction
    Ashkenazim in, 162, 164, 168
    audience for, 136
    Benzinger in, 231–233
    Christianity related to, 135, 136–137, 141–142, 147, 149–152, 162, 168–169

    "Court of Priests" in, *133–134, 134*
    "Division of Fields in Modern Palestine" in, 158–159, *160*
    editors of, 136–137
    encyclopedias and, 137–138
    Estrugo on, 166, 168
    evidence in, 136
    "General View of Rehoboth Colony, Palestine" in, 158, *159*
    Jewish race in, 164–165, *167*
    "Jews of Tunis in Native Costume," *163*, 164
    Kohler, K., in, 232–233
    middle class related to, 137
    Moore, G. F., and, 136–137
    mystification in, 136
    the Orient and, 169–170, 235
    photographs in, 168–169
    "Plowing in Palestine" in, 160, *161*
    "Polish Coins with Jewish Inscriptions," 158
    politics of, 135
    Singer for, 136
    synagogues in, 135
    visual culture in, 135
    World's Fair compared to, 174
    ZOA compared to, 135
Jewish Enlightenment (*Haskalah*), 157
"Jewish gentleman," 79
"Jewish Girls of Tunis," 164
Jewish heritage
    art calendars and, 92–93
    authenticity in, 14
    democracy in, 12
    grammars in, 14–15
    images in, 13–14
    memory in, 12
    myths in, 15
    visual culture in, 13–14, 15

Jewish history
  Americanization scene and, *190*, 190–191
  Arabs in, 192–193
  Battle of Tel Hai in, 191
  diaspora in, 191–192
  Hasidism in, 188–190, *189*
  Jewish Americans and, 192
  languages of, 192
  martyrdom in, 191–192
  Russian Cossack in, 187, *188*
  symbols of, *189*, 189–190, 192
  violence in, 187
  Zionism in, 192
Jewish men, 180
  bodies of, 79–80
  feminism of, 208
  stereotype of, 166, 185, 222
  strength of, 200
Jewish National Fund, 68
Jewish Orientalism, 10, 235–237. *See also specific topics*
"Jewish People's Day," 199–200
Jewish race, 57, *58*, 164–165, *167*
Jewish self-identity, 79
Jewish soldiers, 76
"The Jewish Type Composite Portraits of Ten Jewish Boys, New York," 166, *167*
Jewish types, 164, 166, *167*
Jewish youth. *See* Jewish children
Jewishness, 13, 202
  disputes about, 173–174
Jews. *See also specific topics*
  Arabs compared to, 161–162
  Muslims compared to, 102
  as a people, 197
"Jews of Tunis in Native Costume," *163*, 164
Jews Taken Captive into Babylon, 111, *112*, 114
Jim Crow Laws, 39

Jochebed, 109, *110*, 111
Johnson-Reed Act, 22
"Join the Circle of Palestine's Children," 205–207, *206*, *207*
Joselit, Jenna Weissman, 228
Journal of the Anthropological Institute, 166, *167*
journalistic photography, 62, *63*, 64, 75
Judaism, 182. *See also* Reform Judaism
  democracy from, 213
  Jewishness compared to, 13
  Zionism compared to, 79
Julius II (pope), 89, *90*
Junker, Hermann, 76

kabbalah, 81, 119, 149
kaffiyehs, 29, 68, 73
Kallen, Horace, 10–11, 41–42, 194
Kalmar, Ivan Davidson, 8–9
Katz, Emily, 37–38
Khleifi, George, 240
Kingsley, Charles, 48
Kirshenblatt-Gimblett, Barbara, 10, 50
Kishinev pogrom (1903), 61
Klaber, J. J., 19
Kohler, Johanna, 109, 111
Kohler, Kaufmann, 232
Koltun-Fromm, Ken, 14

languages, 17
  Hebrew, 1, 3, 4
  of Jewish history, 192
League of Nations, 75
legal pluralism, 21
Levi, Gerson, 176–177, *177*
Levin, Shmarya, 64, 66–67
Leviticus, 190–191
Levy, David, 45
Librett, Jeffrey, 35
Lilien, Ephraim, 55, *55*

Lincoln, Abraham, 183
Lowenthal, David, 12–13
Lubin, David, 180, *181*

The Maccabaean (*TM*), 1, *54*, *63*. See also *The New Palestine*
 "For Whom?" in, 64, 66, *66*
 "HOW UNJEWISH!" in, 61, *62*
 "Zion: Out of the Jungle!" in, *67*, 67–68
The Maccabees, 100
Mahmood, Saba, 17
Mann, Louis, 176–177, *177*
Marcus, Ivan, 108
Martin, Meyer, 152, *153*
martyrdom, 191–192
Martyrdom of the Seven Maccabees, 100
Mary, mother of Jesus, 109, 111
masculinity, 18–19, 204, 222
Maskilim, 60, 157
material culture, 51, 97–98, 176, *177*, 202
material gospel, 31
maternalism, 207–208
Mauretania, 29, *30*, 31
McCune, Mary, 211
medical campaigns, 228–229
memory, 103. See also nostalgia
 in Jewish heritage, 12
 Romance press reception and, 195
Mendelsohn, Felix S., 171, 173–174
Meyer, Martin, 152, *153*, 156–157
Michelangelo, 89–90, *90*, 91, 104–105
 prophets and, *106*, 106–108
Michelangelo's Moses
 horns on, *90*, 91
 Shavuot and, 89, *90*, 91, 108
Middle Ages, 33
middle class, 137
Midnight Prayer, 114, *116*
Mikveh-Israel, 1, *2*

Mintz, Elinor, 129
Mitnagdim, 60
Mizrahim, 38, 40, 47, *50*, 50–51
 Arabs and, 73–74
 Muslims and, 74
 in NP, 68, *69*, 70
 "Modern Jewish Farming Methods," 70, *71*
modernity, 152, *153*, 156–159, *160*
 agricultural, 70, *71*, 72–73
 fundraising related to, 52
 as a sociopolitical condition, 51–52
 tradition compared to, 51–52
Moore, Deborah Dash, 239
Moore, George Foot, 136–137
Morgan, David, 13–14
Moses, 184
 Lincoln as, 183
Moses, 89–90, *90*, 91
motherhood
 art calendars and, 109, *110*, 111, 218
 Doorway to Life . . . and, *216*, 216–217
 exoticism and, 220
 family and, 217–218
 feminism and, 213, 214
 Hadassah Mothers the Children of Erez-Israel on, 218, *219*, 220
 happiness and, 216–217
 Health Welfare and, *215*, 215–216
 hypermasculinity and, 222
 Jewish American women and, 93, 111, 221, 230
 Orientalism and, 214–215, 220–222
 "propaganda" and, 214, 221–222, 235
 science and, *215*, 215–216
 secularism and, 217–218
 Stowe on, 217
 visual culture and, 218
Mount of Olives, 33, 49

Muhammad (Prophet), 162
Muscular Christianity, 18, 47–48, 182
Muscular Judaism, 182
music, 3, 183, 192, 199
Muskeljudentum (New Jew), 182
Muslim Empire, 150–152
Muslims
   as Arabs, 76, 193
   Jews compared to, 102
   Mizrahim and, 74
   Western Wall and, 76
Mystic Safed, 119–120, *120*, 121–122
myths, 15

National Council of Jewish Women, 211
national epic, 198–200
National Federation of Temple Sisterhoods (NFTS), 17, 25–26, 89. *See also* art calendars
   activities of, 95
   Christian Americans and, 90–91, 93–94
   ZOA and, 233–234
National Workmen's Committee, 61
nationalisms, 46. *See also* transnationalism
   American, 186–187
   art calendars and, 126–129, *127*
   performance of, 175–176
Nazism, 234–235
   art calendars related to, 123
"New Jew," 79–80, 82, 182
The New Palestine (NP), 29, 31, *59*
   ad in, *30*
   art in, 68, *69*, *70*
   cover of, *43*, *44*, 45
   head coverings in, 73
   Jewish Americans in, 83
   Mizrahim in, 68, *69*, *70*
   modernization in, 72–73
   time related to, 43

New Testament, 48, 108
New Year of the Trees, 3
New York, 182
   Romance in, 185–186, 196
Newman, Paul, 239
NFTS. *See* National Federation of Temple Sisterhoods
Nordau, Max, 79, 182
nostalgia, 14, 29
   in art calendars, 102, 103
   of FAZ/ZOA, 45–46
NP. See *The New Palestine*

Obshchestvo Rasprostranenia Truda (Association for the Promotion of Trade and Agriculture) (ORT), 198–199
O'Donnell, James, 184
Old Jewish Quarter, 123, *123*
Oman, Samuel S., 198
"On the March," *63*, 63–64
the Orient, 242–243
   exploration of, 5
   at Hall of Religion, 174
   heritage of, 5, 126–127, 203–204
   idealization of, 1, 4
   imagination and, 31–32
   JE and, 169–170, 235
   in Jewish American imagination, 40–42
   representations of, 23, 24, 202
   in Temple reconstruction, 143–144
the Orient multiplicity, 34–38
"Oriental" relics
   Jerusalem in, 48–49
   Temple in Jerusalem in, 49
   Western Wall in, 49
Oriental Village, 200–202, *201*
Orientalism, 10, 34, 235–237
   antisemitism related to, 221–222
   Arabs in, 35–36, 121, *121*
   category of, 24

as cognitive process, 35
definition of, 10
in gender and Jewish American visual culture, 18, 20
of Hadassah, 208, 211–212
historicism of, 35–38
in Jerusalem mapping, 151–152
in Jewish American heritage, 242–243
motherhood and, 214–215, 220–222
photographs related to, 168
romantic, 153–155
Said, Edward and, 24, 32, 34–36, 108
Zionism and, 35–36
Orientalism and the Hebrew Imagination (Peleg), 35–36
Orientalism and the Jews (Kalmar and Penslar), 8–9
Orientalism reimagined
American Zionism and, 11–12
categorizations in, 8–9
contemporaneous in, 10
cultural pluralism in, 10–11
heritage in, 9–10, 11
homeland in, 10–11
immigrant status in, 10–11
irredentism in, 10
oldness in, 11
Westerners in, 9
ORT. See *Obshchestvo Rasprostranenia Truda*
Orthodoxy, 94–95. See also Hasidism
Ottoman Empire, 9, 20–21, 27, 52
Ottoman millet system, 20–21

pageants, 182–183. See also World's Fair
Palestine, 243. See also *The New Palestine*
"Agricultural Colonies in Palestine," 158

"Bringing Health to Palestine," 84
"Division of Fields in Modern Palestine," 158–159, 160
historical agriculture in, 158, 158–160, 160, 161
images of, 158, 159
"Join the Circle of Palestine's Children," 206–207
"Plowing in Palestine," 160, 161
SCA and, 203
"Scenes of Palestine Life," 78
"A Survivor of Old Palestine," 50, 50–51
UPA, 43
"Village Wells in Use in Palestine," 162
"We Young Palestinians," 2–3
Palestine Exploration Fund, 146–148
Palestine Royal Commission (Peel Commission), 23, 24
Palestinianism, 12, 79–80
Palestinians, 240
papa ("Abbah"), 3
Peel Commission (Palestine Royal Commission), 23, 24
Peleg, Yaron, 35–36, 72
Penslar, Derek, 8–9
Perrot, Georges, 133, 138, 255n12
photographs, 130. See also Holy Land photographs
of agriculture, 161
as archetypes, 154
Christian Orientalism related to, 168
"Composite Portraits" as, 166, 167
daguerreotypes as, 33–34, 155
didactic related to, 154–155
"documentary," 7
interpretation of, 8
in *JE*, 168–169
Jerusalem mapping and, 152–155

Palestine *(continued)*
  mediation of, 7–8
  Orientalism related to, 168
  recontextualization of, 7–8
  simultaneity of, 6–7
  in Temple reconstruction, 144, *145*, 146
  term use of, 7
photography
  archaeological, 146, 155, 168–169
  arthouse, 155
  journalistic, 62, *63*, 64, 75
"A Picturesque Group in Jerusalem," *69*
Plaskow, Judith, 16
Plate, S. Brent, 13
"Plowing and Hoeing," 160
"Plowing in Palestine," 160, *161*
pluralism. *See also* cultural pluralism
  in Hall of Religion, 178
  legal, 21
Poland, 183
"Polish Coins with Jewish Inscriptions," 158
Polish legends, 258n12
Polish synagogue, 98–100, *99*
politics, 37–38
  of *JE*, 135
  of Jewish children, 222–223
  of speed, 6–7
  in Temple reconstruction, 147
Porterfield, Amanda, 217
Postcards from the Oriental Village, *201*
pre-Christian Greek society, 232
Prell, Riv-Ellen, 17–18
"Pre-Natal and Infant Welfare Station, Jerusalem (Old City)," 220
"Primitive Arab Farming," 70, *70*
Progressivism, 45, 47, 211
pro-life shrine, 237–238, *238*

"propaganda," 27, 207–208, 212–213, 234–235
  on Jewish children, 222, 225, *227*, 227–228, 230
  motherhood and, 214, 221–222, 235
Protestant Americans, 122, 218, 231
protofeminism, 17
Pupils from Poor Homes, 205

race, 39, 40, 87
  Jewish as, 57, *58*, 164–165, *167*
  slavery and, 217
Raider, Mark, 81
recontextualization
  of art calendars, 95, 102, 103–104
  of photographs, 7–8
Reform Judaism, 25–26, 234. *See also* National Federation of Temple Sisterhoods
  kabbalah and, 119
relics, 25, 32, 48–49
"Replica of Western Wall Planned in Kansas," *238*
ritual, 31
  "Tashlik Ceremony in Galicia," 162
  tefillin, 19
ritual practice, 162
The Romance of a People (*Romance*), 56–57. *See also* Jewish history
  American history in, 183
  American nationalism in, 186–187
  audiences for, 171–172, 173, 182, 183–184, 260n53
  Christians and, 194, 195–196
  cultural pluralism and, 186–187
  The Epic of a Nation compared to, 175, 198–199, 203
  Ezekiel 1: 15–21 and, 186
  Hebrew University and, 186
  as heritage, 26–27
  Holocaust related to, 197–198

Jewish Day and, 174
Jewish men in, 184–185
in New York, 185–186, 196
Poland in, 183
symbols in, 185–186
Temple reconstruction in, 172, *172*, 184, 185–186
Torah in, 184
ZOA at, 172
Romance press reception, 197–198
American citizenship and, 193
announcement in, 193–194
Christians and, 194, 195
Jewish American citizenship and, 194–195
memory and, 195
religious cooperation in, 195–196
romantic Orientalism, 153–155
Rome, 236
Roosevelt, Theodore, 48
Rosenthal, Steven, 158, 192
Rosenwald, Mrs. Julius, 234
Rosh Hashanah, 162
Ross, Barney, 200
Russia
Duma in, 64, 66
East European Jews from, 157–158, 161
East European Jews in, 187–188, *188*
"Russian Cossack, in Days of Czar, Beats a Jew," 187, *188*
Russian Jewish liberals, 60–61
"Russia—Poland" (Rosenthal), 158

sacrifice, 81–82
Safed, 119–120, *120*, 121–122
Said, Edward, 24, 32, 34–36, 108
St. Louis World's Fair (1904), 21–22, 182
"Samaria from the South," 59
Sandler, Adam, 239

Sarna, Jonathan, 40–41
SCA. *See* Synagogue Council of America
"Scenes of Palestine Life," 78
Schatz, Boris, 109, *110*, 111, 114, 115, *117*, 118
Schick, Conrad, 146–148
science, 215, 215–216
Science of Judaism. *See Jewish Encyclopedia*
Scott, Blake, 198
Scott, Joan W., 14–15, 17
The Scribe, 114
sculpture, 231–232
Second Commandment, 231–233
Second Temple, 133–134, *134*
secularism, 217–218, 236
Seligsberg, Alice, 210
Shapira, Anita, 79–80
Shavuot, 90, 91, 108
shomrim (guards), 77
sacrifice of, 81–82
youth groups related to, 83
shtetl, 60, 64, 157, 204
Simmons, Erica B., 213
Simons, Mrs. Israel, 89
Singer, Isidore, 136
Sistine Chapel, 107
Six-Day War, 239
slavery, 72, 185, 217
slideshow, 177–178
Smith, Jonathan Z., 73
Sobieszek, Robert A., 154–155
social consciousness, 176–178, *179*
socialism, 61–62
"Son of the Ancient Race," 57, *58*
space
heritage related to, 6
NP related to, 43
time and, 6, 124
in U.S., 37

spectacle, 82
speed
  politics of, 6–7
  threat of, 5
Spirit One Christian Ministry Church, 237–238, *238*
Stage as pictured in Chicago World's Fair guidebook, *172*
Stars of David, 61, *62*, *127*, 128–129, 186
"The Star-Spangled Banner," 199
State of Israel, 24, 38, 240, 241
Statue of Liberty, 43, *44*, 45, 128
stereotype, 61, 79, 80, 81, 82, 156
  agriculture related to, 159–161
  art and, 199
  of JAP, 17–18
  of Jewish men, 166, 185, 222
Stern, Eliyahu, 51–52
Stowe, Harriet Beecher, 217
Struck, Hermann, 68, *69*, 70
Stryowski, Wilhelm August, 162
"Substructure of Temple of Herod, Now Called 'Solomon's Stables,'" *145*
Suleiman the Magnificent (sultan), 33
"A Survivor of Old Palestine," *50*, 50–51
symbols, 81
  of children, 208–209, *210*
  of Jewish children, 222–223, 234–235
  in *Romance*, 185–186
Synagogue Council of America (SCA), 26–27, 173
  Muscular Judaism and, 182
  Palestine and, 203
  unity related to, 202–203
synagogues, 98–100, *99*, 135, 162
Szold, Henrietta, 94, 210, 234

ta'amulah. *See* "propaganda"

Talmud, 13, 49, 134, 136, 142, 149, 214, 263n3
"Tashlik Ceremony in Galicia," 162
technologies, 5–6
  for Holy Land photographs, 34, 130
tefillin, 19
"The Temple at Jerusalem," 140, *141*
Temple in Jerusalem, 49, *145*. *See also* Western Wall
  "Holy of Holies" in, 100, 138, *139*
Temple Mount in Jerusalem, 43, *44*, 49
Temple reconstruction
  authority and, 143–144
  competitions in, 147
  Constantinople and, 141–142
  Haggadahs and, 140, 142, 143–144
  "Holy of Holies of the Temple at Jerusalem" in, 138, *139*
  imagination in, 146–147
  inscription and, 140–142
  liturgy and, 143
  Orient in, 143–144
  Palestine Exploration Fund and, 146–148
  photographs in, 144, *145*, 146
  politics in, 147
  rabbinic text in, 142–144
  in *Romance*, 172, *172*, 184, 185–186
  "Solomon's Stables" in, 144, *145*
  "The Temple at Jerusalem" in, 140, *141*
  "Temple of Herod" in, 144, *145*
  time related to, 140, 142–143
  "View of the Temple of Solomon" in, 144, *145*
  at World's Fair, 172, *172*
  Zionism and, 148
Temple Sisterhoods, 16–17. *See also* National Federation of Temple Sisterhoods

"Three Scenes from the National
    Farm School founded by
    Rabbi Joseph Krauskopf [in]
    Doylestown, Penn," 180
time, 24–25
    NP related to, 43
    space and, 6, 124
    Temple reconstruction related to,
        140, 142–143
Tisha B'Av, 140
TM. See The Maccabaean
"To Liberate the Smaller
    Nationalities," 52, 53
Tomb of Rachel, 33
Torah, 15, 72, 177, 184
    Christians and, 91
    Second Commandment from,
        231–233
Tower of David, 32–33
traditions
    modernity compared to, 51–52
    women related to, 93, 109, 110, 111
transnationalism, 46
    in Hall of Religion, 177–178
transvaluation, 79
Troy, Jean-François de, 100–102, 101
Trumpeldor, Joseph, 52, 191–192
Tsene-Urene. See Ashkenazim
"Tunisian Jewess," 164, 165
"A Typical Street in Jerusalem," 155–
    157, 156

Uncle Tom's Cabin (Stowe), 217
Union of American Hebrew
    Congregations, 95
United Palestine Appeal (UPA), 43
United States (U.S.). See also
    Christian Americans
    agriculture of, 161
    antisemitism in, 22
    democracy of, 128–129
    Emergency Quota Act of, 23
    freedom in, 190–191
    future in, 37
    Hadassah related to, 209
    hypocrisy of, 225
    immigration to, 22, 129, 191, 198
    Muscular Christianity in, 47–48,
        182
    nationalism of, 186–187
    popular culture of, 239
    St. Louis World's Fair in, 21–22
    space in, 37
    Zionism and, 94
United States Capitol Building, 127,
    127–128
UPA. See United Palestine Appeal
Urya, I. B., 198
U.S. See United States
utopias, 38, 41

verbal texts, 166
visual texts with, 26, 143–144, 149,
    159–160, 164, 207, 242
"View of the Temple of Solomon," 145
"Village Wells in Use in Palestine,"
    162
Vishniac, Roman, 60
visual authenticity, 14
visual culture, 23, 31. See also specific
    topics
    of agriculture, 160
    architectural heritage as, 32–34
    art and, 232–233
    chalutzim and, 76–77, 80–81
    of Christian Americans, 90–91, 108,
        109
    definition of, 13
    of FAZ/ZOA, 49–50, 57, 60, 87
    of Hadassah, 212–213
    in JE, 135
    in Jewish heritage, 13–14, 15
    motherhood and, 218
    of Zionism, 49–50, 52

visual religion, 13–14
visual texts, 14–15, 43, 107
　verbal texts with, 26, 143–144, 149, 159–160, 164, 207, 242
Viviani, René, 52, 53
Vizonsky, Nathan, 188–190, 189
Vulgate, 91

"We Young Palestinians," 2–3
"Weary Wanderers," 64, 65
Weisgal, Meyer, 57, 173, 194
Weizmann, Chaim, 23, 52, 54, 56, 56–57, 196
Wenger, Beth, 12, 15, 258n12
West European Jewish Americans, 40
"Western" Jewish types, 164
Western Orientalism, 34
Western Wall
　authenticity of, 32
　Christian American fundamentalists and, 237–238, 238
　image of, 29, 30, 31
　Muslims and, 76
　in "Oriental" relics, 49
　significance of, 33, 49, 76
　Six-Day War and, 239
Westerners, 9
Whitfield, Stephen, 198
"Whither?," 63, 63–64
Wilson, Woodrow, 52, 53
Wise, Stephen, 75
Wissenschaft des Judentums, 157
Wolfenstein, Martha, 57
women, 94, 121, 207–208, 228.
　See also Hadassah Medical Organization
　art calendars and, 93, 131, 229
　inclusion of, 229–230
　traditions related to, 93, 109, 110, 111

Women of Reform Judaism. *See* National Federation of Temple Sisterhoods
The Workers' Village, 129, 130
World War I, 61, 62–64, 63
World War II, 23–24
　Jewish Americans in, 127, 127–128
World Zionist Organization, 23
World's Fair (Chicago, 1893), 182
World's Fair (Chicago, 1933), 237. *See also The Romance of a People*
　cultural pluralism at, 26–27, 175, 186–187
　JE compared to, 174
　New York compared to, 185
　Oriental village at, 200–202, 201
　sources about, 174–175

Yemenite Jews, 68, 69
Yishuv (pre-state Jewish colony in Palestine), 32
YMCA. *See* Young Men's Christian Association
Yom Kippur, 98–100, 99
You Don't Mess with the Zohan (film), 239
Young Men's Christian Association (YMCA), 48
Youth Aliyah, 223–224
youth groups, 83

Zemel, Carol, 60
Zerubavel, Yael, 46
"Zion Gate," 152, 154, 154
"Zion: Out of the Jungle!," 67, 67–68
Zionism, 11–12
　America and, 94
　as conquest, 36
　debate on, 124, 125, 126
　democracy of, 205
　forms of, 176

Hadassah and, 209–210, 212–213
Jerusalem mapping and, 149–150
in Jewish American imagination, 41–42
in Jewish history, 192
Judaism compared to, 79
Orientalism and, 35–36
Orthodoxy and, 94–95
Temple reconstruction and, 148
U.S. and, 94
visual culture of, 49–50, 52
Zionism-as-Progressivism, 211
Zionist artists, 92
Zionist Organization of America (ZOA) (Federation of American Zionists) (FAZ/ZOA), 24–25, 43, 55
    Arabs and, 87
    correctives of, 46–47
    East European Jews and, 47, 57
    guards and, 77
    Hadassah compared to, 27, 234
    history and, 46–47, 87
    JE compared to, 135
    NFTS and, 233–234
    nostalgia of, 45–46
    transnationalism of, 46
    visual culture of, 49–50, 57, 60, 87
    Weizmann and, 56–57
    women in, 229–230
    at World's Fair, 172
Zionist Orientalism, 72
Zionist pioneers. See *chalutzim*
ZOA. *See* Zionist Organization of America